SOCIAL WORK
FOR
WEAKER SECTIONS

Social Work for Weaker Sections

By
Mohammad Naqi

ANMOL PUBLICATIONS PVT. LTD.
NEW DELHI - 110 002 (INDIA)

ANMOL PUBLICATIONS PVT. LTD.
4374/4B, Ansari Road, Daryaganj
New Delhi - 110 002
Ph.: 23261597, 23278000
Visit us at: www.anmolpublications.com

Social Work for Weaker Sections

First Published, 2005

ISBN 81-261-2226-9

PRINTED IN INDIA

Published by J.L. Kumar for Anmol Publications Pvt. Ltd., New Delhi - 110 002 and Printed at Mehra Offset Press, Delhi.

Contents

Preface

Social work and social service are the two modern concepts. But, in fact, these are the new terms for old Indian social practices. In past also the people in authority and power used to take up welfare projects for the common populace, in the country. For instance, the chiefs, dukes and the wealthy people used to build wells, gardens and shelter homes for travellers, on highways. The emperors and kings also built roads, bridges and planted trees on both sides of the pathways for the welfare of their subjects. However, there was no organised effort for the emancipation and empowerment of poor and weaker sections. Whatever was done, was done in the name of generosity and charity. There was no concept of a welfare state.

In modern times, the ideology of human rights, social responsibility and social welfare developed and first, Western and later Asian states began to adopt their citizens, as family members and not merely subjects. With the development of the practice of social welfare, was evolved the new concept of social work.

Now, apart from the official agencies and governmental departments, the voluntary organisations and N.G.Os, are also engaged in social work. These organisations, particularly, target the people at the lower strata of society and all those, who are known as weaker sections.

As per the latest perception and new social philosophy, weaker sections now include OBCs, Scheduled Castes, Scheduled Tribes and the minorities.

This book covers all aspects and areas of social work and examines the basic problems, and fundamental issues in detail. Not only this, it suggests the solutions and remedies also.

The undersigned is confident that this book—with its fresh approach and different treatment of the subject—would be accepted and welcomed by scholars, sociologists and social workers, alike.

—Editor

1

The Have-nots

The magnitude of poverty in our country can be visualised from the fact that as many as 27.10 crore people in the country live below the poverty line as per provisional estimates of 1983-84. Out of this population, 22.15 are from the rural areas and 4.95 crores from the urban areas. The population living below the poverty line, thus forms 37.4 per cent of the total populace. Bihar has 3.65 crores of people living below the poverty line representing 49.5 per cent of its total population. Madhya Pradesh with 2.54 crores of people living below the poverty line has as much as 46.2 per cent of its population in this category. Uttar Pradesh ranks third with 45.3 per cent or 5.30 crores of its people being in this hapless section. Manipur has the least percentage of people living below the poverty-belt -12.3 per cent and in terms of number 1.9 lacs people. The estimates are derived by drawing the poverty line at Rs. 49.9 per capita per month corresponding to a daily calorie requirement of 2400 per person in the rural areas and an income of Rs. 56.64 per capita per month corresponding to a calorie requirement of 2100 per head in the urban areas.

Removal of poverty has been the main plank in the platform of Planning in India and with this objective in view, the Sixth Year Plan had set out a two pronged strategy to deal with this courage. Emphasis was laid on accelerating the pace of agricultural development since it was felt that this would have a beneficial effect on raising the standard of living of the poorer sections of society.

Simultaneously it was felt necessary to strengthen and expand the scope of beneficiary-oriented anti-poverty programmes in rural areas. Consistent with this approach, the Seventh Five Year Plan laid emphasis on accelerated agricultural growth and anti-poverty and employment generation programs mainly in the form of 20 point Programme.

Special Programme

The 20-Point Programme was launched on 1st July, 1975 as a "Garibi Hatao" programme to alleviate the conditions of the poor sections of the society. A revised programme was announced on 14th January, 1982. The basic objective of this programme was to continue its focus on the provision of better living conditions for the weaker sections of the society while aiming at all round improvement in productivity. The revised 20-Point Programme (TPP 1982) has been under implementation from 1982-83 onward. The New 20-Point Programme 1986 (TPP-86), prepared under the guidance of the former Prime Minister Shri Rajiv Gandhi was laid on the tables of both the Houses of Parliament by the Minister of Programme implementation on 20th August, 1986. It was restructured in the light of the experience gained in the implementation of the 20-Point Programmes of 1975 and 1982. While some of the items of the earlier Programmes were dropped, its scope has been extended to bring within its ambit other items having a closer and more direct link with the Nation's assault on poverty.

The Coverage of the Programme has been broadened and includes a number of major areas of social concern such as the provision of clean drinking water, health facilities, acceptance of family planning, expansion of education, equality for women, justice to Scheduled Castes and Scheduled Tribes, new opportunities for youth, housing for the under-privileged sections of the society, improvement of slums and the protection of environment. Besides eradication of poverty, the other important goals sought to be attained relate to enhanced agricultural production and productivity, reduction in income inequalities, removal of social and economic disparities and in general, raising the quality of life. The TTP-86 renews the Government's commitment to the eradication of poverty, the raising of productivity, the reduction of income inequalities and the removal of social and economic disparities; in general it aims at and improving the quality of life of the people. It is not a declaration of intent but Charter of Emancipation for the poor.

"The outlays for different items of the programmes are not fixed separately and specifically and these are derived from the relevant plan heads under States/UTs and Plans of concerned central ministries. The financing of various schemes under the programme shows a close partnership between the Central and State Governments in the spheres of economic planning in general and the implementation, of anti-poverty programmes in particular. The 20-Point Programme forms an integral part of the plans of the State Government/U.T. Administrations and Central ministries. However, some schemes like RLEGP and the family Welfare Programmes are funded entirely by the Central Government. Other Programmes, namely, IRDP, NREP and Bonded Labour Rehabilitation are jointly financed from Central and State Resources on a 50:50 basis.

Out of a total Public Sector outlay of Rs. 1,80.000 crores for the Seventh Plan, the outlay for 20-Point Programme (1986) works out to Rs. 60,500 crores, which represents 33.6 per cent of the total outlay. The share of 20 -Point Programme in the total Central outlay is 22.6 per cent and in the States/UTs outlays 46.1 per cent. The total outlay for 1987-88 is Rs. 44,698 crores, of which the outlay relating to the 20-Point Programme works out to Rs. 13,597 crores, i.e. 30.4%.

Implementation of the Scheme

The administration of the Programme is the responsibility of the 20-Point Programme Monitoring Division of the Ministry of Programme Implementation. The Ministry was formed in September 1985 and prior to that 20-Point Programme Division existed in the Planning Commission. The Ministry is headed by a Cabinet Minister, assisted by a Minister of State. At the Secretariat level it is headed by a Secretary, who is assisted by one Additional Secretary, two Joint Secretaries, one Deputy Secretary, five Deputy Advisers and other supporting staff. Besides, the 20-Point

Programme Monitoring Division, the Ministry has three other Divisions namely the Infrastructure Monitoring Division, Project Monitoring Division and the Administrative Support Division.

Poverty Alleviation Programme Monitoring Division is concerned with the monitoring of the 20-Point Programme. These include Anti-poverty Programme for raising incomes, creating assets and improving the quality of life of the poor, welfare of Scheduled Castes and Scheduled Tribes, some of the minimum needs Programmes like rural water supply, house sites and construction assistance, rural electrification, rural health, nutrition, elementary education, adult literacy and slum improvement as well as other programmes aimed at increasing production and productivity in the economy, efficient distribution of consumer goods, adoption of two child norm, development of youth and women, conservation of environment and making administration responsive to public needs. The TPP-1986 was announced on 20.8.1986 and its implementation and monitoring commenced from 1.4.1987 along with annual Plan 1987-88. The Government of India also set up an Advisory Council under Resolution dated the 12th May, 1987, to advise the ministry on the implementation of the 20-Point Programme.

The success of any programme, however, well formulated and well intentioned, depends on effective implementation. The impact of TPP-86 will, therefore, depend on the earnestness and determination with which it is implemented. Monitoring systems have been developed in different states for keeping a watch on the implementation of Plan projects and schemes. Effective monitoring as a means towards identification of areas requiring corrective action to ensure successful implementation of targets assumes considerable significance with the launching of TPP-86. The primary responsibility of monitoring lies with the agencies entrusted with the execution of the Programme, in this ease the State Governments and, UT Administrations. The Ministry of programmes implementation has been engaged in the exercise of institutionalising an effective monitoring system which would not only motivate effective implementation of the Programme but also bring about speedy communication of dependable information in key areas to enable the monitoring agencies to interpret signals and intervene in a prompt and constructive manner. For achieving this end, the Ministry has been in constant interaction with the nodal Central Ministries as well as the State Governments and UT administrations, both by addressing communications to them and by holding meetings at a personal level both at Delhi and State headquarters. Constant monitoring and review are part of a continuum in any strategy designed to strengthen the implementation of a programme and an effective monitoring system is, thus, a critical pre-condition for effective implementation. In fact, a good monitoring system would provide motivation for implementation of a Programme. With this objective in view, the Ministry of Programme implementation has prepared a comprehensive "Monitoring manual" for the guidance of all concerned.

The charter of the Ministry of Programme Implementation is to closely oversee the implementation of the programme by the State Governments/U.T. administrations and the Nodal Central Ministries/Departments and to initiate action for maximising its effectiveness. This exercise starts with the setting of physical targets on annual, quarterly and monthly basis. The 29-Point Programme 1986 includes 91 sub-points, several of which are further composed of more than one. The Ministry in close consultations with all concerned Central Ministries/Departments, after a series of discussions arrived at a list of items for monitoring under each point and the periodicity of monitoring. The existing Monitoring-cum-Implementation Review System in the Ministry is outlined in the Flow Chart given below :

MPIS On-going Monitoring-Implementation-Review System

Input	: Monthly reports from States/UTs. Quarterly Reports from the Central Ministries based on *Reports from States/UTs.*
Processing	: Compilation and analysis of monthly progress report, compilation and analysis of quarterly progress report after discussion with Planning Commission.
Output	: Monthly Progress report. Capsule report for Prime Minister. Quarterly progress report with Executive Summary.

Follow-up	:	Letters from the Prime Minister/The Minister to the Chief Ministers.
		Discussions with the Chief Ministers, visit to state HQ and field visits.
		Discussion with Chief Secretaries/Development Commissioners. Discussions with the Central Ministries bring major issues to notice of P.M. Office and Cabinet Secretariat.

The two major tools of management information system developed by this Ministry on the implementation of the programme are (i) Monthly Progress Report (MPR) and (ii) Quarterly Progress Report (QPR). The MPR covers achievements during each month against pre-set physical targets under 29 items. The points selected for MPR are those in which achievements can be assessed on a monthly basis such as: Integrated Rural Development Programme (IRDP), employment generated under the National Rural Employment Programme (NREP), Rural Landless Employment Guarantee Programme (RLEGP), Small Scale Industrial Units, Distribution of Surplus land, Bonded Labour Rehabilitation, Drinking Water Supply, Community Health Centres, sub-centres; Primary Health Centres, Immunisation of Children, Family Planning Sterlisation, Equivalence of sterilisation, ICDS Blocks, Anganwadis, SC Families and ST Families Assisted House sites Allotted, Construction assistance, Indira Awaas Yojana for SC/ST, EWS Houses provided, LIG Houses, Slum Improvement. Tree Plantation, Fair Price shops, Village Electrification, Pump sets energised. Improved Chullhas and Biogas Plants (States). While the Monthly Progress report check performance of month to month basis, the quarterly progress report carries out a diagnostic check of the performance on a comprehensive basis covering all the points and include-evaluatory assessments coupled with suggestions for more effective implementation. The performance assessment of each item of the programme is graded as 'Very Good', 'Good' and 'Poor' on the basis of implementation of 90% and above achievement 80% to 90% and below 80% achievement respectively of all the targets.

For the intense ranking of the States on their overall performance, the item-wise achievement is categorised into four parts

A, B, C, and D. Category 'A' includes those items for which achievement of physical targets is 90% and above. Category 'B' and 'C' represent cases of performance superior and inferior to the All India performance. Category 'D' represents 'Nil' performance. Grades are worked out on the basis of 3 points for Category A, 2 points for category 'B', 1 point for Category 'C' and zero for category 'D'. The ranking of the states is done on the performance of 20 selected items namely, (1) IRDP, (2) NREP, (3) RLEGP, (4) Surplus land distribution, (5) Bonded labour rehabilitation, (6) Drinking water problem solved (villages), (7) Immunization of children, (8) Sterilisation. (9) SC families assisted, (10) ST Families assisted (11) Provision of House sites, (12) Construction assistance, (13) EWS Houses, (14) LIG houses, (15) Slum improvement, (16) Tree plantation, (17) villages electrified, (18) Pump-sets energised, (19) improved Chullhas and (20) Bio-gas plants.

For the last few years, Punjab had stood first in the implementation of the 20-Point programme. The components relating to the sectors like the Integrated Rural Development Programme, National Rural Employment Programme, Rural Landless Employment Generating Programme and Small Scale Industries, Immunisation Programme, Justice to Scheduled Castes, Strategies for forestry, Fisheries and Horticulture had done very well according to Mr S.S. Rathi State Governor who had emphasised that the remaining departments should gear up to achieve the targets and maintain their prominent position of the state in implementation of the 20 Point Programme, while addressing a meeting of Senior Officers of various departments for reviewing the progress of the 20-Point programme held on January 9, 1989.

A monitoring machinery has been established in all States/Union Territories and the concerned Central Ministries/Departments. Nodal Officers have been appointed by the respective governments/administrations in all the States/Union Territories and by the concerned Central Ministries/Departments. In the States/UTs, high level implementation and monitoring committees have been set up under the Chief Minister and the Chief Secretary at the State Head quarters. In addition, District and Block level committees have also been set up, which include members of

Parliament and State Legislatures irrespective of their party affiliations and other non-officials people's representatives including minorities. These monitoring bodies suggest measures for removing constraints to speedy implementation of the programme. The existing Programme Management Machinery in the State/UTs is on next page.

Schemes Executed

The 20-Point Programme comprises:

1. Attack on rural poverty;
2. Strategy for rain-fed agriculture;
3. Better use of irrigation water;
4. Bigger harvest;
5. Enforcement of land reforms;
6. Special programmes for rural labour;
7. Clean drinking water;
8. Health for all;
9. Two child norm;
10. Expansion of education;
11. Justice to the Scheduled Castes and the Scheduled Tribes;
12. Equality for women;
13. New opportunities for youth;
14. Housing for the people;
15. Improvement of slums;
16. New strategy for forestry;
17. Prot:ction of the environment;
18. Concern for the consumers;
19. Energy for the villages; and
20. A responsive administration.

The implementation of the different programmes is discussed below in terms of their components, targets and achievements, administrative machinery, deficiencies and suggestions for improvement.

Programme Management in States/Union Territories

Level	*Implementing Agencies*	*Monitoring Agencies*	*Consultative Groups*
State/UT	Concerned Department of the State government/UT administrations	Committee at Chief Minister's level with concerned Ministers and heads of Departments	Consultative groups of Voluntary Agencies have been setup in some states as a follow up of the late Prime Minister Smt. Indira Gandhi's letter dated 4.1.1982 to all Chief Minister.
District	Department disdrict level officers, DRDA in the case of rural allied programmes.	District level committee, in some states : these committees are under the charge of Ministers. Generally District Magistrate/ Collector, Chief Zila Parishad, DRDA District Department Officers are members of these committees. MPs and MLAs irrespective of their party affiliations and non-official people's representative including minorities are also represented.	In some states, District Level Consultative Groups of voluntary agencies are functioning.
Block	Block Development Officer and Department Staff.	Block Level Monitoring Committees. MLAs and Non-official people's representatives including minorities.	

Welfare of the Poor

The Seventh Five Year Plan has set a target of reducing the number of persons living below poverty line in rural areas from 39.9% at the beginning of the Plan to 28.2% in 1989-90 to 10% by 1994-95 and 5% by 1990-2000. In order to bring a ray of hope in the life of every single poor family in every village, it is essential to ensure that one or the other of the anti-poverty programmes reaches every poor person in the country. The major poverty alleviation programmes launched in the Sixth Plan were the Integrated Rural Development Programme (IRDP), National Rural Employment Programme (NREP) and Rural Landless Employment Guarantee Programme (RLEGP). These programmes are being continued with substantial higher out lays and sharper focus during the seventh Plan.

Integrated Rural Development Programme : The IRDP assists families below the poverty line in rural areas by encouraging them to take up self-employment ventures in the primary, secondary and tertiary sectors. Under this programme income generating assets, including working capital, are provided through a package of assistance comprising of subsidy and institutional credit. The programme has been modified suitably in the Seventh Plan in the light of the short-comings found in its implementation during the Sixth Plan. Allocation criteria have been changed from the concept of an uniform amount for every Block to one of selectivity based on incidence of poverty. The programme aims at the "Poorest among the Poor" who will be identified on the basis of an annual household income of Rs. 4800/-which is lower than the poverty line fixed at Rs. 6400/-. In the identification of beneficiaries, guidelines have been issued to involve people's representatives. Supplementary doses of assistance are also given to those families who were covered, during the Sixth Plan but could not cross the poverty line. Further, coverage of women beneficiaries upto 30% of the total is envisaged during the Seventh Plan. To bring about awareness among the beneficiaries, formation of organisations of beneficiaries is being encouraged. The Seventh Plan target is to cover 20 million beneficiary households of which 50% would be those requiring supplementary assistance.

The progress of implementation of IRDP during the Sixth Plan, 1985-86 and 1986-87 is given in the Table:

(Rs. in crores)

Item		Sixth Plan Target	Achievement	Achievement 1985-86	1986-87
1		2	3	4	5
1.	Total allocation	1500	1766.81	407.36	543.83
2.	Total expenditure	1500	1661.17	441.10	604.37
3.	Total Term Credit	3000	3101.61	730.15	997.78
4.	Total investment	4500	4762.78	1171.25	1602.15
5.	Total No. of beneficiaries covered (lac Nos.)	15 (SC/ST:50)	165.62 (SC/ST:64.3)	30.61 (SC/ST:13.23) (Women : 3.03)	37.47 (SC/ST:16.8) (Women :5.67)
6.	Per capita subsidy (Rupees)		1003	1159	1229
7.	Per capita credit (Rupees)		1872.72	2386	2667
8.	Per capita investment		2875.72	3545	3959

A concurrent evaluation of the Programme is being done every month on a random and rotating sample basis by the Department of Rural Development through 29 reputed research institutions in 72 blocks of 36 districts, covering 10 old and 10 new beneficiaries in each block. The findings of the evaluation for the period October 1985 September 86 reveal that, at the national level, pre-dominant coverage (78%) related to the poorest of the poor. At the national level 12% of the old beneficiaries had crossed the revised poverty line of Rs. 6400/-.

National Rural Employment Programme : The Wage Employment Programmes aim at providing supplementary employment opportunities to work-seekers during the lean periods of the year besides creating durable community assets as also improving the quality of life in the rural areas. The Programme operates in conjunction with the on-going developmental works ensuring that employment and development support each other and the benefits flowing to the community are maximised. The guidelines under these programmes accordingly envisage that the rural community should be involved in implementation of the programme from the stage of planning to the stage of execution. The shelf of projects necessary for implementation of the programme are required to be prepared on the basis of the felt needs of the people which would be ascertained in the meetings of Gram Sabhas. The guidelines also provide that the execution of works under the programme should as far as possible, be through Panchayat Raj institutions since these institutions have the capacity, for executing the works and fulfilling the needs of the people. The basic idea behind the employment programmes is that creation of durable assets for strengthening the rural infrastructure will lead to rapid growth of the rural economy as well as generate employment opportunities.

The NREP launched in October 1980 continued even in the Seventh Plan as an important component of the anti-poverty strategy. This programme is being implemented on a 50:50 sharing basis between the Centre and the States. With a view to ensure the creation of durable assets under this Programme, a provision has been made allowing the expenditure on materials to the extent of 50 per cent of the total project cost in a district. The different assets created are social forestry tanks, minor irrigation, soil conservation, rural roads, community buildings and other works.

Against the target of 268 millions man days for 1987-88, the reported achievement upto December, 1987 was 194 million man days. Of this, 59% was provided to SCs and STs, 46% to landless labourers and 19% to women.

In view of the need to encourage afforestation and taking up a massive programme of fodder plantation, 25% of the funds under NREP and RLEGP are being earmarked for social forestry. Further, 10% of the outlay is being earmarked for the maintenance of the works constructed under NREP/RLEGP. 10% of the annual allocations of the States/UTs under NREP and RLEGP are also earmarked for works that exclusively benefit the SCs/STs. Funds at the rate of Rs 6 crores per annum each under the two Programmes are to be utilised for construction of Sanitary latrines. Diversion of resources earmarked year-wise for construction of housing units, social forestry and SC/ST to other sectors is not permitted. Under the Indira Awas Yojana amounts are earmarked for SCs/STs and freed bonded labourers. The amount earmarked for the year 1987-88 was Rs. 125 crores. A target of 1.08 lac houses had been fixed for 1987-88 under this programme.

Programme for Farmers

The Seventh Five Year Plan envisages an annual growth rate of 4% during the Plan period in the case of agricultural production and 3.7% in the case of foodgrains production. One of the important programmes launched during the Seventh Plan is the National Watershed Development Programme (NWDP) for Rainfed Areas for increasing production of rainfed crops like millets, pulses, oilseeds and cotton.

Out of the total net sown area in the country, 72% is rain-fed. The National Watershed Development Programme for Rain-fed Agriculture is being implemented in 16 States covering 99 districts where pilot projects on water conservation/harvesting technology were already in operation. As against a target of 11173 micro-watershed during 1987-88, the cumulative achievement upto December 1987 was 14979. An area of 2.32 lac hectares was estimated to have been covered under rain-fed farming during

1986-87 and it was envisaged that an area of 5.41 lac hectares would be covered during 1987-88.

The Planning Commission has suggested to the State Governments that while preparing the state plans, attention should be paid specifically to the following items as a part of the long-term drought proofing strategy: (a) Priority and stepping up of expenditure on and completion of such irrigation projects as are likely to benefit chronically, drought-prone areas; (b) promote use of water-saving devices like the sprinkler system drip-irrigation; (c) take the help of scientific organisations, like the Department of Space, for identifying water rechargeable locations, digging of tubewells etc., (d) Much greater research and push on dryland farming; and (e) stress on year-round propagation of water management/water conservations method.

The objective of the Drought Prone Area Programme (DPAP) is to have an integrated area development on a mini and micro water shed basis to bring about optimal development of land, water, live stock and human resources for restoration of ecological balance so as to mitigate the effect of drought. Under this Programme, which is in operation in 511 block of 70 districts in 13 States, activities such as afforestation, soil conservation, efficient utilisation of scarce water through surface and ground sources, conservation of scanty rainfall, introduction of dryland farming technology, and suitable agronomic practices are taken up. The allocation per block is Rs. 15 lacs a year which is shared by the Centre and States on a 50:50 basis.

Optimum use of water holds the key to the fulfilment of our needs of food and other agricultural products. Of the diverse purposes for which there is demand for water, irrigation, is the main component. The gap between the potential created and utilised represents a vast resource which must be tapped by efficient management of irrigation water. At the beginning of the Seventh Plan, the cumulative potential created and utilised from all sources was 67.5 millions hectares and 60.6 millions hectares respectively. The Seventh Plan envisages creation of additional irrigation potential and utilisation of 13 million hectares and 11 million hectares respectively. The total potential created and utilised during 1985-86 and 1986-87 was 4.41 millions hectares and 3.50 millions hectares respectively. Targets for the creation of irrigation potential and its utilisation were 2.3 million hectares and 2.05 million hectares respectively for 1987-88. It is reported that the gap between the potential created and utilised is pronounced in the States of Andhra Pradesh, Bihar, Gujarat, Maharashtra, Karnataka and Madhya Pradesh.

The Command Area Development Programme (CADP) aims at bridging the gap between potential created and its utilisation. The Programme, at present, includes 132 projects in 8 States and 1 U.T. with a total command area of 17.3 million hectares. The Seventh Plan envisages construction of field channels covering an area of 6.81 million hectares, land levelling covering an area of 1.82 million hectares and implementation of "Warabandi" system in about 8 million hectares of land. There is a pressing need to improve water management techniques to bring about increased utilisation of created potential. A conjunctive water -use programme which provides for taking up minor irrigation works in the commands of major and medium irrigation projects, would go a long way in the direction of integrated project planning in the field of irrigation. During the years from 1985 to 1987, 1.96 million hectares of field channels, 0.29 million hectares of land levelling and 2.04 million hectares of "warabandi" had been completed. For 1987-88 the targets were 1.27 million hectares of field channels, 0.15 million hectares of land levelling and 1.68 million hectares of "warabandi".

The minor irrigation programme consists mostly of exploitation of ground water potential and small surface water schemes. These are implemented by the State Governments from their resources supplemented by institutions finance and other resources like Tribal Sub-plan, IRDP, NREP, Small and Marginal Farmers, Western Ghat Programme, etc.

In the Plan 1987-88 emphasis had been on speedy completion of on going projects and new schemes had been restricted to medium irrigation projects in drought prone, tribal and backward areas. A new Centrally Sponsored Scheme with 100% central assistance has been introduced for conducting a census of minor irrigation projects in all the States/UTs. The activities of the Central

Ground Water Board have been stepped up with particular reference to ground water investigation and development in the North-eastern States.

Crops at Large Scale

Agriculture continues to be the mainstay of our economy. The Seventh Plan aims at 4% per annum growth of agricultural output and 3.7 per cent annum growth of foodgrains output. The major programme thrusts in the Seventh Plan are: (i) Special Rice Production Programme in the Eastern Region, (ii) National Oilseeds Development Project, (iii) National Watersheds Development Programme for Rainfed Agriculture, (iv) Development of Small and Marginal Farmers and (v) Social Forestry.

Special Rice Production Programme in the Eastern Region : In the Eastern region (Assam, Bihar, Orissa, West Bengal, Eastern U.P. and Madhya Pradesh) the gap between the potential and the actual yield of rice is the highest among the regions. To exploit this potential for higher yields, the Special Rice production Programme has been launched as a Centrally Sponsored Scheme in 430 selected blocks.

National Oilseeds Development Project and Technology Mission on Oilseeds : The main thrust under the National Oilseeds Development Project (NODP) is to intensify efforts at the district level to increase the production of oilseeds, 180 districts have been identified in 7 States covering an area of 146 lacs hectares. This is implemented as a Centrally Sponsored Scheme on 50:50 basis. The important components of the project include production, distribution and buffer stocking of seeds, distribution of minikits, strengthening of fertilisers distribution channels, more effective farm mechanisation as well as marketing and price support. With a view to providing research and technology support and making the country self-reliant in edible and non-edible oils and to reduce imports of vegetable oils, a Technology Mission on Oilseeds Production was set up in May, 1986. The Mission concentrates its activities on the major crops (groundnut, rapeseed, mustard, soyabean, sun-flower, saf-flower, linseed, sesamum and niger) which contribute substantially to the edible oil economy of India.

National Pulses Development Project : Pulses form a rich source of protein and a vital part of the diet of the majority of people. The production of pulses in the country has, however, been stagnant in the range of 10-13 million tonnes. To give a thrust to the production of pulses, a Centrally Sponsored National Pulses Development Project has been launched under which emphasis is given on crop specific and area-specific programmes covering major pulse crops like gram, arhar, peas, lentil, moong and urad. The emphasis is on increasing the area and raising the productivity per unit area. The NPDP was launched in June 1986 covering 13 major pulse growing states.

Horticulture : A number of Central/State sector schemes have been taken up for the development of fruits and vegetables. These schemes are mainly for the production and distribution of planting materials and for the demonstration of improved cultivation practices.

Post Harvest Operations : The Programme envisages creation of facilities for modern storage, processing and marketing. Food Corporation of India (FCI), Central Warehousing Corporation (CWC) and State Warehousing Corporations are engaged in building and maintaining large storage capacities. The Seventh Plan target is creation of 10 million tonnes of additional storage capacity.

Animal Husbandry and Dairy Development : The Animal Husbandry Programmes are aimed at meeting the requirement of milk, eggs, meat, wool, drought-power and rural transport. The Special Livestock Production Programme is, at present in operation in 103 districts in 21 States and 4 U.T.s under which financial assistance is provided to small/marginal farmers, agricultural labourers for rearing cross-bread heifer calves and for establishment of sheep, poultry and piggery production units. Further, 30% of the beneficiaries selected under the Programme are to be from SCs/STs.

Fisheries : A net work of Fish Farmers Development Agencies has been set up in the country which arranges fish-seed, credit, fertiliser, etc. for fish farmers besides imparting training and providing subsidy for tanks and pond development for the first year.

Land Reforms Implemented

Land reforms constitute vital element both in terms of our anti-poverty strategy and for modernisation and increased productivity in agriculture. 'Land to the Tiller' has been a major goal of the government. Land records form the base for all land reform measures. In the Seventh Plan, a Centrally sponsored Scheme for up-dating land records and strengthening of Revenue Machinery has been introduced.

One of the major programme of land reforms has been the distribution of ceiling surplus land. Under a Centrally sponsored scheme, financial assistance is given to the assignees of ceiling surplus land Rs. 2500 per hectare for purposes of land development, provision of inputs as well as immediate consumption needs of beneficiaries. This expenditure is shared on 50:50 basis between Centre/States.

Laws on the imposition of ceilings on agricultural holdings were introduced, in several states during the 1950s and 1960s. As there are many loopholes in these laws, effective implementation has been hampered.

Upto March, 1987, 77.75 lacs acres were declared surplus, out of which, 58.36 lac acres were taken under possession. Only 45.38 lac acres were distributed. The balance of 28.35 lac acres was not distributed for such reasons as litigation, unsuitability for cultivation, reservation for public purposes, etc. Vigorous legal action is required to release the land locked up in litigation. Again a target of 0.8 lac acres for 1986-87, the achievement was reported at 0.5 Lac acres upto December, 1987.

Farm Workers

Enforcement of Minimum Wages for Agricultural Labour : The Central Government (in respect of 42 employments) and the State Governments (in respect of 210 employments) are required to revise the minimum wages once in two years or on the rise in the Consumer Price Index of 50 points. There is a Centrally sponsored Scheme launched in 1984-85 on a pilot basis for strengthening the enforcement machinery for implementation of the minimum wages in Madhya Pradesh, Rajasthan, Orissa and,

Manipur. This scheme envisages appointment of 200 Rural Labour Inspectors (RUs) in blocks where the population of SC and ST agricultural workers is 70 per cent or more. Enforcement of minimum wages has been unsatisfactory in rural areas and an effective implementation machinery does not exist at the block/Taluka levels in many suites. It is essential that minimum wages are revised on time so that entitled benefits are not denied to unorganised rural labour by mere process of delay in the revision of minimum wages. Amendments to the Minimum Wages Act are also required to make punishment more determent and to enable launching of prosecutions by the affected persons or associations of workers/voluntary organisations. Voluntary agencies should be encouraged and involved so that unorganised labour is made aware of their rights to be received under the law.

Rehabilitation of Bonded Labour : The effective implementation of the Bonded Labour System (Abolition) Act, 1976 involves identification and release of bonded labour and action against offenders. Under a Centrally Sponsored Scheme initiated in 1978-79, matching grant assistance from the Centre to the extent of 50 per cent of the total cost is provided. The overall amount of assistance for rehabilitation is Rs. 6250 per bonded labour w.e.f. February, 1986. Of this amount Rs. 500 is released to the beneficiary immediately on his release from bondage. Presently, Vigilance Committees consisting of officials and non-officials have been constituted under the provisions of the Act at the district and sub-divisional levels to over see the implementation of the Scheme. The Scheme for involving Voluntary Agencies has been prepared by the Ministry of Labour as per the aspirations of the 20-Point Programme 1986. This scheme envisages identification of bonded labour by Selected Voluntary Agencies in those states where the problem is acute. More concerted efforts are required on the part of the State Governments for satisfactory implementation of this Programme.

The over all position reveals that as on 31 November, 1987, 2,22,691 bonded labourers had been identified and released. Of these, 1, 93,002 were rehabilitated. As against a target to rehabilitation of 18,202 bonded labourers during 1987-88, 10,273 had been rehabilitated upto December, 1987.

Essential Facilities

Provision of safe drinking water to the entire rural population is envisaged in the Seventh Plan. Supply of drinking water is also included in the Minimum Needs Programme (MNP) in the state plans. Considering the magnitude of the problem and its overriding priority, a Centrally Sponsored Scheme—Accelerated Rural Water Supply Programme (ARWSP) was launched to supplement the efforts of the States/UTs. To help the process of providing adequate safe drinking water in the rural areas, a "Technology Mission on Drinking Water in villages and Related Water Management" was launched in August 1986, with a view to developing low cost solutions for providing adequate quantities of drinking water of acceptable quality in rural areas through the application of available scientific and technological inputs from various national laboratories and by promoting better water management.

The thrust of the Programme will be to provide drinking water facilities to the spill-over problem villages from the Sixth Plan, numbering 39,000 on a priority basis and to villages subsequently identified as problem villages as on 31st March, 1985, based on the criteria adopted during the Sixth Plan.

Once a water supply scheme is implemented in a village, it is of the utmost importance that adequate arrangements are made to ensure its proper maintenance so that the assets created continue to provide water to the target population without breakdown or fault in its designed capacity. In securing this objective it is essential to involve local communities through panchayats, cooperatives and other groups. The local communities would have to be assisted in maintaining the water supply sources in good condition through financial supports as well as technical training. A provision under M.N.P., to the maximum extent of 10 per cent of the M.N.P. outlays, has been allowed to the Plan to supplement the efforts on the non-plan side for the operation and maintenance of rural water supply systems. It has been reported that the one tier maintenance system with caretakers appointed at the Panchayat level has proved its efficacy in certain areas. Training of caretakers will have to be imparted under TRYSEM programme and they will have to be equipped with necessary tools and spare parts.

Medical Facilities

India is committed to attain "Health for all by 2000 AD." and population stabilisation by reaching "Net reproduction rate of unity". This has been reiterated in the country's National Health Policy adopted in 1983 and in the Seventh Five Year Plan.

In the over all health development programme, emphasis is laid on preventative and promotive aspects of Health Services and of organising effective and efficient services which are comprehensive in nature, freely accessible and generally affordable by the people. The major thrust areas are (i) Promotion of Primary Health Measures backed up by adequately strengthened infrastructure facilities. (ii) Close coordination with health related services and activities like nutrition, safe drinking water supply and sanitation, (iii) involving active participation of voluntary organisations. (iv) qualitative improvement in health and family planning services, (v) provision of essential drugs and vaccines. (vi) provision of adequate training and direction of medical research relevant to common health problems of the people.

Considerable emphasis has been laid on the control of communicable diseases and the augmentation of Maternity and Child Health services. Under the control of communicable diseases, the programmes include National Malaria Eradication, National Tuberculosis Control and the National Programme for Control of Blindness communicable diseases account for more than 2/3rd of the total morbidity and mortality in the country. For their control and eradication, the Primary Health Care system is being utilised for delivering comprehensive front-line care of better disease survival and control. In the case of National Leprosy Eradication of the main objective is to ensure early case detection and domiciliary treatment of cases along with health education. For the control in of blindness, intensive health education of "Eye Health Care" is given and eye-care services in rural areas are being extended through mobile units and the organisation of camps as well as the establishment of infrastructure of eye health care as an integral part of the general health services.

In establishing the above infrastructure a phasing pattern has been adopted to ensure even spreading of adequate and appropriate health service facilities. A network of sub-centres, Primary Health

Centres and Community Health Centres have been set up in the country.

Immunisation Programme : The Major causes of sickness and death of children in India are communicable diseases many of which are preventable by immunisation. To achieve this goal: a "Technology Mission on Immunisation" has been launched. The Mission covers all aspects commencing from research and development to actual delivery of services to the affected population in the fields, due to diptheria, tetanus, polio-myelitis, tuberculosis, measles and typhoid and to achieve self-sufficiency in vaccine production. The aim is to achieve 100 per cent coverage of pregnant women with two doses of tetanus-toxide vaccination and 80% of infants with the DPT, Polio, BCO and Measles, Vaccines by 1990. Two sub-missions have been set up, one for immunisation and vaccination and the other for production of vaccines and Research and Development on the new and improved vaccines. Till 1987-88, 182 districts and 106 medical colleges with larger catchment areas were covered. During 1988-89, 120 more districts had been identified and the rest of the districts were to be covered during 1989-90.

Sanitation : Lack of an adequate sanitation system is one of the factors affecting the quality of life of the rural population and the dignity and privacy of women. It has been reported that only 40 lakhs of rural population out of 56 crores were provided sanitation facilities till the end of Sixth Plan. The objective stated in the Seventh Plan is to cover 25% of the rural population with sanitation facilities in line with the objectives laid down for the "International Drinking Water and Sanitation Decade." Sanitation facilities are provided under the State Sector Minimum Needs Programme. Since January 1986, construction of sanitary latrines was taken up under NREP, RLEGP and the Indira Awaas Yojana. A Centrally Sponsored Rural Sanitation Programme was introduced in 1986-87 with the main objective of covering the Scheduled Castes/Tribes population below the poverty line and others. The funds under this scheme are subject to the condition of matching provision of the States under their Minimum Needs Progra-mme. A review of the programme indicates that the coverage of 25 per cent of the rural population would not be realised and the target may have to be reduced to 5 per cent. A review of the various programmes under rural sanitation is required to be undertaken to adopt a coordinated approach to this problem. Further steps should be taken to streamline the monitoring system for this scheme.

Rehabilitation of Handicapped Programme for the rehabilitation of the Handicapped include (i) Assistance to disabled persons for securing aids and appliances, (ii) Scholarships to disabled persons to pursue education, (iii) Assistance to voluntary organisations to promote education, training and rehabilitation of disabled persons and (iv) reservation of jobs for the handicapped in the public sector. To deal with the multi-dimensional problems of the handicapped population, institutions like the National Institute of Visually Handicapped (Dehradun), National Institute of Orthopaedically Handicapped (Dehradun), National Institute of Mentally Handicapped (Hyderabad), Aliyavar Jung National Institute for the Hearing Handicapped (Mumbai) have been set up. To improve the quality of life of handicapped persons of all categories and to enable them to have access to the fruits of modern technology and with a view to develop aids and appliances which are cost effective and are suitable to Indian conditions. A Technology Development Project in the Mission Mode has been established by the Ministry of Welfare. With a view to enable placement of handicapped, special employment exchanges and special cells in normal employment exchanges for the handicapped have been set up. The National Policy on Education also stresses the need for education of the handicapped in normal schools and the establishment of special schools for the severely handicapped.

Family Welfare

The importance of the Family Welfare Programme in our socio-economic development plans is well established and the promotion of responsible parenthood in its broad perspective is essential to the success of the concept of a "Two Child Norm". Family Planning Services are offered through the total health care delivery system. People's participation is sought through all institutions voluntary agencies, opinion leaders, people's representatives and Government functionaries. The policies and programmes initiated in the Seventh Plan aim at achieving a birth rate of 27 per thousand population, death rate of about 10 per thousand population, and a "Couple Protection Rate" of 42 per cent by 1989-90. The family welfare strategy includes health, child survival, women's status and employment, literacy, education and socio-economic development. It seeks to streamline the entire spectrum of Programme management, adopt a multi-disciplinary and integrated network of all relevant developmental agencies and escalate the Programme in to a genuine voluntary people's movement.

The Seventh Five Year Plan envisaged a target of 31 million sterilisations, 21.25 million IUD insertions in the five year period and increasing the annual number of CC/OP Users to 14.50 million in the last year of the Plan. The number of acceptors of all methods of family planning increased to 20.43 million during 1986-87. An achievement of 5.03 million sterilisations, 3.94 million IUD insertions and 11.60 million CC/OP Users was reported in the year 1986-87. While there was a shortfall achievement against the target of sterilisation, the achievement against targets of IUD and CC/OP users were slightly higher. The Maternity and Child Health (MCH) programme has been geared up to achieve the objective of reducing infant mortality rate to below 60 by 2000 A.D.

Integrated Child Development Services (ICDS Projects) : To ensure proper physical, psychological and social development of infant and pre-school children an integrated package of health, nutrition and educational services is provided through the ICDS. The beneficiaries of ICDS are children below 6 years of age, pregnant women and lactating mothers. In the location of Integrated Child Development Services (ICDS) Projects, priority is given to tribal development blocks, rural blocks having a substantial scheduled castes population, drought prone areas, other backward rural areas and slums in large cities.

The focal point for the delivery of the services is the "Anganwadi" (Child Care Centre) which is manned by an honorary worker. One 'Anganwadi' generally caters to a population of about 1000 in a Rural/Urban area and 700 in tribal areas. During 1989-90, the progressive total of centrally sponsored and state sector ICDS projects came to 2286 and 202 respectively i.e. a total of 2438.

Schools for Children

The National Policy on education 1986 envisages a National System of Education and seeks to provide all students, irrespective of caste, creed, location or sex, access to education of comparable quality. The most important measure for achieving the goal is the achievement of universal elementary education for all children upto 14 years of age, 3 goals which has been enshrined in our Constitution as one of the Directive Principles of State Policy. Another major objective is to reorient the contents and process of education at all levels to raise its standards and to make education a key instrument of social transformation, modernisation and economic growth as well as a powerful tool for inculcating social, moral and cultural values. The national policy on Education further enjoins on the entire nation to pledge itself to the eradication of illiteracy particularly in the 15 to 35 age group. It also aims at making the programme of literacy meaningful by combining it with practical information and skills relevant to the day-to-day needs of the learners.

The objectives stated above are to be achieved through an array of strategies including combination of formal and non-formal methods, educational technology, teacher-training, the improvement of physical resources and involvement of the community. The major programmes already initiated in this regard are: (a) Every habitation with a population of 3000 (200 in hilly, desert and tribal areas) above will have a primary school; (b) Enrolment Drive will be launched to achieve the enrolment target, (c) A comprehensive system of incentive and support services will be provided for girls and children of economically weaker sections of society and scheduled castes/scheduled tribes; (d) For school drop-outs and unenrolled and working Children, a system of non-formal education will be organised with flexibility with a relevant curriculum and diversity, learning activities; (e) Operation Black Board has been launched ensure provision of minimum essential facilities as well as learning equipment, minimum essential accommodation and at least two teachers in every school and (f) The programme of in-service teacher training has been intensified.

The core curriculum at school stages would include those

contents essential for nurturing national identity. A mass programme for functional literacy has been launched involving students in the National Service Scheme, National Cadet Corps and non-student youth in Nehru Yuva Kendras. The existing programme of Rural Functional Literacy will be reoriented by introducing greater use of spoken languages, better method of training of functionaries, increasing the number of women instructors and continuing linkage with post literacy and continuing education. Jana Shikshan Nilayams will be established for providing continuing education to neo-literates and school drop-outs and for retention of literacy skills to enable them to apply their learning to improve their living standards. Shramik Vidya Peeths will be strengthened to improve occupation skills and technical knowledge.

A 'Technology Mission for Eradication of Illiteracy' (National Literacy Mission) has been launched with the support of all available technologies and improved pedagogical inputs to make the teaching learning process more effective, quicker and easier and to promote a more attractive learning environment.

Welfare of the Weaker Sections

The Scheduled Castes population accounts for 16 per cent of the total population and they suffer from social discrimination as well as economic deprivation. The Scheduled Tribes population accounts for 8 per cent of the total population and though they are at various stages of socio-economic progress, they face handicaps on account of isolation. The major goals of growth and development of the country are to remove the handicaps and impediments to the advancement of Scheduled Castes and Scheduled Tribes so as to bring them at par with the rest of the society. Special provisions have, therefore, been made in the Constitution to safeguard their interests and secure socio-economic justice to them.

The Protection of Civil Rights Act, 1955 provides for punishment for preaching and practising untouchability. Various State Governments have set-up legal aid schemes for the victims of untouchability, appointed Prosecuting Officers and created Special Police Cells/Squads for exercising supervision over prosecutions for the contravention of the provisions of the Act;

special courts and special mobile courts have been set up 'for speedy trial of untouchability offences; identifications of untouchability prone areas have been undertaken; encouragement is provided for inter-caste marriages and awards have been instituted for this purpose. Publicity and other measures for removal of untouchability have also been undertaken. Committees with official and non-official members have been set up in 18 States/UTs to review/supervise the working and implementation of the PCR Act.

The Education Policy 1986 makes a specific mention for remedial coaching at all stages of school education and special coaching for classes 9-11 for preparing the SC/STs children for professional courses.

The Centrally Sponsored Scheme of post-matric scholarships to Scheduled Castes and Scheduled Tribes enables a considerable number of them to go into the fields of higher education. Under this scheme, hundred per cent Central Assistance is provided to States/UTs. The Scheme has two components, namely, (i) Maintenance Allowance and (ii) Reimbursement of Compulsory non-refundable fees. A high-level official Committee reviews the working of this Scheme.

Pre-matric scholarships for children of those engaged in unclean occupations, namely, scavengers, tanners and flayers are also in operation.

Central Assistance is also provided on 50:50 basis to State/UTs for construction of hostel buildings with the object of providing hostel facilities to Scheduled Castes girls studying in middle, high school, higher secondary institutions, colleges and universities.

To improve the representation of SCs and STs in various posts and services under the Central/State Governments and public sector undertakings, pre-examination coaching centres for SCs/STs have been set up in the various parts of the country, the objective being that this would enable them to secure the full benefits of quotas reserved for them in the various services.

There are 21 Scheduled Castes Development Corporations in the country which work as an interface between the SC families and financial institutions in respect of bankable schemes. They function as guarantors/promoter and act as catalysts by providing missing inputs by way of contributing margin money.

Socio-economic programmes for the development of Scheduled Castes envisage the strategy of using a Special Component Plan for 20 states and 4 UTs which have a relatively large Scheduled Castes population. The Special Component Plan for Scheduled Castes is not linked to any specific scheme and it is for the totality of the State's effort for the furtherance, especially, economic development of the Scheduled Castes. The objective is to give thrust to programmes like Animal Husbandry, Agriculture and Village and Cottage Industries. This grant is meant to supplement a much larger flow of funds earmarked from the State Plans. 50 per cent of the Special Central Assistance is distributed to States/UTs on the basis of SC population and relative backwardness and 50 per cent on effort-based criteria.

For the "Liberation of Scavengers Programme," conversion of existing dry latrines into low-cost 'pour flush' latrines and schemes for providing alternative employment to the unemployed scavengers are undertaken. Under this Programme, financial assistance is given to the State Governments on the basis of a 'Whole Town' approach. So far work in 116 selected towns in various States had been undertaken and of these, 25 towns had been made scavenger free and 4000 unemployed scavengers had been rehabilitated in alternative employment upto March, 1987. The then Prime Minister had also addressed letters to all the Chief Ministers and Central Ministers in February, 1987 emphasizing the need for giving high priority to this programme. Central assistance is also extended for low-cost sanitation schemes under the Centrally Sponsored Programme of Integrated Development of Small and Medium Towns. The Housing and Urban Development Corporation (HUDCO) also extends finance to the extent of 50 per cent of low cost latrine projects.

The Tribal Sub-plan is in operation in 17 states and 2 U.T.s. This, however, does not cover the tribal majority states and UTs of Arunachal Pradesh, Meghalaya, Mizoram, Nagaland, Lakshadweep and Dadra and Nagar Haveli as the respective state/UT Plans are already for a majority tribal population. The Tribal Sub-plan approach covers 184 integrated Tribal Development projects, 284 pockets of tribal concentration and 73 primitive tribal group projects. The five sources of financing Tribal sub-plan programmes are: (i) Flow of funds from State Plans; (ii) Flow from central Sponsored Scheme; (iii) Special Central Sponsored Scheme; (iv) Special Central Assistance; and (v) Institutional Finance. For the development of Scheduled Tribes, the three centrally sponsored Programmes are: (i) construction of hostels for tribal girls; (ii) research and training; and (iii) Aid to voluntary organisations. A Central Tribal Research Advisory Council has been set up by the Ministry of Welfare under the Chairmanship of the Deputy Minister, Ministry of Welfare. A Tribal Cooperative Marketing Federation of India (TRIFED) has been registered to improve marketing of tribal produce, to eliminate intermediaries and to obtain better value for tribal produce so as to augment the incomes of tribal families.

The Bureau of Public Enterprises has issued guidelines which inter-alia, require measures to be taken for the proper rehabilitation of tribals displaced by major projects. A committee under the Chairmanship of the Deputy Minister in the Ministry of Welfare reviews the progress in this regard.

Women Welfare

The major thrust of the programmes of Women's Development concentrates on the economic and social status of women in the country. The basic approach is to make them economically independent and self-reliant so that 'equality of status' for women is ensured. This would help in achieving the goal of integrating them into the mainstream of development as equal partners along with men. The programmes for securing equality for women focus their attention of creating awareness amongst women themselves of their rights, role and status in society, generating mass consciousness in the society about their being equal partners and contributors in all endeavours and on securing their educational advancement and economic independence.

The lower status of women in India compared to that of men is reflected in various socio-economic indicators like an adverse sex ratio, lower female life expectancy, high female infant mortality rate, low female literacy rate, poor enrolment, high drop out rates of girls, lower female work participation rates, low-access to existing and emerging technologies, vulnerability to violence, social disabilities, etc. This requires continuous and coordinated efforts on the part of the various governmental and non-governmental organisations in areas of health, education, vocational training, employment, legislation etc. In order to assess the overall impact of various government efforts in raising the status of women, various beneficially oriented programmes, exclusively meant for women, are being monitored on a half yearly basis.

A National Commission of Self-employed Women was set up in January 1987 to examine the constraints of women workers, in the unorganised sector and to suggest measures for their integration in the national development process. The Dowry Prohibition Act was amended in September 1986 to make the provisions therein more stringent and effective. A new criminal offence of "Dowry Death" has been incorporated in the Indian Penal Code. The "Immoral Traffic Act' 1986 rectifies the existing inadequacies and makes its provisions more stringent so that the problem of immoral traffic amongst human beings could be dealt with effectively in all its dimensions. A new legislation namely "Indecent Representation of Women (Prohibition) Act, 1986 has also been passed.

To enhance awareness and to create mass consciousness of women's problems and rights, a programme of educative publicity has been launched through seminars, workshops, debates, exhibitions, films and other means of mass media.

The Central Social Welfare Board has evolved various programmes for sustaining the growth of voluntary organisations for taking up a variety of welfare programmes concerned with children and women. Hostels for working women, women's training centres, institutes for rehabilitation of women in distress, shot-stay homes for women and girls are also being set up to meet their specific needs.

Programmes designed to improve the training and employment for women include Condensed Course of Education for Adult Women and Vocational Training, support to Training and Employment Programmes for Women (STEP), setting up of Women's Development Corporations in the States, Training-cum-

Employment and Income Generating Production Centres, etc. Representation of women at the decision making advisory levels in public and official bodies, agencies and organisations is being encouraged as their involvement is crucial in ensuring their equal participation in nation building.

Youth Welfare

About 32 percent of our population are in the age group of 15-35 years and they constitute a vital and vibrant human resource of the nation. Further, as per the 1981 census, 73 per cent of our youth population of 221 million lives in rural areas. An integrated strategy for harmonious development of youth for meeting the national aspirations has been adopted. Efforts are made to create in them an awareness of their potential and social responsibility, creating conditions conducive to their participation in the development process and to involve voluntary organisations effectively in youth work and to give recognition to outstanding performance of young persons in different endeavours.

Character building and promotion of physical fitness has been made an integral part of the youth programmes. The National Policy on Education, 1986 envisages that sports and physical education are an integral part of the learning process with emphasis on building a nation-wide infrastructure for physical education, sports and games consisting of play fields, equipment, coaches and teachers of physical education as part of a skill improvement programmes. Special thrust has been given to the teacher training programmes in physical education and in promotion of mass participation of students in physical education and sports programmes.

National Service Scheme (NSS) with the objective of "Service to the Community" is under implementation through universities and colleges. It renders useful service to the community as well as develops the personality of students. NSS undertakes activities like environment enrichment and conservation, health and family welfare, social service in welfare institutions, non-formal and adult education, functional literacy programmes, etc. During 1986-87, special camps of NSS for cleaning of the Ganges and waste lands development were also undertaken. Every year 12th to 19th January is observed as a National Youth week and 15th January as "NSS Day". The scheme which was started in 1969-70 with a coverage of 40,000 students, had increased to 9.35 lakhs during 1988-89.

The programme of Nehru Yuva Kendras (NYK) was started in 1972 with the object of serving the interests of non-students youth, mainly in the rural areas. District level NYKs are established as constituent units. The total number of NYKs in the country is 401. It is envisaged that all districts in the country would be covered by Nehru Yuva Kendras by the end of the Seventh Plan. The responsibility of running the programme has been given to an autonomous organisation called Nehru Yuva Kendra Sangathan. The strategy of NYKs has been to generate awareness, organise and mobilise rural youth for development work in the villages with emphasis on values, vision and voluntary action. In terms of organisation at grassroots level, the goal has been to inspire youth to form village level voluntary action of groups of youth. An estimated two lakh villages have been covered so far. The target is to cover all 5.7 lakhs villages in a couple of years.

The National Cadet Corps (NCC) develops leadership and character amongst the youth and creates a force of disciplined and trained manpower which would render assistance in times of need. Training through adventure is a very important facet of the NCC Programme and this enables the cadets to overcome fear and develop self-confidence and leadership. Parasailing mountaineering, tracking, sailing expeditions and cycle/moped expeditions are organised for the NCC cadets.

The Government of India adopted a National Sports Policy in 1984 which has imparted a new thrust to sports activities in the country. Priorities have been accorded to the provision of infrastructure for sports and games both in towns and villages, identification of talent, etc.

The National Service Volunteer Scheme (NSVS) started in 1977-78, provides opportunities to young people, generally those who have completed their first degree course, to involve themselves on a voluntary basis in nation building activities for a specific period and on a whole-time basis. It seeks to provide young people avenues for doing constructive work suited to their educational background and aptitude during the inter-regnum between their leaving studies and entering the world of work. National Service Volunteers are deployed to work with NYKs, NSS units, etc.

Financial assistance is given to voluntary agencies engaged in youth work. With a view to giving recognition to the outstanding work done by young persons and voluntary youth organisations for national development and/or social service, the National Youth Award Scheme was launched from 1985. Under this Scheme upto 50 awards are given each year for achieving excellence in different fields of social service or national development. With a view to encouraging voluntary efforts at the grass-roots level in building a healthy society contributing to national development, assistance is provided to Youth Clubs for activities like library and reading facilities, sports activities, cultural programmes etc.

National Integration Camps and Inter-state visits of young persons are organised for promoting national integration and for inculcation of secularism among youth. NYKs universities and voluntary organisations are provided financial assistance for organising such camps. Efforts are made to provide opportunities to persons belonging to SCs and STs, minorities, those in the border areas and disadvantaged youth to participate in these camps. Seminars on various themes of National Integration are also organised. To bring about general awareness about the customs, traditions and ways of life of people under different parts of the country and promoting increasing understanding among the youth, exhibitions for youth are being organised from 1985-86. To ensure that the exhibitions actually create an impact on the public at large, the agencies entrusted with the task of organising exhibitions are advised to hold these exhibitions at the time of local festivals, fairs, cattle fairs, etc.

Settlement of Poor

At the beginning of the Seventh Plan it had been estimated that the shortage of housing was 24.7 million units (18.8 million in rural areas and 5.9 million in urban areas). During 1985-90, 16.2 million units (12.4 million in rural areas and 3.8 million in urban areas) were programmed to be constructed. The aim is to step up the ongoing programmes of allotment of house-sites and provision of construction assistance to landless families, increasing the pace of construction of houses for Economically Weaker Sections and Low Income Groups, raising the availability of finance for house construction through banks etc. and intensifying research with a view to developing low cost building material and technologies.

As per the recommendations of the UN Commission of Human Settlements, the first Monday of October every year has been designated as the "World Habitat Day". This day is reminder to all 10 make positive efforts to provide shelter to the needy. In India, it is estimated that around 2.3 million people, living both in rural and urban areas have no shelter. Further a sizeable number of families become homeless every year due to natural calamities such as cyclones, floods, land-slides, etc.

In order to meet the particular requirements of the poorer sections belonging largely to Scheduled Castes and Scheduled Tribes, the Indira Awass Yojana has been launched from 1985-86 under RLEGP for the construction of houses and micro-habitants for them. The target is to construct 1 million houses during the Seventh Plan period. The outlays for rural house-sites and construction assistance are provided in the State Plans and these are covered under the Minimum Needs Programme.

Reforming Living Conditions

In the formulation of the strategy for urban development, improvement of slums has acquired a special place. As a long term measure, planned house building with particular focus on meeting the needs of the poor sections of society alone holds the key for curbing the twin problems of squating and proliferation of slums. The development of small and medium towns as well as big towns in the vicinity of large metropolises in regarded as an instrument for retarding migration to large towns. Reservation of sufficient land, for provision of affordable shelter in the form of "Sites and Service" and "Core Housing" are important elements of this strategy. There is a centrally sponsored scheme providing matching assistance to the State/UTs for strengthening the infrastructural facilities and civic amenities in selected small towns. In the short-term, the only practical way of ameliorating the sub-human living conditions in slum areas is to improve their environment by, providing basic amenities. The scheme of Environment Improvement of Urban Slums (EIUS) is being implemented under the Minimum Needs Programme. It envisages provision of a package of basic service for removal of the unhygenic environment prevalent in the slums and for the provision of minimum civic facilities to the slum dwellers, namely; drinking water, community bathrooms and latrines, street lighting, open sewers, storm water drains and street paving. The cost of providing these services has been revised to Rs. 300/per capita during the Seventh Plan. The scale of services provided, varies from state to state. The guidelines do not, however specify the facility of services to be provided. A proper mechanism should be evolved for ensuring qualitative assessment of the work, done by the state authorities in improving the slums. For this purpose, field visit should be intensified and improvement brought about in the system of reporting progress.

Protected Forests

Against the target set out by the National Forest Policy of bringing one-third of the geographical area of the country under forest, only 23 per cent is classified as forests. Since a large, part of the area classified as forests does not actually have proper tree cover, the actual area under forests is much smaller. Estimates made by the National Remote Sensing Agency during the 1980-82 mapping cycle estimate the area under forests to a mere 46 million hectares and an alarming rate of loss of forest cover at 1.5 million hectares annually. The focus on the forestry, should therefore be one of involving a massive afforestation drive though co-operation of the public. The programmes involved include social forestry farm forestry, reclamation of wastelands, plantation of appropriate vegetation in hills, deserts and coastal areas. This programme takes full note of the welfare of tribal and other community, traditionally dependent upon forest.

There are afforestation programmes in the State Sector including the externally assisted social forestry projects in several states as well as the centrally assisted schemes of the National Wastelands Development Board. This Board was set up in May 1985 with the major objectives of formulating consistent and coordinated policies for massive afforestation with special emphasis on fuel-wood; fodder and the involvement of people in afforestation of wastelands. Recognising the role that voluntary agencies and NGOs can play in this area, grants-in-aid are provided to voluntary agencies. The assistance is mainly given for activities connected with afforestation such as nursery raising and for evaluation studies.

A scheme of decentralised nurseries is in existence since 1985-86 wherein involvement of people has been encouraged. The scheme involves setting up village, level nurseries from 0.125 acre to 0.25 acre, each producing 25,000 to 50,000 seedings annually to progressively replace departmental nurseries. The "Nursery Men" will be small farmers, schools women's groups, voluntary agencies, and co-operatives. In 1986-87, 22.10 crores seedings were raised and the target, for 1987-88 was of 28.70 crores. The "Tree Pattas Scheme" has also been introduced in a number of states. A scheme of "Indira Priydarshini Vriksha Mitra Awards" has also been' instituted to encourage afforestation programmes.

In order to promote integration of various afforestation programmes and to increase the forestry component in rural development programmes, funds for forestry under the NREP and RLEGP, have been earmarked to the extent of 25 per cent. One of the important elements under the afforestation programmes is that of survival of trees/saplings. A survey to assess the survival rate of trees/saplings is being organised by the National Wastelands Development Board.

Pollution Control

The main thrust in the field of environment, initiated in the Seventh Plan include environment protection and conservation; education and awareness; pollution control; environmental impact assessment; ecological research; organisational and regulatory measures for hazardous substances. Ganga Action Plan, etc. As environment is all pervasive, its protection requires deep involvement of the people at all levels and public awareness of the dangers of environmental degradation is of the utmost importance.

Necessary institutional mechanism are being evolved to ensure the implementation of the Environment (Protection) Act; 1986, which came into force from 19th November, 1986. Environmental education and training programmes have been taken up particularly development of educational kits, setting up of environmental clubs, all India essay competitions on environment education and National Environment Awareness Campaign.

Through active State intervention, the interests of the consumers in regard to availability, quality, weight and price of goods are protected. Supply of essential consumer goods, in rural and urban areas, at reasonable prices and on a reliable and regular basis is to be assured particularly for the weaker sections of society. Standardisation and quality control is being extended to increasingly cover more items of daily consumption. The Public Distribution System has to play an active role in making available essential commodities. Consumers should be fully involved in the distribution of essential commodities. People's participation has to be ensured through formation of Consumer Advisory vigilance Committees at all levels.

In December, 1986, the Consumer Protection Act, 1986 was passed, which envisages setting up of a Central Consumer Protection, Council and State. Consumer Protection Councils as well as estblishment of consumer Disputes 'Redressal Agencies'. Many states have set up State Consumer Protection Councils. The Act is an important step in the history of the consumer movement in the country.

With a view to encouraging youth in the consumer movement, a 'National Youth Award for Consumer Protection has been instituted. Consumer awareness, campaigns are launched through publicity media, as well as through publication of brochures and pamphlets for consumer education.

To bring about quality control, testing facilities of the Bureau of Indian Standards are being expanded. Enforcement of important consumer protection laws such as the Essential Commodities Act. Prevention of Food Adulteration Act. Standards of Weights and Measures Act are being closely monitored to ensure their implementation. The Department of Civil Supplies closely monitors the availability of essential commodities at reasonable prices.

Sources of Energy

The backwardness of our villages is characterised by low levels of availability of energy for productive purposes. Supply of energy in the form of electricity, biogas and other non-conventional energy sources have become an imperative need to prevent large scale deforestation, electrification of villages and energisation of pump-sets also form part of the minimum needs programme. The Seventh Plan envisaged electrification of 1.18 lakh villages out of 2.07 lakh villages which is to be electrified at the beginning of the Plan. It is also to energise 23.9 lakh pump sets out of a balance of the beginning of the Seventh Plan. During 1986-87,21 villages were electrified against the target of 21.6 thousand villages were electrified against the target of 21.6 thousand and 5 lakh pump sets were energised against a target of 3.9 lakhs. While the overall performance was in excess of the target there was shortfall in States like Assam. Bihar, Gujarat, Jammu and Kashmir. Meghalaya and West Bengal. The main reasons attributed are inadequate transmission systems and unwillingness of farmers to go in for pumpsets because of poor electric supply and consequent dependence on portable diesel pumpsets. The National Project for Biogas Development (NPBD) caters to family type biogas plants. It is estimated that the total potential for family size biogas plants in the country is about 16 million and that the total number of plants set up so far is about 8 lakhs. The Seventh Plan target is 7.5 lakhs against Sixth Plan achievement of 3.6 lakhs. The Biogas programme has multiple benefits and helps in improving rural sanitation and environmental hygiene. Setting up such plants also reduces ecological disturbances and deforestation.

There is a National Programme for Improved Chullhas for providing domestic cooking energy. This is part of the Minimum Needs Programme. The Programme consists of providing subsidy for promotion of different models of fixed and portable chullhas. This programme has an impact in improving the health and sanitation in rural households as well as on the conservation of fire wood. The potential is estimated at 150 million improved chullhas in the country and only about 3 millions have been covered so far.

During the sixth plan period Integrated Rural Energy Planning Programme (IREP) was started on a pilot basis in 20 blocks in eight States. This programme involves developing planning capability in the States and UTs for preparing and implementing area based integrated rural energy plans and projects through which the optimum mix of all types of energy sources, conventional and non-conventional, would be provided to the rural areas for improving diverse energy needs for domestic purposes as well as productive activities. From 1986-87 a Centrally Sponsored Scheme has been started with provision of Central assistance for development of this capability in the States and UTs. The target for 1987-88 was 38 Blocks. It is proposed to establish 100 IRDP blocks by the end of Seventh Plan.

The Authorities

To bring about an optimal productivity of output at various administrative levels and to eliminate harassment to the public, the role of a responsive, understanding and helpful administration becomes important. To achieve this objective Action Plans at different administrative levels are being drawn up incorporating in specific terms, steps to be taken for making the administration result-oriented and responsive. Machinery has been created at various levels for prompt redressal of public grievances and special emphasis has been given to the simplification of procedure in various ministries of the Central Government and also in the States.

To bring about decentralisation in decision making, delegation of powers has been reviewed and further liberalised. For enforcement of accountability, the major steps taken include: (a) preparation of Action Plans and monitoring the implementation of these Plans on a monthly/quarterly basis, (b) fixation of levels for taking decisions in various categories of cases and the channel of their submission and (c) revision of the format of Annual Confidential Reports to provide for objective appraisal of the performance of the Officer reported upon.

The State Governments are also actively involved in making their administration responsive to public needs and many State Governments have adopted/extended the system of 'Single

Window Clearance' (Ahmedanagar experiment). These various measures are expected to bring about a more sympathetic and helpful interaction between the Government and the public.

Poverty in Towns

India has witnessed population explosion after independence. During the past four decades the total population of the country had doubled from 350 million in 1947 to 800 million in 1980. During the same period, the urban population had increased four-fold from 50 million to 200 million. By the turn of the century total population crossed 1000 million and urban population 350 million. Though there are many challenges posed by urbanisation trends, the most demanding of them is urban poverty.

According to official estimates approximate 27.7 percent of the urban population lived below the poverty line in 1987-88; it meant at least 5.7 crore people or more than one out of every four urban citizens. The National Commission on Urbanisation has drawn pointed attention to the most brutal and inhuman living conditions in urban areas with large sections of people living in squatter settlements. According to a study conducted by National Institute of Urban Affairs 68 per cent of the urban poor were women and children. If one added to this the aged and the disabled, the customary perception of the urban poor changes. More recently, this aspect has been forcefully brought out by a distinguished authority on human settlements from Argentina, Mr. Jorge E. Hardoy in one of the publications of the International Child Development Centre of UNICEF based in Florence (Italy). According to him, the most vulnerable urban group in future will be children. Tens of millions of children will be struggling to survive alone or with their families unless a massive effort is launched to create conditions that substantially reduce the number of house-holds leading lives of deprivation, without stable or adequate income without access to the most indispensable services and constantly facing fear as urban violence grows.

The UNICEF expert says: " The future cities of the third World will be very different from the cities we know. They will be different not only in size and population but also on account of their age and labour structures. These will be cities of adolescents and children. Many will work before the minimum age established by law because their incomes are crucial for their families and for their own survival. Most will not complete primary school even though completing school is a family aspiration. Many will die young or live in poor health and will abandon their homes and live on their own on the city streets threatened by violence and the process of de-humanisation. Different values and codes resulting from poverty and unemployment, combined with the massive presence of children and adolescent and of households headed by single woman, will give rise to a mixture of aggressiveness and solidarity of expectations and frustrations".

The signs of what Mr. Hardoy has observed are already visible in Indian cites. The phenomenon of urban poverty has altered the landscape, the social fabric and overall character of Indian cities.

Policies and Programmes for Urban Poverty Alleviation : Poverty removal, as a dominant objective in India's development strategy appeared initially in the Fifth Five Year Plan (1974-79). It recognised the existence of large-scale poverty in India and observe that, despite the sizeable gains of economic development and improvement of living standards over the two decades of planning, large numbers have remained poor. The Fifth Plan however, made no distinction between rural and urban poverty. It was the Sixth Five Year Plan (1980-85) which marked, in a sense, the commencement of a definite approach to poverty issues. It approached the problem in three stages: (a) Identification and measurement, (b) Developing realistic targets, and (c) formulation of specific programmes. Like the preceding Five Year Plan, the Sixth Plan also did not directly address urban poverty issues. The Sixth Plan, however, did provide for moving nearly 61 lakhs of the total urban poor above the poverty line, essentially through the provision of Additional consumption benefits' and better and more equitable distribution of health, education, sanitation, housing and drinking water, and slum upgrading, and environmental improvement programmes. The Seventh Five Year Plan (1985-90) constitutes the first conscious attempt to address urban poverty issues directly. It takes explicit note of the growing incidence of poverty in urban area and points out that the persistent migration from rural areas had led, on the one hand, to rapid growth of slums in many cities and towns, and, on the, other hand to over crowding in relatively unskilled and low-paid jobs in the informal sector. The Seventh Plan accordingly places considerable emphasis on improvement in the living conditions of slum dwellers. It further notes that, in order to be effective, the problem of urban poverty would require a major thrust towards employment generation and creation of productive jobs. In line with this major thrust, the Seventh Plan has proposed a strategy that includes provision of gainful employment to the unemployed, particularly women and youth, raising the earnings of those in low-paid jobs, stepping up the productivity and earnings of self-employed workers, and improving the access of the urban poor to basic amenities such as education, health care, sanitation and safe drinking water.

The National Commission on Urbanisation has examined the available evidence on the impact of the various programmes-centrally sponsored, state sponsored and locally initiated. It has also reviewed some of the programmes in the field. The results are mixed but the overall conclusions are: the reach of the programmes is limited; there is a high degree of inflexibility; there is a lack of convergence of programmes; even the main targets are often missed; and barring the Hyderabad/Vizag UCD Projects, the programmes are still working on a laboratory scale. At the same time the Commission is aware of the highly effective and innovative programmes in some cities such as the Sites and Slum Improvement Projects in Chennai the Small Loan Programme and Community Health Scheme of the Kolkatta Metropolitan Development Authority; the Urban Community Development Projects in Hyderabad and Visakhapatnam the Low Cost Sanitation-Schemes in Patna and other cities.

The major programmes for amelioration of the conditions of the urban poor may be discussed as follows:

Shelter-related Programme : Among the shelter related programmes; slum eradication had featured as a key approach during the First and Second Plans. In view of resource limitations, resistance of local populations, to shifting and maintenance failures, the approach was abandoned in favour of Slum Improvement and Sites and Services Schemes. About 15.3 lakh slum dwellers are believed to have benefited already under the "slum improvement scheme. The Seventh Plan aims at securing coverage of about 90 lakhs slum dwellers.

The Economically Weaker Sections (EWS) Housing Programme had succeeded in construction of 65,432 shelter units in the public sector during the Sixth Plan period (1980-85). The National, buildings organisation has estimated that, as on March 1981, about 24 lakhs units were needed for houseless, who should be given first priority, while about 31 lakhs units were needed for those who live in Kutcha units. Besides, the urban poor are concentrated in bastees and chawls and whole families of 6-7 persons live in congested, one room tenements. The congestion is increasing owing to growing impoverishment, immigration, and population growth from within. Thus, even though the public policy response to the housing needs of the urban poor has improved, it cannot meet more that 10 per cent of the backlog.

Nutrition Supplement Programmes : Programmes of nutrition have been significantly expanded in the Seventh Plan. The Special Nutrition Programmes (SNR) and Mid day Meal (MDM) are proposed to be integrated with Integrated Child Development Scheme (ICDS). The expected coverage of beneficiaries is likely to be 1.1 core children and pregnant mothers under SNP and about 50 lakhs children under MDM by the end of 1990.

The public distribution system also aims at providing a balanced diet at reasonable prices in the endemically poverty stricken malnourished and under-nourished parts of the country. Even this limited concept of public distribution is not realised in practice. A review of the literature shows that off take from the public distribution system is greater in urban areas than in rural areas in per capita terms. Andhra Pradesh has used its public distribution system both extensively and intensively to distribute about 5 kg. of rice per capita per month to an individual family, subject to a ceiling of 25 kg. along with other essential goods such as sugar, wheat, palm oil (upto a ceiling of 2 kg.) coarse cloth, kerosene, etc. A review of case studies of the public distribution system of Andhra Pradesh shows that the urban poor families meet about 40 per cent of their needs from the public distribution system.

Child Development : Among the general programmes of child development, the spread of free education has certainly brought benefits nearer to the urban poor. However, owing to economic and social conditions, the school drop-out rate is higher among the urban poor than the rest of the urban population. Health services have improved in pilot project areas, thanks to intensive efforts of Integrated Child Development Scheme (ICDS); Urban Basic Services (UBS) and Urban Community Development (UCD) projects, but these have still not approached national coverage.

Employment Generation and Employment-oriented Training Programmes : Recently the Government of India have started a Self-employment Programme for the Urban Poor (SEPUP) by earmarking a sum of Rs. 200 crores to be distributed to poor urban entrepreneurs whose income does not exceed Rs. 600 per month. The maximum credit available is Rs. 5000. The list of economic activities for which loans are available contains 35 items covering activities like hawking on hand cart, laundering, welding, cycle rickshaw operation, shoe making, hairdressing etc.

Participatory Programmes : Urban Community Development (UCD) was started as a pilot project as early as 1959. However, only very few pilot projects survived. In 1981, the Urban Community Development, Low Cost Sanitation and Small and Middle Town Development Projects supported by UNICEF were merged into a new service called Urban Basic Services (UBS). Its aim is to promote citizen participation, strengthen the service capabilities of the local bodies in working with people on commonly felt needs, bring about convergence of services and coordinate resources of various agencies for the purpose.

Indian policy-makers have not been unaware of the problems of urban poverty but according to NCU, their response has been generally unimaginative, inadequate, half hearted and narrowly sectoral. The urban poors are usually equated with slum dwellers. Housing is perceived to be the slum dweller's main problem. Till recently, providing pucca houses was perceived as the solution (until the money ran out and it was realised that, in the numbers game, there was no chance of winning). Recent new responses like Sites and Services Slum Improvement, Urban Community Development Projects (UCD), Integrated Child Development Services (ICDS), Basic Services Approach, Mid day Meal Scheme for the school children and Small and Medium Towns Development Programme, reflect a relatively better assessment of the situation, a more realistic attitude to resource constraints, and probably a new awareness of social responsibility. However, most of these programmes are at their early, experimental stage covering not even a small fraction of the people they are meant to benefit. Many are floundering in implementation, and some are already showing signs of malfunction. However, these approaches certainly merit proper trial, careful monitoring and evaluation, followed by redesign and strengthening as may be seen to be necessary. Nevertheless, considering the scale, complexity and gravity of the urban poverty situation and threat it poses to the social fabric and economic well-being of our cities, these measures are woefully inadequate and more effective measures will have to be sought if alleviation of urban poverty is to be achieved within reasonable time span.

Suggestions for Improving the Lot of the Urban Poor : According to the National Commission on Urbanisation bold, intensive and coordinated efforts are needed to improve the income and consumption level of the bottom 30 per cent of our population to extend their access to basic environmental and social services, and to ensure their better utilisation and for this purpose it has suggested a thirteen-point programme package for implementation which comprises: (i) National Programme of employment training for urban poor youth; (ii) National Programme of credit support for expanding micro-enterprises and technological upgradation; (iii) Micro enterprise infrastructure development support (marketing and production centres); (iv) Marketing development supports; (v) New Programmes of public assets creation for promoting wage employment for the urban poor; (vi) Universalisation of Urban Community Development (UCD) and Urban Basic Services (UBS) activities; (vii) Educational support for extension of family planning and maternal and child health services; (viii) Intensification of non-formal education for school drop-outs and working women; and (ix) Slum Improvement shelter upgradation, sites and services schemes, land supply, tenurial security and facilitation through participatory approaches and NGO involvement; (x) Extension of public distribution system; (xi) Extension of the family security programme; (xii) Support for innovative programmes of voluntary agencies; (xiii) Support for training and action research in urban poverty.

Administrative Set up : Urban poverty removal is going to be a long term task. Long term perspective planning, sectoral and spatial coordination and cumulation through continuity of policies over successive phases will be necessary to make a real impact on the poverty situation. Alleviation of poverty is not the function of a single department. It has to become an orientation for all development departments so that each project which is accepted, and every outlay which is provided is examined in the light of what it means for both the urban and the rural poor. The role of the nodal organ is to provide a common framework for the realisation of all sectoral initiatives.

At the implementation level, the nodal ministry is likely to be the Ministry of Urban Development. While this ministry can provide coordination of habitant inputs to support the anti-poverty programme, the inputs have to come from many departments and many agencies. The only poverty alleviation services which the Urban Development Ministry was helping state and local governments to establish and monitor were UBS and UCD. They received scant attention because of their mini scale size. A national programme with responsibility for co-ordinating programme outlays amounting to hundreds of crores every year cannot be accomplished without a strong structure. The minimum which would be necessary is a separate department of Urban Basic Services and UCD, within the ministry, with an additional or full secretary at its head. Not only are the tasks to be tackled variegated and challenging, requiring induction of new forms of socio-economic expertise at the central level, but the sheer financial magnitude of the National Urban Works Programme and National Agency for UBS/UCD as citizen participation would also require the support of a full-fledged department. At state level, it might be necessary to designate a senior commissioner to coordinate services for alleviation of rural and urban poverty. At local government level, the Department of Urban Basic Services and Citizen Participation may be placed under the charge of an Additional Commissioner. In middle sized towns, a project officer, co-ranking with executive officer, may be needed. In smaller towns, the differentiation is not necessary. An orientation, however, will be needed.

The nodal ministry will be responsible for urban poverty alleviation programmes and will be mainly responsible for administering the National Programme for Wage Employment for the Urban Poor, setting up and coordinating the National Agency for Urban Basic services and Citizen Participation and the interest subsidy schemes for shelter upgradation programmes and micro enterprises development. As the nodal ministry, it will monitor and coordinate (through inter-departmental committees of secretaries preferably) the entire urban poverty alleviation effort. Its partners will be the Ministry of Labour, Ministry of Commerce and Industry, Ministry of Health, Ministry of Human Resource Development, Ministry of Civil Supplies and Ministry of Social Welfare. To coordinate financial institutions must direct their loan operations towards the needs of the urban poor.

The implementation of poverty alleviation programmes has brought down the number of the poor living below poverty line from 48% in 1977-78 to 37% in 1984-85 and this percentage has come down to 26% in 1989-90. In absolute terms the number of poor persons has down from 373 million in 1984-85 to 211 million in 1989-90. These objectives are laudable and can be achieved if the adequate financial allocations are made for various welfare programmes and are properly utilised, and the pace of their implementation is accelerated.

Job Opportunities

The Youth are the most vulnerable to economic problems and suffer due to unemployment and underemployment. The government could not of course guarantee government employment to every one as the right to work would imply. It should however grant unemployment allowance to the educated youth at least. Haryana state is the first to have introduced the scheme of unemployment allowance @ Rs. 15/-p.m. for Matriculates and @ Rs. 100/-p.m. for graduate and post-graduate unemployed youth. The other states should also follow suit. Some states grant free travel to youth appearing for interviews for public jobs. But these are no substitutes for employment. The government should generate employment opportunities for youth to the maximum. Some of the recent plans and programmes to achieve this end are:

Jawahar Rozgar Yojna : The Congress (I) government had launched Jawahar Rozgar Yojna an ambitious employment guarantee programme envisaging Rs. 2625 crores financial assistance to village panchayats in 1989-90 to guarantee employment to at least one person in a rural family living below the poverty line, for 50 to 100 days a year at a workplace near his or her residence. The then Prime Minister Shri Rajiv Gandhi had observed that the Yojna would reach out to all 440 lakh families in rural India living below the poverty line and that all existing rural wage/employment programmes like the Indira Awaas Yojna, the Rural Landless Employment Guarantee Programme, the National Rural Development Programmes and the Integrated Rural Development Programmes would automatically be merged into the Yojna. Under the Programme panchayats with a population ranging between 3,000 to 4,000 would get annual financial assistance from Rs. 80,000 to Rs. 1 lakh. A highlight of the scheme was that 30 per cent of the jobs would be reserved for women. The government hoped to incorporate in the programme integrated schemes to provide employment to the nomadic tribes. The Government expected that through the devolution of this programme to panchayats, the benefits of the programme directly reaching the people would be significantly greater than in the past, as thus far, too large a proportion of the funds for such programmes had gone to contractors and intermediaries there have also been other leakages. Besides, there is scope for economising on the costs of administration. Central assistance could finance 100 per cent of the programme, the government was structuring the finances in such a way that the States would get their allocation in proportion to the size of their population below the poverty line.

The scheme suffers from some snags. The impressive figure of Rs. 2625 crores is not the fresh outlay. As much as Rs. 1711 crores has been transferred from National Rural Employment Project and Rural Landless Employment Guarantee Scheme which have been merged in the Yojna and thus Rs. 389 crore is all that is actually fresh outlay; out of the total outlay, Rs. 2100 crores or 80% is to come from the Centre and the remaining from the States. It is to be watched how the additional amount of money will be arranged by the Centre and the States. The Yojna is to be implemented by panchayats and each with a population of about 4000 is to be given Rs. 1 lakh to offer jobs. If these villages have only 40 percent of the residents living below the poverty line-which is the national average then at least 320 families of five members each will need immediate help. Distributing Rs. 1 lakh evenly will mean an annual earning of Rs. 1250 for each family of five or Rs. 250 per year per individual which is ridiculously an insignificant amount to ensure removal of poverty. Even this calculation may be grossly un-optimistic as a substantial portion of funds will be expended on providing administrative infrastructure and paraphernalia to manage the scheme and it is the local elite which will benefit from the plans and also a plan share will go to the undeserving sections as has been the experience in the execution of Integrated Rural Development Programmes. Lastly panchayats which have been entrusted with the responsibility of implementing the Yojna dominated as they are by local landlords administered as they are by village officials will not be in a position to hand out justice even handedly as the elite and the officials will join hands to deal roughly with the lowest of the lowly. It is only the actual working of the Yojna which will prove how its benefits have reached the poor including the rural youth.

Nehru Rozgar Yojna : Complementary to the Jawahar Rozgar Yojna, Nehru Rozgar Yojna was launched by the Government of India in October, 1989 to provide various employment avenues to the urban poor mainly the urban youth. The Yojna consists of three components: (i) Scheme for setting up of micro-enterprises and providing training and infrastructure setup, (ii) Scheme for wage employment for public assets creating and (iii) Scheme of employment through Housing and Shelter upgradation.

The total financial outlay for the Yojna is of the order of Rs. 650 crores out of which the institutional finance amounts to Rs. 432 crores. The subsidy element is estimated at Rs. 218 crores for which Rs. 150 crores and Rs. 68 crores are to be provided by the centre and State/U.T. governments and urban Local. Bodies respectively. The share of subsidy between Government of India and the State Governments is 50:50 in the case of micro-enterprises schemes and 80:20 in the case of wage employment and employment through Housing and shelter upgrading schemes respectively. Allocation of the Central funds to the state/UTs is on the basis of urban population and incidence of urban poverty. States/UTs are in turn responsible to disburse them to different districts and local bodies/implementing agencies on the basis of the urban population of each district. Nehru Rozgar Yojna expects the municipal bodies as Jawahar Rozgar Yojna expects the Panchayats to play key' role in the entire process which includes selection of employment oriented activities, identification of beneficiaries, provision of necessary infrastructure, assistance in procurement/supply of raw material, facilitating the banks in the recovery of loans through neighbourhood/mohalla committees, liasion with technical agencies etc.

The Yojna is expected to provide direct employment opportunities to about 10 lakh persons in five years and to open up additional employment avenues in newly established enterprises, service centres, public works programmes, training and shelter upgrading activities etc.

The objectives of the Yojna are indeed laudable but it suffers from some lacunae: the local bodies may not be able to perform their pivotal role in fulfilling the objectives of the Yojna as constituted as they are at present are not able to discharge their present responsibilities because of their weak financial and personnel base and to expect them to perform additional responsibilities requiring higher managerial skills is unrealistic and unimaginative; except the major municipal corporation they may not be able even to comprehend the problem and the issues involved in planning and execution of the Yojna. The local bodies are notorious in failing to collect their own revenues at reasonable level, one wonders how they can be expected to help other agencies in their recoveries. Again the finances to be contributed by the states and local bodies of their own share, will also pose a serious problem due to their incapacity to raise their funds. The beneficiaries will have to raise loans also to provide the 'needed capitals for their enterprises and it is doubtful if they will be happier or sadder depending upon their capacities to pay back the principal with interest; finally the proposal to set up District Urban Development Agency as an autonomous body to mobilise, administer and account for Yojna funds does not appear to be viable from the institutional and financial points. This job can be easily entrusted to District Rural Development Authority which has the requisite experience of implementing the rural development programs and thus the present rural-urban dichotomy which constitutes a major impediment in the process of comprehensive district development can also be avoided.

The success of this Yojna non-withstanding the financial allocations will to a large extent depend on the strength of the institutions concerned with its implementation. We can only hope that it will go along way in affording enormous opportunities for employment to the urban youth resulting in the alleviation of their poverty.

Other Employment Generating Proposals : National front Government had approved a specific action plan to create additional three million jobs by 1994-95. The total un-employed youth with at least matriculation qualification was put at five million in 1987-88. This included about 1.5 million unemployed graduates. The action plan aimed at to create 2.5 million additional jobs for non-graduates and five lakh jobs for graduates outside the government sector and to reformulate economic policies to make it conducive for employment in the private sector. The specific time bound action plans had been proposed to increase seats in ITIs and Polytechnics by 10,000 annually. This was in addition to the annual increase of about 16,500 in these vocational training institutions.

These additional 1 0,000 seats would be created by introducing one more shift in 120 ITIs to train persons. It would involve a recurring cost of Rs. 4 crores. There are 903 government ITIs and 1167 non-government ITIs in the country with a total seat capacity of about 3.5 lakh. A high powered committee has to be appointed to draw up plans for implementing the government decision.

An action plan was also being drawn to create self-employment opportunities for the educated unemployed. These included facilitating entrepreneurship in the private sector self-employment opportunities through public sector and expansion of self-employment opportunities under the existing schemes. The measures for entrepreneurship facilitation include arranging finance, providing various inputs and facilitating licensing and the like.

The Public Sector would reserve some proportion of dealership contracts and service agencies for the educated unemployed. There were several general suggestions to create immediate employment opportunities without incurring additional capital expenditure. These were increased use of cloth made by handloom weavers for uniforms, increased use of shoes made by artisans, use of locally made cane basket instead of metal ones. Works in railways and other agencies will be integrated in right to work programme. Shifts in factories will be increased by reducing the hours of working. Entrepreneurs would be encouraged to use more labour and less capital.

Poverty has assumed serious dimensions in India. It is not confined to rural areas alone. There are stark manifestations of poverty in our cities also. Cities like Mumbai, Chennai and Kolkatta has such a large proportion living in slums, shanties and pavements that almost one-third of these big cities are nothing but slums where the urban poor live. It is estimated that about half of our people are living below the poverty line which may be defined as one where the human-being gets the wherewithals of living which are consistent with the dignity of man, where, for example, the minimum nutritional standards are fulfilled. Task Force on Projections of Minimum Needs and Effective Consumption Demand set up by the Planning Commission 1977 had defined poverty line as mid point of the monthly per capita expenditure having daily calorie intake of 2000 per person in rural areas and 2100 per person in urban areas.

Ever since our country embarked a planning process in 1951. Our principal objective has been improving the pace of economic development so as to increase the gross national product by increasing output in all sectors of the economy the underlying assumption was that if development takes place, its fruits will percolate to all sections of our society including the poorer. But the trickle-down effect of development has not reduced the incidence of poverty. Therefore the policy makers, social scientists and other thinkers had started thinking that normal process of development could not be depended upon to make a dent on poverty and we must have a direct assault on poverty. Similar feeling permeated our slogan "Garibi Hatao". Accordingly programmes to deal with poverty such as Integrated Rural Development Programme (IRDP), National Rural Employment Programme (NREP), The Rural Landless Employment Guarantee Scheme (RLEGS) and Training for Rural Youths for Self-employment (TRYSEM) were initiated as part of strategy of removing poverty. And earlier programmes of poverty alleviation such as Drought Prone Area Programme (DPAP), Community Development Programme (CDP), Small Farmers Development Agency (SFDA) and Marginal Farmers and Agricultural Labourer Development Agency (MFALDA) were merged in IRD. All the existing rural wage employment programmes like the Indira Awas Yojna, RLEGP, NRDP and IRD were merged into the Jawahar Rozgar Yojna in 1989. As the basic objective of the Sixth Five Year Plan is the diminishing or reduction of poverty, if not its total elimination and the concern of the Seventh Five Year Plan has also been to reduce poverty further by 14 per cent, it is imperative that the anti-poverty programmes should register significant success.

These programmes have however, not been able to achieve the desired results due to the deficiencies they suffered from. There has been dominance of the Central Government in initiating and planning these programmes as reflected in the Centrally sponsored schemes allowing for little freedom and flexibility at the local level; gaps in planning are reinforced by an administrative system which has yet to demonstrate its capability to respond adequately and effectively to new challenges; the responsibility is diffused in establishing accountability for the achievement of several development schemes at the district level; there is no single ministry or agency within the Planning Commission and even at state level which integrates the various programmes to form a co-ordinated whole. Over-reliance on bureaucratic administrative machinery to implement anti-poverty programmes has led to the gradual erosion of people's participatory institutions; the failure of the state to implement land reforms, to promote tiny and cottage industries sector; anti-poverty activity was confined to the governmental bodies without participation of either public or other public agencies and voluntary organisations, middlemen exploiting the beneficiaries, swallowing the reliefs and not letting them reach the poor people concerned, corrupt practices, lack of adequate facilities for training for different vocations and income generating schemes, job opportunities, menace of population explosion, illiteracy, unemployment and underemployment leading to migration of rural population to cities, black market, inflation and corruption. Factors which can substantially contribute to the success of anti-poverty programmes should include decentralised planning as Jawaharlal Nehru, the architect of the planning process had rightly emphasized the significance of the grass-root level institutions at the district level, at the block level and at the village level for channelising the development programmes not only for plan implementation but ISO for plan formulation; greater devolution of authority for poverty removal at the district and sub-divisional level, evolving a suitable administrative machinery with simpler procedure to avoid middleman and corrupt practices, highest standard of devotion, efficiency and integrity from the bureaucracy at both higher and lower levels; proper coordination and cooperation amongst the different agencies concerned with implementing the programmes and also the normal government agencies to avoid duplication and diffusion of responsibility, linking of IRDP with cooperative sector, strengthening of the role of voluntary agencies and social workers, greening the waste land which constituted one third of India's land resources, exploiting the employment potential of land reclamation through land army, implementation of land reforms, initiating programmes for the landless such as those of improvement of public works, for the artisans for raising their skills, of agro industrialisation and establishment of ancillary industries for minimum consumption including that of provision of drinking water, intensifying special programmes for the scheduled castes/tribes and backward classes for the promotion of education, health and population control, an attack on black money and corruption, a programme of anti-inflation because inflation leads to the erosion of whatever resources the poor possess finally it is imperative that the weaker sections of the community-the tribals, the poor in the urban areas, landless labourers, marginal farmers etc., should be awakened and their organisations should be involved in the process of implementation of anti-poverty programmes. Removal of poverty is a herculean task but given the implementation of measures suggested above, and the political will, it can be mitigated to a very great extent, if not completely eliminated in not far distant future.

2

Forced Workers

A man keeping another man in perpetual bondage for his selfish and personal designs is the type of man's cruelty to man which is not confined to a particular country or a particular region but is found as a global phenomenon for hundreds of years, right from the Biblical days to the present era. The nomenclature changed from period to period and place to place: slave, serf, villein, and bonded labour. In India, this type of exploitation of man remained prevalent in the name of Begar and Ryot for years. The term 'bonded labour' or bandhua mazdoor is of recent origin. Despite the abolition of the zamindari system, land reforms, Bhoodan movement, enactment of legislation (Bonded Labour Abolition Act, 1976), establishment of Panchayati Raj', interest shown by Social Action Groups, spirited individuals, and even the Supreme Court, we have not been able to scrap this evil from our society. Lakhs of bonded labourers continue to be exploited and carry the yoke of neglect, suffering and frustration in abject silence. In fact, the system of bonded labour, as prevalent in Indian society, is a relic of feudal hierarchical society. A considerable interest has come to be shown in the bonded labour during the past two decades by the social workers, social scientists and the government because it is considered incompatible with our social ideal of egalitarianism and human rights. The magnitude of bonded labour is just baffling as lakhs of adult males and females as well as children are condemned to be suffering under its yoke.

Bonded Labour

We have to understand two terms: 'bonded labour system' and 'bonded labour'. The 'bonded labour system' refers to the relationship between a creditor and a debtor who obtains loan owing to economic compulsions confronting his day-to-day life and agrees to abide by the terms dictated by the creditor. The important term of the agreement is that the debtor agrees to mortgage his services or the services of any or all the members of his family, for a specified or unspecified period. The relationship built on the agreement is on such unequal terms that while for every labour or service, there must be some fair remuneration equivalent to the price of labour in the market, under the bonded labour system, the service is rendered for the debt or in lieu of the interest accruing to the debt. The debtor either works without receiving any remuneration or if at all there is any remuneration it is much less than the minimum wage (notified under the Minimum Wages Act) or the prevailing rate of market wage.

The 1976 Bonded Labour (Abolition) Act defines 'bonded labour system' as the system of forced labour under which a debtor erlters into an agreement with the creditor that he would render service to him either by himself or through any member of his family or any person dependent on him, for a specified or unspecified period, either without wages or for nominal wages, in consideration of loan or any other economic consideration obtained by him or any of his ascendants, or in pursuance of any social obligation, or in pursuance of any obligation devolving on him by succession. The agreement has other consequences too, such as, forfeiting the debtor the freedom of employment, denial of freedom of movement in any part of the country, and denial of the right to sell at market value any of his property or product of his labour.

The term 'bonded labour' has been defined by the National Commission on Labour as "labour which remains in bondage for a specific period for the debt incurred". The Commissioner for Scheduled Castes and Scheduled Tribes explained the term bonded labour in its 24th Report as "persons who are forced to work for the creditors for the loan incurred either without wage or on nominal wage" (Sharma, 1990:52).

The 'bonded labour' is different from 'contract labour' employed in industries, mines, plantations and docks, etc. The contract labour includes workers who are not directly recruited by the establishment, whose names do not appear on the pay-roll, and who are not paid wages directly by the employer. In theory, the contract labourers in India are covered by the Factory Act, 1948, the Mines Act, 1952, the Plantations Labour Act, 1951 and the Dock Workers Act, 1948 so as to give them benefits as are admissible to labour directly employed. However, the advantages of employing both bonded labour and contract labour are the same: (i) the labour is engaged at the lower cost, (ii) the employers have not to extend the fringe benefits to the workers, and (iii) the employers are not under any obligation of providing welfare and security measures to the workers as stipulated in various Acts. The system of contract labour in our country was abolished in September 1970 by an Act called "Contract Labour (Regulation and Abolition) Act".

The two basic features of bonded labour are: indebtedness and forced labour. The forced labour can hereditarily descend from father to son or be passed on for generations together. During the period of bondage, the debtor cannot seek employment from any other person. In economic terms, this means that he cannot "sell his labour in the market at market value". The bonded labour system is mostly found among agricultural labourers in villages, though today it has extended to workers working in stone quarries, brick kilns, bidi factories, glass factories and in detergent, carpet, gem stones and many other factories.

The bonded labourers are known by different names in different parts of India. For example, in Andhra Pradesh and Karnataka they are known as 'Jeethams', in Gujarat and Madhya Pradesh as 'Halis', in Bastar district in Madhya Pradesh as 'Kabadis', in Hyderabad as 'Bhageld', in Rajasthan as 'Sagris' in Bihar as 'Kamias' or 'Kamiantis', in Orissa as 'Gothees', in Tamil

Nadu as 'Pandiyals', in Kerala as 'Adiyas', 'Paniyas' and 'Kattunaikens' and in Uttar Pradesh as Koltas.

Reasons for Exploitation

Though the main causes of origin, growth and perpetuation of bonded labour system are economic but the social and religious factors too support the custom. The economic causes include: extreme poverty of the people, inability to find work for livelihood, inadequate size of the landholdings to support family, lack of alternative small-scale loans for the rural and urban poor, natural calamities like drought, floods etc., destruction of the standing crops, plague and other diseases leading to death of men and animals, absence of rains, drying away of wells, meagre income from forest produce, and inflation and constant rising prices. The social factors include: high expenses on occasions like marriage, death, feast, birth of a child, etc., leading to heavy debts, caste-based discrimination, lack of concrete social welfare scheme to safeguard against hunger and illness, non-compulsory and unequal educational system, and indifference and corruption among government officials. Some times, the exploitation by some persons in the village also compels people to migrate to some other place and seek not only employment on the employer's conditions but also get protection from the influential persons. The religious arguments are used to convince the people of low castes that religion enjoins upon them to serve people of high castes. Illiteracy, ignorance, immaturity and lack of skill and professional training sustain such beliefs. Broadly speaking, it may be maintained that bondage originates mainly from economic and social pressures.

Laws Enacted

The pernicious and fastidious practice of bonded labour existed in many states in India. After independence, it could not be allowed to continue to blight the national life any longer. As such, when the Constitution of India was framed Article 23 was enshrined in it which prohibited 'traffic in human beings', begar and other similar forms of forced labour. However, no serious effort was made to give effect to this Article and stamp out the shocking practice of bonded labour. The Forced Labour (Abolition) Convention adopted by the International Labour Organization (ILO) in 1919 was ratified by India only in November 1954. Some states in India had also enacted laws for abolishing the bonded labour. For example, the Bihar Kamianti Act was passed in 1920, the Madras Agency Debt Bondage Regulation in 1940, Kabadi System Regulation in Bastar in Madhya Pradesh in 1943, Hyderabad Bhagela Agreement Regulation in 1943, Orissa Debt Bonded Abolition Regulation in 1948, Rajasthan Sagri System Abolition Act in 1961 (which was amended in 1975), and Bonded Labour System (Abolition) Act, Kerala in 1975. It was specifically laid down in most of these regulations (like those of Madras, Orissa, Bihar and Hyderabad) that the agreement between the creditor and the debtor entered into after the commencement of the regulation was to be wholly void if (a) the full terms of the agreement were not expressed in writing and a copy thereof was not filed with the designated authority, (b) the expressed and implied period of labour exceeded one year, (c) the interest provided for was not simple interest over one year, and (d) the interest exceeded 6.25 per cent per annum. But it was after the announcement of the 20-point programme on July 1, 1975 that the legislative exercise at the national level began with some amount of seriousness and urgency. The ordinance was enacted in October 1975 which was later replaced by the Act passed in February 1976, called the Bonded Labour System (Abolition) Act. All the state laws became inoperative after the enactment of the Act by the union government in 1976.

The Act implies: (i) identification of bonded labourers; (ii) release of bonded labourers; (iii) action against offenders, i.e., creditors who had forced agreement upon the debtor; (iv) holding of regular meetings of the vigilance committees at the district and tehsil level; (v) maintenance of the prescribed registers; and (vi) conferring of judicial powers to executive magistrates. The Act also provides for the rehabilitation of the bonded labourers who are freed from their creditors. The 1976 Act was : amended in 1985 in which it was clarified that the contract workers and interstate migrant workers, if they fulfil the conditions laid down in the

Bonded Labour System (Abolition) Act, 1976, will be considered as bonded labour.

The main problem that is faced in the implementation of the 1976 Act is the identification of the bonded labourers. Neither the administrators at the district and tehsil levels admit the existence of the bonded labourers in their areas nor the creditors accept that any bonded workers are serving them, nor the workers themselves are willing to give statements that they are being forced to work as bonded labourers since long. It is the social workers attached to non-political social action groups and voluntary organizations who identify the bonded labourers. The other handicap which aggravates the problem is the economic rehabilitation of the released labourers. The economic rehabilitation includes: finding jobs for them, getting them minimum wages, giving them training in skills, horticulture, animal husbandry, etc., promoting their traditional arts and crafts, allotment of agricultural land, helping them in developing the allotted land, helping them in getting the raw material, providing them either land for constructing houses or low-cost dwelling units, arranging bank loans or credit for them, helping them in the processing of forest produce, educating them and their children, arranging for their medical care, etc. All these are herculean tasks. Besides ensuring the economic rehabilitation, the State Governments are also expected to arrange for their psychological rehabilitation and integration of various schemes of central and State Governments. In chalking out plans and strategies of rehabilitation, the freed labourers are to be given the choice between various alternatives.

State of Plight

One Chief Justice of the Supreme Court (Justice P.N. Bhagwati) described the bonded labourers as "non-beings, exiles of civilization living a life worse than that of animals, for the animals are at least free to roam about as they like and they can plunder or grab food whenever they are hungry, but these outcastes of society are held in bondage and robbed of their freedom even. They are consigned to an existence where they have to live either in hovels or under the open sky and be satisfied with whatever unwholesome food they can manage to get, inadequate though it may be to fill their hungry stomachs. Not having any choice, they are driven by poverty and hunger into a life of bondage, a dark bottomless pit from which, in a cruel exploitative society, they cannot hope to be rescued" (Yojana, May 1-15, 1987:32-33).

It is estimated that there are about 32 lakh bonded labourers in India. Of these, 98 per cent are said to be bonded due to indebtedness and 2 per cent due to customary social obligations. The highest number is believed to exist in three states of Andhra Pradesh, Karnataka and Tamil Nadu, followed by Orissa, Uttar Pradesh, Bihar, and Madhya Pradesh. According to the recent figures released in May 1997 on the basis of a State Government sponsored survey (conducted as per the Supreme Court direction), Tamil Nadu has the maximum number of 24,000 bonded labourers in the country, engaged in 30 different occupations (The Hindustan Times, May 13, 1997). It has been pointed out that the majority of the bonded labourers work as agricultural labour in villages and belong to the outcaste or tribal communities. Of the total labour force in the rural areas, about 33 per cent are engaged in non-agricultural activities, 42 per cent work as cultivators, and 25 per cent as agricultural labourers. Of those who work as agricultural labourers, 48 per cent belong to Scheduled Castes and 33 per cent to Scheduled Tribes. Being unskilled and unorganized, the agricultural labourers have little for their livelihood other than personal labour. The bonded agricultural labourers occupy the lowest rung of the rural ladder. Social and economic stratification in a village is linked with land and caste which in turn govern the economic and social status of the people. The bonded labourers thus live in pitiable and miserable conditions. They are socially exploited because though in theory they are assured food, clothes, free tobacco, etc., but in practice they get the food that is left over, and clothes that are discarded by family members. They are made to work for 12 to 14 hours a day and are forced to live with cows and buffaloes in shed. If they fall ill, they may be procured some medicines from the local Hakim depending the sweet will of the employer.

The picture of sufferings of the bonded labour may be depicted by citing the example of the shackles of bonded repatriates from Sri Lanka in Kodai Kanal district in Tamil Nadu in 1984. Under the Sirmavo-Shastri Pact of 1964 and Sirmavo-Indira Gandhi Pact of 1975 pertaining to the repatriation of persons of Indian origin in Sri Lanka, 1.11 lakh families consisting of 4.45 lakh persons were repatriated to India by mid-1984. Of these, 1.07 lakh families (or about 4 lakh persons) settled down in Tamil Nadu. Most of these were plantation labourers in Sri Lanka and as such, being unskilled workers, became homeless wanderers in Tamil Nadu in search of a living. They were politically disorganized, economically dependent, culturally unaware of their rights, and organizationally lacked leadership and initiative. A large number of about eight thousand repatriates who settled in labour camps in Kodaikanal were engaged in the construction of roads and buildings, or worked as quarry workers or landless agricultural labourers. About two and a half thousand repatriates worked as labourers in two companies engaged in the production of synthetic fibre, etc. Soon, because of their pauperization, these labourers fell prey to the contractors and moneylenders and became bonded labourers. They lived under in human conditions in thatched huts. Provisions were supplied to them from designated shops weekly. There was no provision for their medical care. There was so much water scarcity that children seldom bathed and always remained dirty. Working conditions were hazardous and they were made to work for 10 to 14 hours a day. Certain surveys conducted at that time showed that average gross earnings per individual varied between Rs. 240 and 290 for those working in the two companies. The elements of bondage existed in initial travel advance, intermittent cash advances for the day-to-day expenses, debt owned to contractors, giving blankets which were to be returned on quitting, and forcing them to sign blank papers to be used later by contractors at their will. Uncooperative workers were roughed up by the hired hooligans of the contractors. On the appeal of the Bandhua Mukti Morcha under the leadership of Swami Agnivesh, the Supreme Court appointed a three-member commission in April 1986 to inquire into the conditions of this 'coupe labour' in Kodaikanal.

The commission found the working and the living conditions so horrible that the Supreme Court directed the Tamil Nadu government to abolish the contract system which was responsible for all the evils of exploitation of the workers, to strictly enforce the Plantation Labour Act, 1951, and to provide adequate relief to the bonded labourers till they were freed and rehabilitated under the Bonded Labour System (Abolition) Act. The Tamil Nadu government was thus forced to chalk out the rehabilitation programme.

The total number of bonded labourers identified and freed in India by March 1989 was 2.42 lakhs, of whom 2.18 lakhs (i.e., 90%) were said to be rehabilitated also (Pais, Yojana, May 1987:23). Thus, hardly 8 per cent of the total bonded workers in India have been identified so far, in-dicating lack of interest of the State Governments in solving the problem of the bonded labour.

At least four reports submitted to the Government of India in between 1979 and 1983 pointed out how the disgusting and squeamish practice of bonded labour existed in India and continued to disfigure the social and economic life of the country. These reports were: (a) the Report of the Centre for Rural Develop-ment to the Ministry of Labour, Government of India, on "Rehabilitation of Bonded Labour in Monghyr District, Bihar", (b) the Report of the Public Policy and Planning Division of the Indian Institute of Public Administration to the Ministry of Labour, Government of India, on "Evaluation Study of Bonded Labour Rehabilitation Scheme in Tehri Garhwal, Uttar Pradesh", (c) the Report of Laxmi Dhar Misra, the Director General (Labour Welfare) of Government of India based on the "Spot Studies Regarding identification, Release and Rehabilitation of Freed Bonded Labourers in Uttar Pradesh, Madhya Pradesh, Andhra Pradesh, Karnataka, Orissa, Bihar, Rajasthan, Tamil Nadu and Kerala", and (d) the Report of the National Seminar on "Identification and Rehabilitation of Bonded Labour" held from February 7-9, 1983.

Of the 2.42 lakh bonded labourers identified and released up to March 1989, 26 per cent were got released in Karnataka, 20 per cent in Orissa, 16 per cent in Tamil Nadu, 14 per cent in Andhra

Pradesh, 11 per cent in Uttar Pradesh, 5 per cent in Bihar, 4 per cent in Madhya Pradesh, 3 per cent in Rajasthan, 0.5 per cent in Maharashtra, 0.3 per cent in Kerala and 0.2 per cent in Haryana (Yojana, Ibid.:23).

Resettlement

Getting the bonded labourers identified and freed was the statutory obligation of the State Governments only but from November 1987 onwards, the voluntary organizations also came to be authorized both for identification and rehabilitation. Of the 2.18 lakh bonded labourers rehabilitated up to March 1989, three-fourths were in four states of Orissa (23.8%), Karnataka (23.3%), Tamil Nadu (17.1%) and Uttar Pradesh (12.1%), in three states of Andhra Pradesh (11.1%), Bihar (5.2%) and Madhya Pradesh (3.5%), and the remaining 4 per cent in three states of Rajasthan (3.2%), Maharashtra (0.4%) and Kerala (0.4%) (Indian Labour Journal, August 1989:1277). There is also a provision in the 20-point Programme of 1986 regarding the identification and rehabilitation of the bonded labour. Point 6 of this programme covers bonded labourers. Under this programme, the Government of India issued instructions in August 1986 to the Deputy Director General (Labour Welfare) of all the states to take follow-up action. Since then, the Union Ministry of Labour has been monitoring and evaluating the programme of identification, release and rehabilitation of bonded labourers from time to time.

Rehabilitation is both physical and psychological. Physical rehabilitation is essentially economic whereas psychological rehabilitation has to be built up through a process of assurance and reassurance. The two must go side by side. The first prerequisite of psychological rehabilitation is that the freed bonded labourers must be wrenched away from the old habitat and be rehabilitated at a place where they will no longer be subject to the ruinous influence of the erstwhile bonded labour-keepers. Unless they are psychologically assured that after release from bondage, debt will not regulate their destiny any longer, there is every possibility that they may slide back to debt bondage.

Basically, there are three phases of rehabilitation: (i) immediate physical subsistence after release; (ii) short-term measures to help the freed workers to start a new life (for example, allotment of a house site, assistance for construction of a house, allotment of a plot of agricultural land, supplying a pair of bullocks and agricultural implements, or provision of avenues of gainful employment, etc.); and (iii) long-term measures (such as, arranging credit, training in new skills, developing existing skills, providing a remunerative price support, ensuring non-formal literacy of adult members and formal literacy for children, securing medical care, protection of civil rights...). It is thus the rehabilitation which will give the freed bonded labourers the status of beings so that they may be able to identify themselves with the mainstream of a civilized human society and realize the dignity worthy of human existence.

Recently (1994-95), a voluntary organization—named Action for Community Organization, Rehabilitation and Development (ACCORD)—helped five tribes in the Nilgiris in Tamil Nadu (Paniyas, Bettakurumbas, Kattunaickens, Motukurumbas and Irulas) in getting them freed from the agony of bondage and land deprivation (The Hindustan Times, May 13, 1995). It took ACCORD ten years of toil to bring about this change. The tribals, many in slavery since the eighteenth and the nineteenth centuries, had become bonded labourers after slavery was abolished. During the annual Onam festival, the landlords would fix yearly bondage for the tribals who would get paddy and two sets of clothes along with few basic things. The death-knell of bondage was sounded in the mid-sixties when grow-more food campaign resulted in Malyali settlers from neighbouring Kerala coming to lower Nilgiris. The positive offshoot of this development was that the system of people working for one year for meagre paddy was stopped. However, its negative aspect was that the settlers started cheating the tribals and taking over the forest land gradually. The ACCORD helped the tribal tea plantation growers not only in getting loans but also in forming in December 1988 a Sangam with the participation of about 20,000 tribals to foster the concept of tribal unity. This Sangam has reduced their sufferings, protected them from exploitation of bondage, helped them in asserting their rights, and establishing schools, health centres, hospitals, etc., ACCORD is now planning to pull out, handing over all the development activities to the Sangam.

The Drawbacks

Qualitatively reviewing the implementation of the rehabilitative programmes for the bonded labourers in different states, we find that some states, like Orissa, Uttar Pradesh, Kerala and Andhra Pradesh point out the welcome features of identification and rehabilitation but some need to introduce many innovative changes. The following visible lacunae in the implementation of the programme need to be dealt with immediately: Firstly, instead of treating the programme in isolation as the programme of a particular ministry/department, there has to be coordination among various concerned ministries/departments like those of agriculture, animal husbandry, irrigation, forest, fisheries, etc., so that the programme is dealt with as an integrated national programme. Secondly, since the social milieu and the social structures which promoted the bonded labour system in the past continue to dominate the village life and the economy even today, they need to be probed into and changed with commitment. Thirdly, the development departments are so much burdened with schemes like IRDP, JRY, TRYSEM, etc., that their programmes mostly remain time-bound and target-oriented without taking into account the needs, aptitudes and preferences of the beneficiaries. The need is, therefore, to design programmes in such a manner that they serve as target-group oriented rather than target-oriented. Fourthly, with poor infrastructure and lack of qualified and committed staff and resources, the beneficiaries are not provided protective covers on a long-term basis with the result that very often productive assets turn into liabilities. Fifthly, middlemen operate like parasites and take away the limited fruits and benefits of rehabilitation to their advantage. What is required, therefore, is carefully and rationally formulated scheme with varied linkages, keeping an eye on the type of infrastructure already available. Sixthly, the freed bonded labourers who come from the lowest strata of the society and represent the extremes of poverty and destitution are unable to exercise the choice of a particular scheme which may be most profitable to them. Their dependence on the concerned officials in selecting a particular scheme for them deprives them of the real benefits of rehabilitation. This dependence needs to be reduced. Lastly, the attitude of the erstwhile bonded labour keepers, people at large, and officials in various departments has not changed at all towards the poor bonded labourers. Even when the labourers are assaulted by their erst while masters and landlords, their land is forcibly taken away, their children are not permitted to pass through the paddy fields of the landlords to reach schools, their animals are whisked away by their exploiters, and they complain to police, approach doctors for help, lodge complaints with the officers of the concerned departments, they (officers, police, doctors, etc.), are not at all moved by their pathetic stories and remain callous, unresponsive, insensitive and ineffective to help them. Without change in the attitude of the people and the officials, the freed labourers cannot withstand the organized onslaughts against them by the more influential sections of the society. Their ignorance, illiteracy and lack of capacity to fight for their rights will always hamper them to enjoy the gains of freedom and development.

Changing social systems and social structures as to benefit the poor who become the bonded labourers is not easy. Let us take two illustrations. A tribal needs money to pay bride-price for his own or his son's marriage. He obtains loan by mortgaging his services and thus becomes a bonded labourer. Similarly, suppose an individual is convicted by court for illicit distillation and is heavily fined. Since he has no money to pay fine, he takes loan from an influential person by pledging his labour and becomes a bonded labourer. Now, is abolishing the custom of bride-price possible? Is imposition of fine by the court for an illegal action wrong? Many economic needs can not be gratified by the poor individuals without seeking loans. In such cases, what is needed is careful scrutiny of the agreements for obtaining loans so that pledging the labour as security may be prevented and the system of bonded labour may be controlled.

The group approach to development will bring the freed bonded labourers together, enable them to pool their resources, get help from various agencies, departments and banks, and integrate themselves for a common purpose for a qualitative and permanent rehabilitation. Such a 'group effort' can be land-based, craft-based or asset-based for success. This requires proper selection of beneficiaries, the place where they are to be rehabilitated, selection of skills to be taught to them, and building awareness among the beneficiaries themselves and converting them into willing partners in a joint venture for their rehabilitation, progress and advancement.

The crucial problem is that if the freed bonded labourers are not rehabilitated, they will suffer more. The question before them would be: should they choose hunger or slavery, freedom or security, hard work in serfdom or crime to support family and the resultant fear of imprisonment? While the rehabilitation work was totally assigned to State Governments till about a decade ago, in 1983 the Central Government also sponsored the scheme through the Ministry of Labour. The central scheme provides for four to five crore rupees a year to the State Governments for formulating specific schemes on a matching grant basis. A Planning Commission report says that the progress of rehabilitation work is very slow. The State Government officials lack initiative or remain indifferent to identification and rehabilitation programmes. The social workers too face many handicaps in their work. It is hoped that the central aid and the involvement of voluntary organizations will make the identification and rehabilitation programmes of the bonded labourers more effective.

In 1982, the Supreme Court also declared 'forced labour' as violation of fundamental rights of such labourers, and in 1983 described labour with below the prescribed minimum wages as 'forced labour'. In 1984, it further described the failure of the State Governments to implement the provisions of the Bonded Labour (Abolition) Act, 1976 as violation of the Constitution. It also described rehabilitation after release as obligatory so that freed labourers are not driven by poverty, helplessness and despair into serfdom once again (Sharma, 1990:56). Such judicial interpretations are expected to strengthen the efforts of the State Governments and the voluntary organizations in getting the bonded labourers freed from the clutches of their employers.

Conscious Efforts

The plight of the bonded labourers continues to be a serious social problem and a matter of concern for public, government, judiciary, social scientists and social workers. If between 16 and 17 lakh crimes in a year, for which about 25 lakh persons are arrested under the IPC, are considered a serious issue for the Indian society, freeing of three million bonded labourers must be viewed as a very crucial issue. For this purpose, it is necessary that researches be sponsored by different funding agencies to ascertain the extent and the nature of the problem, examine handicaps in identification, utility of various rehabilitation schemes, co-ordination of activities between Central Government, State Governments and voluntary organizations, necessity of amending the 1976 Act, determining responsibilities and accountability of the concerned officers, and introducing after-care programmes for the freed bonded labourers. Unless serious efforts are taken to save the bonded labourers from ruthless exploitation by the vested interests, the problem will continue to be a social menance. The total abolition of the system of bonded labour through legislation may not be feasible in the foreseeing future, yet doing away with the legislation may cause further distress to the victims. Removing poverty, unemployment and illiteracy, which are believed to be the three basic causes of the bonded labour system, is also not easy. The formulation of future plans, programmes and projects for the bonded labourers would require a broad approach and action at various levels.

The problem of bonded labour has, thus, to be fought at various fronts–social, psychological and legal. We have to educate the exploited not to succumb to pressure tactics. We have to tell the exploiters that law cannot be circumvented and has to take its course in democratic India. We have to create committed opinion among the masses. We have to involve not only intellectuals but also the enlightened citizens to carry the message to those who matter. We have to enforce laws rigidly. We have also to impress upon the politicians to tackle the issue with concerted interest and a missionary zeal. The system based on exploitation by a few socially and economically powerful persons, trading on the misery and suffering of large numbers of men, and holding them in a bondage constitutes a shameful feature of our national life. The bondage of the economically impoverished segments of society for a small debt is totally incompatible with the egalitarian socio-economic order promised to Indians. Wiping out this system is basic and crucial to human dignity and conformity to constitutional values.

3

The Labourers

Labour Welfare

The term "Labour Welfare" eludes a precise definition applicable to all countries and even to the same country for all times. The Royal Commissions on Labour had therefore remarked, "Welfare must necessarily be elastic, bearing a somewhat different interpretation in one country from another, according to different social customs, the degree of industrialisation and the educational development of the worker". The National Commission on Labour had observed that the Concept of Welfare is necessarily dynamic, bearing a different interpretation from country to country and from time to time, and even in the same country, according to the value system social institutions; degree of industrialisation and general level of social and economic development. Even within one country its context may be different from region to region".

There is no unanimity on the concept of labour welfare. The International Labour Organisation (I.L.O.) in its resolution of 1947 had defined labour welfare as the provision of such services, facilities and amenities which may be established in the vicinity of undertaking to enable the persons employed in them to perform their work in healthy, congenial surroundings and provided with amenities conducive to good health and moral. A resolution adopted by ILO in June 1956 enumerates some of these services and amenities. These include adequate canteens, rest and recreation facilities, sanitary and medical facilities, arrangements for travel to and from work and the accommodation of workers who are employed at a distance from their homes.

Labour Investigation Committee of the Government of India had observed in 1945; " For purpose we prefer to include under welfare activities, anything done for the intellectual, physical, moral and economic betterment of the workers, whether by employer by Government or by other agencies, over and above what is laid down by law or what is normally expected as part of contractual benefits for which the worker may have bargained."

The study team on Labour Welfare appointed by the Government of India in 1950 to review the existing welfare facilities had divided welfare activities into three groups: Welfare facilities within the establishment such as medical aid, creches, canteens supply of drinking water, etc.; welfare facilities outside the establishment such as recreation, housing, education, etc., and social security.

In 1963, the ILO constituted a Committee of experts on welfare facilities for industrial workers which divided welfare services into : (a) Welfare amenities within the precincts of the establishments; latrines and urinals, washing and bathing facilities, creches; rest shelters and canteens; arrangements for drinking water and prevention of fatigue, health services including occupational safety; administration arrangements within a plant to look after welfare; uniforms and protective clothing, and shift allowances and (b) Welfare outside the establishment: maternity benefit, social insurance, medical facilities, educational facilities, recreational facilities, holiday homes and leave, travel facilities, workers' cooperatives, vocational training for dependents of workers, other programmes for women, youth and children and transport to and from the place of work.

In 1966, the Government of India constituted a Committee on Labour Welfare. This Committee felt that a scientific definition of labour welfare should take cognizance of the perspective of economic development as well as the future aspirations of labour. It realised that it was logical to classify social security measures also -as labour welfare. It thus, modifying the definition of labour welfare prescribed by the ILO in the context of social and economic conditions in our country, the Committee included under the term labour welfare such services' facilities and amenities as adequate canteens, rest and recreation facilities, sanitary and medical facilities, arrangements for travel to and from work and for the accommodation of workers employed at a, distance from their homes and such other services, amenities and facilities including social security measures as contribute to improve the conditions under which workers are employed.

The need for labour welfare is too obvious to require any elaboration. The provision of welfare measures mentioned above will grant them minimum standards of work and living conditions and thus contribute to increase the productive efficiency of workers and infuse in them a new spirit of self-realization and fulfilment. Investment in labour welfare will thus be conducive to greater production which would be in the best interests of employers and the nation at large. It will also help in creating a healthy atmosphere in the work place, keep the labour force satisfied and contented and promote industrial peace.

Welfare Laws

The beginnings of labour welfare legislation and programmes go back to the period after the first world war, but it was after independence that the country entered a new phase of intensive labour legislation and welfare programmes.

The Preamble to the Constitution affirms the resolve of the people of India "to constitute India into Sovereign, Democratic Republic and to secure all its citizens justice—social, economic and political; Liberty of thought, expression, belief, faith and worship; Equality of status and opportunity; and promote among them fraternity assuring the dignity of the individual and the unity of the nation".

Article 23 of the Indian Constitution prohibits traffic in human beings and beggar and other similar forms of forced labour. Any contravention of this provision is an offence punishable in accordance with law.

Article 24 of the Constitution prohibits employment of children in factories, etc., below the age of fourteen years.

Part-IV of the Constitution lays down certain Directive Principles of the State Policy. These principles are not justiciable but they are fundamental in the governance of the country. It is the duty of the State to apply these principles in making laws.

Article 39, 41, 42 and 43 of Part -IV of the Constitution refer to the labour policy. Article 39 lays down that the State shall, in particular, direct its policy towards securing: that the citizens, men and women equally have the right to an adequate means of livelihood; that the ownership and control of the material resources of the community are so distributed as best to subserve the common good; that the operation of the economic system does not result in the concentration of wealth and means of production to the common deferment; that there is equal pay for equal work for both men and women; that the health and strength of workers, men and women and the tender age of children are not abused and that citizens are not forced by economic necessity to enter a vocation unsuited to their age and strength; the childhood and youth are protected against exploitation and against moral and material abandonment.

Article 41 provides, "The State shall, within the limits of economic capacity and development make effective provision for securing the right to work, to education and to public assistance in certain cases of unemployment, old age, sickness and disablement and other cases of undeserved want.

Article 42 says that the state shall make provision for securing just and human conditions of work and for maternity relief.

Article 43 stipulates, "The State shall endeavour to secure, by suitable legislation or economic organisation or in any other way to workers, agricultural, industrial or otherwise, work, a living wage, conditions of work ensuring a decent standard of life and full enjoyment of leisure and social and cultural opportunities and in particular the State shall endeavour to promote cottage industries on an individual or co-operative basis in rural areas.

In pursuance of the directives of the constitution, the Central and State Governments have enacted the following legislations since independence:

During the pre-plan (1946–51) the Central Government passed the Mica Mines Labour Welfare Fund Act (1946), the Industrial Disputes Act (1947), Coal Mines Labour Welfare Fund Act (1947), the Employees State Insurance Act (1948), Coal Mines Provident Fund Act (1948), the Factories Act (1948), the Dock Workers (Regulation of Employment) Act (1948) and the Plantations Labour Act (1951). The Uttar Pradesh Government passed the U.P. Sugar and Power Alcohol Industries Labour Welfare Development Fund Act, 1950.

During the First plan period (1951–56), Parliament enacted the Mines Act, 1952, the Coal Mines (Conservation and Safety) Act, 1952 and, the Salt Cess Act, 1953. State Legislatures of Bombay, Assam and Uttar Pradesh passed the Bombay Labour Welfare Fund Act, 1953, the Assam Tea Plantations Fund Scheme Act, 1955 and the Uttar Pradesh Labour Welfare Fund Act, 1956 respectively.

Under the Second Plan (1956-61), seamen and motor transport workers were also brought within the purview of labour laws through enactments by the centre of the Merchant Shipping Act (1958) and the Motor Transport Workers Act (1961), Assam also enacted the Assam Tea Plantations Employees Welfare Fund Act, 1959.

The Central legislation enacted in the Third Plan (1961-66) includes the Iron Ore Mines Labour Cess Act (1961), the Maternity Benefit Act (1961), the Payment of Bonus Act (1965), the Beedi and Cigar Workers (Conditions of Employment) Act (1966) and the Seamen's Provident Fund Act (1966). The Mysore Labour Welfare Fund Act; 1965 and the Punjab Labour Welfare Fund Act. 1965 also came into being in the same period as state legislations.

The Payment at Gratuity Act, (1972) the Limestone and the Dolomite Mines Labour Welfare Fund Act were passed, as central legislations in the period covered by the Fourth Plan (1969-74). Besides, the family pension scheme was also included the Provident Fund Act consequently the Act came to be known as the Employees' Provident Funds and Family Pension Act, 1952.

During the Fifth Plan period (1974-78), the new enactments passed included: the Equal Remuneration Act (1976), Bonded

Labour System (Abolition) Act (1976) the Sales Promotion Employees (Conditions of Service) Act (1976) and the Beedi Workers Cess Act (1976) and Beedi Workers Welfare Fund Act, 1976. Besides, some of the existing legislations were amended to increase the number of beneficiaries and the extent of benefits by raising the wage limits as in the ESI and Workmen's Compensation Acts the Employees' Provident Fund Act was amended to provide for 'deposit linked insurance' for workers covered either by the Provident Fund or the Coal Mines Provident Funds Schemes. This amended Act is known as the Labour Provident Fund Laws (amendment) Act, 1976.

In 1952, a subsidized housing scheme for industrial workers was introduced by the Centre. State Governments set up Housing Boards to carry through the central scheme and to implement their own schemes. In 1956, a subsidised housing scheme for plantation workers was launched by the Central Government.

Apart from these statutory provisions, the Central government has also set up non-statutory welfare funds for public undertakings, excluding the railways and major ports. Many State Governments also provide welfare amenities on an adhoc basis through welfare centres. Some enlightened and progressive employers have also been providing welfare amenities over and above the statutory provisions.

Government's Role

The legislations pertaining to labour policy and labour welfare are administered by the Ministry of Labour, Government of India and the Departments of Labour in the State Government.

The Ministry of Labour is under the charge of Cabinet Minister/ Minister of State holding independent charge. A Secretary of the Government of India is the administrative head and he is assisted by an Additional Secretary, four Joint Secretaries, and one Director General and other senior and junior officers.

The Ministry is responsible for laying down policy in respect of labour matters including industrial relations, cooperation between labour and management, regulation of wages and other conditions of work and safety, labour welfare, social security etc. Implementation of labour policy is the responsibility of State Governments, subject to control and direction of the Central government, exception case of labour employed in railways, mines, oil fields, major ports, banks, Insurance companies (having branches in more than one state) and others which appear in the Union list. The ministry has also taken responsibility for the implementation of social security schemes under the Employees State Insurance Act, 1948, Provident fund schemes under the Employees' Provident Funds and Miscellaneous Provisions Act. 1952 and administration of welfare funds in respect of workers in the 'beedi' industry and mines other than coal mines. It also coordinates the activities of State Governments in labour matters and tenders advice as and when necessary. The Ministry also provides training facilities to persons to improve their skill for greater employability. It also functions as the model organisation for all activities relating to the International Labour Organisation and the International Social Security Association. It coordinates the participation in the meetings and conferences of the organisations and implementation of international labour standards and other recommendations of these bodies.

Structure of the Ministry of Labour : The organisation of the Ministry of Labour (main Secretariat) is reflected in the enclosed chart. The Ministry is assisted by four attached offices, 22 subordinate offices and six autonomous organisations :

Attached Offices : (i) Director General of Employment and Training is responsible for laying down the policies, procedures, standards and over-all coordination of employment service procedures and of vocational training programmes throughout the country. (ii) Chief Labour Commissioner (Central) is responsible for the prevention, investigation and settlement of industrial disputes under Industrial Disputes Act; 1947 and the implementation of labour laws in industries and establishments in respect of which the Central Government is the appropriate authority and the verification of membership of the unions affiliated to the Central Workers' organisations. (iii) Directorate General of Factory Advice Service and Labour Institutes is concerned with the safety, health and welfare of workers in factories and docks. It is responsible for coordinating the implementation of the Factories Act, 1948 by the State Governments and formulation of Model Rules thereunder. It is also concerned with administration of the Dock Workers (Safety Health and Welfare) Act, 1986. It undertakes research in industrial safety, occupational diseases, industrial hygiene, and industrial physiology. It also provides training in productivity, industrial engineering techniques and management services and conducts diploma course of one year duration in industrial safety. (iv) Directorate of Labour Bureau is responsible for collection and publication of statistical and other information regarding employment, wages, earnings, industrial disputes, working condition and publication of statistical and other informa-tion regarding employment, wages, earnings, industrial disputes, working conditions, etc. It also compiles and publishes the Consumer Price Index numbers for industrial and agricultural workers.

Subordinate Offices : The functions of some of the subordinate offices are :

(i) Directorate General of Mines Safety is entrusted with the responsibility of enforcing the provisions of the Mines Act, 1952 and the Rules and Regulations framed thereunder. Besides, the Maternity benefit Rules framed under the Maternity Benefit Act, 1961 in respect of non-coal mines are also administered by this Directorate. The provisions of the Indian Electricity Act, 1910, as applicable to mines and oil fields, are also enforced by this Directorate.

(ii) The nine offices of Welfare Commissioners are responsible for providing welfare facilities to the workers employed in the mica mines lime stone and dolomite mines, iron ore, manganese and chrome ore mines and in the beedi and cinema industries.

(iii) The eleven Industrial Tribunal cum Labour Courts have been set up under the provisions of the Industrial Disputes Act, 1947 for adjudication of the Industrial Disputes act 1947 in which the Central Government is the appropriate Government; and

(iv) The Board of Arbitration (JCM) has been set up under the Scheme for Joint Consultative Machinery and Compulsory Arbitration for resolving differences between the Government and the general body of its employees on pay and allowances, weekly hours of work and leave of a class or grade of employees.

Public Sector Establishments

The following are the autonomous organisations under the Ministry of Labour :

Employees' State Insurance Corporation is responsible for the implementation of the Employees' State Insurance Act, 1948, which provides for medical care and cash benefits in cases of sickness, maternity and employment injury.

Employees Provident Fund Organisation is responsible for implementing provident fund, family pension and deposit linked insurance scheme under the Employees' Provident Funds and Miscellaneous Provisions Act, 1952.

The National Safety Council was set up the 4th March, 1966. The main objective of the Council is to generate, develop and sustain safety awareness at the national level. The Council conducts a variety of educational training and promotional activities. These activities include holding of specialised public training courses, inplant training courses, seminars, and conferences on industrial safety and health screening of safety films in the factories, conducting fire safety and health surveys, providing free technical advice-cum-information service, publishing the Industrial Safety Chronicle (Quarterly), the Industrial Safety News (Monthly Newsletter), technical booklets, multi-coloured safety posters, Chemical Safe Practice Pamphlets, National Safety Calendars and a variety of other promotional literature and utility articles with safety slogans.

Central Board for Workers' Education Society deals with the scheme of training workers in the techniques of trade unionism and in bringing about consciousness among workers about their rights arid responsibilities. The Board also undertakes programmes for rural workers' education and functional adult education.

National Labour Institute conducts action oriented research and provides training to grass root workers in the trade union movement, both in urban and rural areas, and also to officers dealing with industrial relations, personnel management, labour welfare, etc.

The National Council for Safety in Mines was established in July, 1963 with a view to enhancing safety consciousness among miners.

Steps for Welfare

Apart from fixing minimum wages, the 'ministry' of labour is also concerned with the payment of reasonable wages and bonus to various sections of workers. The Payment of Bonus Act, 1965 provides for a minimum statutory bonus of 8.33 per cent to eligible workers. Bonus can be paid upto 20 per cent subject to availability of allocable surplus. The limit of salary for eligibility, under the Act is Rs 2,500 per month. The payment is subject to the stipulation that the bonus in respect of employees drawing wages or salary between Rs. 1600 and Rs 2500 per month would be calculated as if their salary or wages is Rs 1600 per month.

Fiscal Support

The Ministry of labour attaches great importance to the welfare of workers. To provide welfare facilities to the workers employed in certain mines and in the Beedi and Cinema industries and to supplement the efforts of the employers and the State Governments in this regard Welfare Funds have been established under the following Acts:

(a) The Mica Mines Labour Welfare Fund Act, 1946; (b) The Limestone and Dolomite Mines Labour Welfare Fund Act, 1972; (c) The Iron Ore, Manganese Ore and Chrome Ore Mines Labour Welfare Fund Act, 1976; (d) The Beedi Workers Welfare Fund Act, 1976; and (e) The Cine Workers Welfare Fund Act, 1981.

The Funds are generated by levy of cess in the manner indicated as follows :

S. No.	Fund	Cess	Collected by
(i)	Mica	@ 3.5% ad valorem on export	Custom authorities
(ii)	Iron Ore/ ManganeseOre	@ Rs. 3 per Metric tonne of chrome ore	Customs authorities on export
		@ 50p. per metric tonne or iron are	Welfare Commissioners on internal consumption
		@ Re. 1 per metric tonne of Manganese Ore-produced/consumed	Welfare Commissioners on Internal Consumption
(iii)	Limestone & Dolomite	@ 50* per metric tonne of Limestone/dolomite	Welfare—Commissioners
(iv)	Beedi	@ 30 p** per one thousand @ manufactured beedis	Central Excise authorities
(v)	Cine Workers Welfare Fund	Rs. 1000/-per feature film	Central Board of Film Certification

* Before 1.5.1988 the rate was 20 p. per metric tonne only.

** Before 1.3.1987 the rate was 10 p. per one thousand manufactured beedis.

The welfare measures financed out of the funds relate to provision of medical, housing, drinking water, educational recreational and family welfare facilities, etc. While most of the activities are administered directly by the Welfare Organisation under the Ministry, loans and subsidies are also provided to the State Governments, local authorities and to the employers for implementation of approved prototype schemes.

Health Care

Besides 12 hospitals with a capacity of 425 beds and 236 dispensaries set up till March 1989, wherefrom free treatment is provided to eligible workers and their families, some of the other schemes for the Mine and the Beedi workers are: Reservation of beds in T.B. and General Hospitals; Supply of artificial limbs; Reimbursement of cost for treatment of cancer; Treatment of workers suffering from mental diseases; provision of ambulance van to managements; Provision of spectacles to mine and beedi workers; Leprosy relief for mine and beedi workers; Maternity benefit scheme for female beedi workers; Group Insurance scheme for Beedi workers through Cooperative Societies; Family Welfare Programmes -A scheme for payment of extra monetary compensation for sterilisation to beedi workers; Grant-in-aid to managements for managing dispensaries; Financial assistance for provision of dispensary service; Fatal and Serious Accident Benefit Scheme; and Domiciliary Treatment to T.B. Patients.

Rehabilitation

For providing housing facilities to iron, manganese, chrome, limestone, dolomite and mica miners and also beedi workers, the following schemes are in vogue:

Type-I Housing Scheme : Under this scheme, the mine managements are given a subsidy of Rs 10,000 per tenement or 75 per cent of the actual cost of construction, whichever is less. In addition, development charges at the rate of Rs 1,000 per tenement for ordinary areas and Rs 1,500 per tenement for black cotton or swelly soil areas or actual cost of development, whichever is less, are also paid to the mine managements. Under this scheme, 13,467 houses had been sanctioned out of which 11,850 houses have been constructed so far.

Type-II Housing Scheme : Under this scheme, the mine managements other than mica, are reimbursed a subsidy of Rs. 20,000 per tenement or 75 percent of the actual cost of construction, whichever is less. In addition, development charges at the rate of Rs. 1,500 per tenement for ordinary areas and Rs. 2,250 per tenement for black cotton or swelly soil areas or actual cost of development whichever is less are also paid. Under this scheme 6,770 houses had been sanctioned out of which 5,890 houses have been constructed so far.

Build Your Own House Scheme : Under this scheme, workers employed in limestone, dolomite, iron, manganese, chrome and mica mines are given a subsidy of Rs. 1,000 and an interest free loan of Rs. 4,000. For beedi workers the loan component is Rs. 6,000 while the subsidy is Rs. 1,000. Under this scheme 2,196 houses had been sanctioned so far out of which 1,750 have been constructed.

Housing Scheme for Economically Weaker Sections : Under this scheme, the land is provided and houses are constructed by the state Government for allotment to the beedi workers. The State Governments are paid subsidy at the rate of Rs. 5,000 per tenement or 50 percent of actual cost of construction, whichever is less. Development charges at the rate of Rs. 800 and Rs. 1,000 per tenement for ordinary and swelly soil or black cotton areas respectively are also paid. Under this scheme, administrative approval had been issued for the construction of 7,481 houses out of which subsidy has been released of 4,452 houses so far.

Scheme for Grant of Subsidy : With a view to encourage workers to form cooperative societies, financial assistance to the extent of 75 per cent of the cost of construction of a workshed or godown or both or Rs. 75,000 for each, whichever is less is paid to societies having a minimum membership of 100 provided ownership of the land is vested in them. So far 8 worksheds have been sanctioned under this scheme out of which 2 have been constructed.

Group Housing Scheme : The scheme aims at encouraging the workers to form Cooperative Group Housing Societies of at least 50 workers which would build tenements for their members with their own resources supplemented by financial assistance from the welfare funds and other sources. The Society will be allowed to negotiate second mortgage (in addition to mortgage to Fund) of the tenements in favour of a Financial Institution or any other person. The Government will sanction from respective welfare funds the loan and subsidy at the following rates:

(a) Loan: (i) for mine workers at rate of Rs. 4,000 per house

(ii) for beedi workers at the rate of Rs. 6,000 per house

(b) Subsidy at the rate of Rs. 1,000 per house for both the mine and beedi workers

Schooling for Children

(i) A Scheme for award of scholarships to the sons and daughters of mine/beedi/cine workers studying in Class V and above in recognised institutions is in operation. The amount of scholarship ranges from Rs. 15 to Rs. 125 per month. Scholarship at an enhanced rate of Rs. 200 per month is given to students pursuing courses in medicine, engineering, etc. An amount of Rs. 114.35 lakhs was disbursed as scholarship to 36,083 students in the year 1987-88. (ii) A Scheme for financial assistance for provision of one set of school uniform each to the wards of mica miners (upto Class IV) and beedi workers (Class I only) at the rate of Rs. 50 per head per annum is also in operation. 6,099 Children had benefited from the scheme of a cost of Rs. 3.05 lakhs in the year 1987-88. (iii) Financial assistance for purchase of Text Books/ Slates/Notes Books to the wards of mine workers studying upto Class IV at the rate of Rs. 10 to 25 per annum is given. 2,740 children had benefited from the scheme at a cost of Rs. 0.47 lakh in the year 1987-88. (iv) Financial assistance upto 50 per cent of the cost of a bus is given to mine managements for purchase of school buses subject to a maximum of Rs. 1.25 lakhs for a normal bus and Rs. 60,000 for a mini bus. During the years 1987-88 and 1988-89, seven buses had been purchased. (v) Financial assistance is given to mine managements for maintenance of libraries at the rate of Rs. 2,000 per annum. (vi) Under the scheme for establishment of Central Library cum reading rooms in Iron ore, Manganese Ore and Chrome Ore Mines the accommodation is made available by the mine owners on a nominal rent. Staff and furniture are provided by the Labour Welfare organisation. An initial grant of Rs. 5,000 and a recurring grant of Rs. 2,000 per annum for purchase of books and Rs. 100 per month for purchase of periodicals, magazines and newspapers is also made available. A further grant of Rs. 1,000 per annum is made available for binding of books and other miscellaneous expenditure. (vii) A scheme for grant-in-aid to recognised schools in the iron are mining areas upto 50 percent of the cost of purchase of furniture and equipment is in operation. (viii) A mid-day meal scheme provides for refreshments at the rate of Rs. 0.75 per day per child attending primary classes at recognised schools in mica and iron ore mining areas, 215 children had benefitted from the scheme at a cost of Rs. 0.8 lakh in the year 1987-88.

Essential Commodities

A scheme for financial assistance for implementing water supply schemes in iron are, magnese ore/chrome ore/limestone and dolomite mines is in operation. Under this scheme financial assistance not exceeding 75% of total estimated cost is payable. Scheme for sinking wells in the mining areas is also in operation. An amount of Rs. 4.50 lakhs under the above mentioned schemes has been approved by the Central Government during the year 1988-89.

Entertainment

The following prototype scheme are in operation under various Welfare Funds:

Excursion-cum-study tour scheme for mine workers provides for a grant-in-aid to the mine managements payable on matching basis subject to a maximum of Rs 10, 000 per tour for tours sponsored by them upto 3,000 kms, to and, from anywhere in India. An amount of Rs 1.48 lakhs was spent in the, year 1987-88 for the purpose. A Scheme for provision of Audio-Visual Sets (16 mm projectors) and Mobile Cinema Units is in operation. There is also a provision for reimbursement upto Rs 20,000 per annum film hire charges to the mine managements. A Scheme for supply of TV sets to the mine managements/beedi cooperatives societies provides for reimbursement of Rs 10,000 per colour TV set and Rs 4,000 per, black and white TV set. There is also a scheme for organisation of games and sports, social and cultural programmes for the mine/beedi workers. A scheme for purchase of buses for transportation of mine workers to and from their places of work provides for payment of grant-in-aid at the rate of Rs 1.25 lakhs for a normal bus and Rs 0.60 lakh for a mini bus. Under Mica Mines Labour Welfare Fund 6 Schools in Andhra Pradesh and 2 Schools in Bihar are also functioning.

Receipt and Expenditure under the Labour Welfare Funds for the years 1986-87 and 1987-88 was as indicated below:

(Figures in Rs lakhs)

Name of the Fund	*Income*		*Expenditure*	
	1986-87	*1987-88*	*1986-87*	*1987-88*
(i) Mica	128.28	120.51	123.23	139.37
(ii) Iron Ore/Magnese Ore/ Chrome Ore	435.45	257.03	235.09	243.74
(iii) Limestone and Dolomite	170.00	113.34	131.23	158.87
(iv) Beedi	416.98	1102.04	323.82	419.47
(v) Cine	—	27.67	—	1.49

The Officials

The Labour Welfare Organisation which administers these funds is headed by Director-General (Labour Welfare). Each State/ Union Territory has been put under the jurisdiction of one of the 9 welfare Commissioners for the purpose of administration of these funds. The 9 regions, have their headquarters at Bhilwara, Allahabad, Karma, Kolkatta, Nagpur, Jabalpur, Bhubaneswar, Hyderabad and Bangalore. To advise the Central Government on matters related to administration of funds, tripartite Central Advisory Committees (Central Advisory Board for Mica Fund) have been set up. Similarly, tripartite Advisory Committees in the con-cerned states, headed by, Labour Minister of the State, have been set up. The Advisory , Committees in the State approve the budget under each fund for the State whereafter it is sent to Central Government for sanction.

Safety for All

The responsibility of the State towards weaker sections of the community is well recognised and is embodied in the Constitution itself as one, of the Directive Principles. Article 41 of the Constitution specifically provides that "The State shall within the limits of its economic capacity, and development make effective provision for securing the right to work to education and to public assistance, in cases of unemployment, old age, sickness and disablement and in other cases of undeserved want. As Welfare State, India has been striving to provide certain measures of social security through: The Workmen's Compensation Act, 1923; The Employee's State Insurance Act, 1943; The Maternity Benefit Act, 1961; The Employees' Provident Funds and Miscellaneous Provisions Act, 1952; and The Payment of Gratuity Act, 1972.

The Workmen's Compensation Act, 1923 provides for payment of compensation to workmen or their dependents, as the case may be, in case of industrial accidents (including certain occupational diseases) arising out of and in the course of employment and resulting in disablement or death. The Act applies to all railway, servants (other than employed in administrative work) and persons employed in any such capacity as is specified in Schedule II to the Act which includes persons employed in factories, mines, plantations, mechanically propelled vehicles, construction, works and certain other hazardous occupations. There is no wage limit for coverage, under the Act. The Act is however, not applicable to the persons who are covered under the Employees State Insurance Act, 1948.

The Act provides for payment of compensation to the workman in cases of disablement (temporary as well as permanent) and to his dependents in case of death. The minimum amount of compensation for death is Rs. 20,000 and for permanent disablement Rs 24,000. The maximum amount of compensation for permanent disablement can 99 upto Rs 1,14,000 while that for death can go upto Rs 9,000 depending on the wages and age of the workman at the time of his death. In case of temporary : disable-ment, compensation at the rate of 50 per cent of wages is payable for a maximum period of 5 years.

Administration: The Act is administered by the respective State Governments/Union Territory Administrations.

The Employees' State Insurance Act, 1948: Provides for free medical treatment to insured, persons and their dependants and cash benefits in contingencies such as sickness maternity and employment injury, that result in loss of wages. The Act also ensures economic relief to the dependants of an injured worker in case of death clue to employment injury in the form of dependants' pension. The provisions of the Act are initially applicable to perennial factories using power and employing 20 or more persons. Most of the State Governments have extended the application of the Act to smaller power using factories, employing 10-19 persons and non-power using factories, 'shops, hotels, restaurants, cinemas including preview theatres, road motor' transport companies and newspaper establishments employing 20 or more persons. The coverage under the Act is at present restricted to employees drawing wages not exceeding Rs 1,600 per month. During 1988-89, the Act was implemented in 24 new industrial centres covering about 54,256 additional workers, raising the total number of centres to 580 as on 31st December 1988. The total number of employees and the beneficiaries covered was 61.68 lakhs and 272.59 lakhs respectively. The reduction in coverage is due to gradual decoverage of employees consequent on their wages exceeding Rs 1,600 per month.

Administration: The Employees' State Insurance Scheme is administered by a corporate body, called the ESI Corporation (ESIC) which has members representing employees, employers, Central Government, State Governments, Parliament and medical profession. The Director General functions as the Chief Executive of the Corporation and is also an Ex-officio member of the Standing Committee and the Corporation.

During 1988-89, the Corporation commissioned three new hospitals with a total bed strength of 262 beds and 25 new dispensaries. The total number of hospitals has gone up to 103 and the beds to 18,803. The number of dispensaries has increased to 1,266. In addition, there are 42 ESI Annexe with 842 beds. Besides, 4,445 beds have been reserved in Government and other hospitals, for the use of ESI beneficiaries.

The Corporation disbursed a total sum of Rs 104.22 crores during 1987-88, as against Rs 103.34 crores during 1986-87 for payment of sickness, maternity and employment and injury benefits.

The Maternity Benefit Act, 1961 : Regulates the employment of women for certain period before and after child birth and provides for maternity and certain other benefits. The Act applies, in the first instance to mines, factories, plantation and circus industry. The provisions of the Act can be extended to any other establishment or class of establishments by the State Government. There is no wage limit for coverage under the Act. The Act does not, however, apply to women employees who are covered under the Employees' State Insurance Act.

The Act provides for payment of maternity benefits at the rate of average daily wages for the period of actual absence upto six weeks immediately preceding and including the date of delivery and for six weeks immediately following that day. In order to qualify for maternity benefits the women employees should have rendered 160 days service during preceding 12 months period. The Act also provides for grant of six weeks maternity benefit in case of mis-carriage. The Act was amended in 1988 by the Maternity Benefit (Amendment) Act. Some of the important amendments are: The provisions of the Act are being extended to shops or establishments employing ten or more persons: The qualifying period for grant of maternity benefit is being reduced from 160 days of actual work in the preceding 12 months to 80 days of actual work in the preceding 12 months; The rate of medical bonus payable to women employees in case the employer does not provide pre-natal confinement and post-natal care free of charge, is being raised from twenty five rupees to two hundred and fifty rupees; A provision is being made for filing of complaint with the competent court by the aggrieved woman or an office bearer of a registered trade union of which such woman is a member or a voluntary organisation or an Inspector. At present, complaints can be filed only with the previous sanction of the Inspector; and The rate of maternity benefit is being fixed at average daily wages for three calendar months or minimum wages fixed or revised under the Minimum Wages Act or rupees ten per day, whichever is higher.

The above provisions have been brought into force with effect from 10.1.1989.

Administration: The Central Government is responsible for administration of the provisions of the Act in mines and circus industry while the State Governments are responsible for the administration of the Act in factories, plantations and other establishments. The Central Government has entrusted the administration of the Act to the Central Labour Commissioner in respect of Circus Industry and to the Director General of Mines Safety in respect of mines.

The Employees Provident Funds and Miscellaneous Provisions Act, 1952 : Provides for compulsory provident fund, family pension arid deposit linked insurance.

The Act which initially applied to six major industries in 1952 is now applicable to 173 industries/classes of establishments employing 20 or more persons. By the end of September, 1988, 1.72 lakh establishments had been covered and the number of subscribers was 140 lakhs. The coverage under the Act is at present restricted to employees drawing pay not exceeding Rs 2500 per month.

The statutory minimum rate of provident fund contributions payable by the employers and the employees, which was or 6% of basic wages, dearness allowance including the cash value of any food concession and retaining allowance (if any) of the employee had been raised to 8.5% of basic/wages, dearness allowance including cash value of any food concession and retaining allowance (if any) of the employees, with effect from 1st August, 1988. The rate of interest to be credited to the members' provident fund accumulations (unexempted) for the year 1988-89 has been raised to 11.8 per cent per annum as against 11.5% for 1987-88.

The provident fund contributions are invested as per the pattern of investment prescribed by the Central Government, from time to time through the Reserve Bank of India, Bombay which holds the securities in safe custody. Other banking arrangements have been assigned to the State Bank of India. As on 30th Sept. 1988 the total investment amounted to Rs. 18,716;80 crores out of which Rs. 8,574.21 crores pertained to unexempted establishments and Rs. 10,142.59 crores to exempted establishments.

The Employees' Provident Fund Organisation provides non-refundable withdrawal to workers from their provident fund accumulations for financing of life insurance policies, house building, illness of members/family members, marriage and higher education" temporary closure. During 1987-88, a total amount of Rs. 145.27 crores had been sanctioned and paid as withdrawal to the subscribes covered under unexempted establishments. In cases where the employers' contribution are not payable to the out-going members of the unexempted establishments in full, the unpaid part together with interest is credited to the Reserve and Forfeiture Account. During 1987-88, the amount forfeited was Rs. 11.18 crores. The accumulations in this Fund are utilised for meeting the liabilities under Special Reserve Fund and Death Relief Fund. The money in the Special Reserve Fund and Death Relief Fund is utilised for paying the provident fund accumulations to the outgoing members of the unexempted establishments or their nominees/heirs where the employers failed to remit to the Fund, the whole or part of the provident fund contributions deducted from the wages of the members. Out of a total amount of Rs. 354.51 lakhs transferred to this Fund from the Reserve and Forfeiture Account upto 31.3.1988 including the recoupment of Rs. 44.51 lakhs made on recovery of arrears from the employers of unexempted establishments, a sum of Rs. 365.41 lakhs had been paid upto 31st March. 1988. The Fund was thus over-drawn by a sum of 10.90 lakhs during 1987-88. Financial assistance out of Death Relief Fund upto Rs. 1,250 is available to the survivors of deceased members whose pay did not exceed Rs. 1000 per month at the time of death and whose balance in the Provident Fund accounts than Rs. 1250 so as to bring the total to the figures of Rs. 1250. Out of a total sum of Rs. 181 lakhs transferred to this fund from the Reserve and Forfeiture Account, a sum of Rs. 161.27 lakhs had been utilised upto the end of March, 1988.

The total amount of Provident Fund arrears recoverable from the defaulting unexempted establishments as on 30 Oct. 1988 was Rs. 85.3 crores, out of which Rs. 30.85 crores was due from the establishments lying closed, under liquidation arrears stayed due to courts orders, pre-taken over and pre-nationalisation dues of nationalised units or taken over and assisted by Industrial Reconstruction Corporation in which cases there were limited options for recovery. The balance of Rs. 54.28 crores represented the effective amount of arrears. The arrears of provident fund dues from the exempted establishments was Rs. 117.04 crores. The Employees' Provident Fund authorities have been taking action for recovery of dues against the defaulting employers (unexempted) under Section 8 and for prosecutions under Section 14, 14 A and 14 AA of the Act. Action for prosecutions under section 406/409 I.P.C. is also taken in cases where employers deduct employees' share of provident fund contributions from their wages but do not remit the same to the Provident Fund authorities.

The Employees' Family Pension Scheme, 1971 : Provides the family pension and life assurance benefits. The scheme is compulsorily applicable to all employees who have become members of the Provident Fund on or, after 1st 1971 but is optional to those who had become members of the provident fund prior to that date. The total number of subscribes as on 30th Sept. 1988 was 95.46 lakhs.

The scheme is financed by diverting 1.6% of pay of, the employees from out of their share of contributions towards provident fund with an equal amount from employers' share of provident fund contributions. The Central Government also contributes to the Family Pension Fund at the rate of 1.6% of the pay of the members. The contributions received during 1987-88 amounted to Rs 256.63 crores. All money belonging to Family Pension Fund is kept in deposit in the public account. The interest allowed on this deposit which was 5% per annum initially, was raised to 7½% per annum with effect from 1 April, 1988.

The benefits extended of this scheme are family pension life insurance benefits and retirement cum withdrawal benefits. The total amount paid in settlement of claims under this scheme during 1987-88 amounted to Rs 18.95 crores.

The Employees' Deposit or Wage Insurance Scheme, 1976 : It is applicable to all factories/establishments to which the Act applies. All the employees who are members of the provident fund in both the exempted and un-exempted establishments are covered under this scheme. The main feature of this scheme is that the workers are not required to pay any contributions. The employers are required to pay contributions to the Insurance Fund at the rate of 0.5% of the total emoluments, i.e. basic wages and dearness allowance, including cash value of any food concession and retai-ning allowance if any, of the employee. The Central Government also contributes to the Fund at the rate of 0.25% of the total emolu-ments of the employees. All money belonging to the Insurance Fund are kept in deposit with the Central Government in the Public Account. The interest allowed on this deposit, which was 7 % per annum, has been raised to 8% per annum with effect from 1st April 1988.

Benefits: On the death of an employee (while in service) who is a member of the Employees' Provident Fund or of the exempted Provident Fund, the person is entitled to receive the Provident Fund accumulations is paid an additional amount equal to the average balance in the provident fund account of the deceased during the proceeding three years or during the period of his membership of the fund whichever is less, if such average balance was not less than Rs 1000 at any time during the said period. The maximum amount of benefit payable under Scheme is Rs 10,000.

The Act was last amended in 1988. The Amendment Act provides inter-alia for raising the minimum rate of provident fund contribution from 7% of pay and dearness, allowance to 8% of pay and Dearness Allowance; increasing the number of represen-tatives of the organisations of employers and employees on the Central Board of Trustees from 6 each to 10 each; making the existing penal provision more stringent; Extending the existing legal and penal provision to the exempted establishments; Setting up of an independent machinery for recovery of arrears of provident fund dues; Setting up of one or more Tribunals for hearing appeals filed against the orders of the Provident Fund authorities in the matters of applicability of the provisions of the Act, assessment of dues, etc. ; and authorising establishments employing 100 or more persons to maintain provident fund accounts of their employees at the establishment level.

Administration : All the three schemes, namely the Employees Provident Funds Scheme, 'the Employees' Family Pension Scheme and the Employees Deposit Linked Insurance Scheme are administered by the Central Board of Trustees which is a tripartite body. The Central Provident Fund Commissioner is the Chief Executive Officer of the Organisation and Secretary to the Board. Apart from the Central Office, the organisation has at present more than 16 Regional Offices and 45 Sub-Regional Offices functioning in various States for implementing the provisions of the Act and the three Scheme framed there under.

The cost of administration of the Employees' Provident Fund Scheme is met out of the levy of administrative/inspection charges from the employers of covered establishments. The cost of administration of the Employees Family Pension Scheme is borne entirely by the Central Government while the cost of administration of the Employees' Deposit Linked Insurance Scheme is borne partly by the employers of covered establishments and partly by the Central Government.

The Payment of Gratuity Act, 1972 : Provides for a scheme for payment of gratuity. The Act applies to every factory, mine, oil field, plantations, port, railway company and shop or establishment in which 10 or more persons are employed. Under the Act, the Central Government is empowered to extend the provisions of the Act to any other establishment or class of establishments in which 10 or more persons are employed. In exercise of there powers, the Central Government has so far extended the provisions of the Act to Motor Transport Undertakings, Inland Water Transport Establishments, Local Bodies, Chamber of Commerce and Industry, Solicitors, Office; Companies, Societies and Associations or group which give any circus performance in any arena and required payment for admission into such exhibition from spectators or audience. The Act is applicable to employees other than apprentices drawing wages not exceeding Rs. 2,500 per month.

The Act provides for payment of gratuity on termination of employment on superannuation, retirement or resignation or death or disablement subject to completion off continuous service of not less than 5 years. The condition of continuous service of 5 years does not apply in to case of death or disablement. The Act provides for the payment of gratuity at the rate of 15 days wages for every complete year at service of part thereof in excess of 6 months. The maximum ceiling for payment of gratuity is Rs. 50,000.

Administration : The Central Government is responsible for administration the provisions of the Act in establishments under its control, establishments having branches in more than one State, major ports, mine, oil fields and railway company. In all other cases, the responsibility for administration of the Act is that of the respective State Governments.

Central Board for Workers Education : The Central Board for Workers Education was set up in 1958 for imparting education to workers. The Board implements the workers Education Scheme through its 43 Regional Centres in four zones with offices at Bombay, Calcutta, Delhi and Madras. The Board is a tripartite body comprising the representatives of the workers, employers and Government. The Board has its own training Institute in Mumbai i.e. Indian Institute of Workers Education (IIWE). The objectives of Central Board for Workers Education Programme is to increase awareness among workers with a view to enabling them to effectively participate in the social and economic development and developing among them understanding of their problems, environment, responsibilities and promoting leadership among the rank and file of workers. The Government expects that through labour education, the trade unions will develop into strong and responsible labour organisations, collective bargaining would gain greater acceptability and spread to large segment of the work force.

Functional Adult Literacy Classes : During the year 1988-90, 9732 workers successfully completed the course in 424 sessions of Functional/Adult Literacy Classes. These included 2695 from plantation, 2116 from mines, 4921 from other areas.

The break-up is as follows:

	SC	ST	Others	Total
Male	1203	536	6410	8149
Female	380	488	715	1583
Total	**1583**	**1024**	**7125**	**9732**

Training of Women Workers : Greater emphasis was given to the participation of women workers in various programmes of the Board. During the period 1988-90, 40 women workers teachers, 365 women workers at unit level classes, 38 women workers teachers in Refresher Courses, 1512 women workers in Functional Adult Literacy Classes, 25, 106 in rural Programme, 3,324 in unorganised sector and 204 quarry workers were trained.

Refresher Courses : During the period 1988-89, 52 refresher courses were organised for worker teachers in which 1002 worker teachers participated including 38 women worker teachers. In these refresher courses topics like Concept of Workers' Participation in Industry, Collective Agreements. New Culture in Industrial relations, Developing Skills of Communication, recent amendment in Labour Legislation, etc. were covered.

Rural Workers : Starting with Seven Pilot Projects in 1977-78, rural workers education programme of the Board has now become regular and continuing feature of the Board's major activities. By the end of December, 1988, the Board had trained 765 Rural organisers sponsored by the State Governments and 699 Rural educators.

Unit Level : During the period 1988-89, 28613 workers were trained in unit level classes. The Board gives financial assistance to the extent of 90% of the total admissible expenditure to the trade unions for conducting short-term programme of 1-4 days duration. Since inception till 31.12.88 an amount of Rs. 102.54 lakhs had been paid by the Board to unions/institutions who trained 4,67,549 workers.

The Board produces training aids in the form of textual and pictorial booklets in English on topics like Trade Unions, Industrial Relations, Labour Laws, Labour Economics, Productivity, Family

Welfare, Safety, etc. These booklets, written by eminent persons in respective fields in simple and lucid style, have been considered use full literature an study material in the training programme conducted by the Board. These are also available in Hindi, Assamese, Tamil, Nepali and Urdu.

To facilitate teaching, the Board brings out learning materials in regional languages for use in different training programme. During 1988-89 the standard material for education was brought out in Gujarati. With this addition, standardised material in now available in eight regional languages.

Forced Labour

The system of Bonded Labour constitutes a great slur on our society. It is an outcome of certain categories of indebtedness which have been prevailing for a long time involving certain economically exploited helpless and weaker sections of the society. This system originated from the uneven social structure characterised by feudal and semi-feudal conditions. According to National Commissions on Labour, "Bonded labour can best be described in terms of debt bondage fixed for a time or a life time or hereditarily descending from father to son in some cases". The Indian School of Social Science has defined bonded labour as a social agreement between a debtor and creditor under which the debtor agrees to render labourer personal services to the creditor without remuneration in lieu of the satisfaction of the debt or part of debt or interest on principal amount for a specific period or till the debt is satisfied or repaid. The Commissioner for Scheduled Castes and Scheduled Tribes in its twenty-fourth report had used the term 'bonded labour' to mean, "Persons belonging to any particular caste or community forced or partly forced to work for a creditor under an agreement either without wage or for nominal wage which was less than the prescribed minimum wage". The Bonded Labour System (Abolition) Act, 1976 defines, bonded labour as "the system of forced or partly forced labour under which a debtor enters, or has, or is presumed to have entered, into an agreement with the creditor to the effect that: (i) in consideration of an advance obtained by him or by any of his lineal ascendants or descendants (whether or not such advance is evidenced by any document) and in consideration of the interest if any, due on such advance, or (ii) in pursuance of any customary or social obligation or (iii) in pursuance of an obligation devolving on him by succession, or (iv) for any economic consideration received, by him or by any of his lineal ascendants or descendants, or (v) by reason of his birth in any particular caste or community, he would render by himself or through any member of his family, or any person dependent in him, labour or service to the creditor, for specified period or for an unspecified period, either without wages or for nominal wages, or forfeit the freedom of employment or other means of livelihood for a specified period or for an unspecified period, or forfeit the right to move freely throughout the territory of India or forfeit the right to appropriate or at market value any of his property or product of his labour or the labour of member of his family or any person dependent on him. The two essential ingredients of bonded labour thus are: (1) indebtedness and (2) forced labour. The National Commission on Agriculture has accordingly observed: "The prominent feature of the system of bonded labour is that a man pledges his person or sometimes members of his family against a indebtedness has rightly, labelled as "the mother of the problem of bonded labour". Being compelled by the exigencies of the situation the bonded labourer is compelled to take loan and do forced labour in lieu thereof.

According to the finding of a survey jointly undertaken by the Gandhi Peace Foundation and the National Labour Institute in 1978, the number of agricultural bonded labourer is estimated to be 26.17 lakhs. The largest concentration is in Uttar Pradesh (5.50 lakhs); followed by Madhya Pradesh (5 lakhs), Orissa (3.50 lakhs), Andhra Pradesh (3.25 lakhs), Tamil Nadu (2.50 lakhs), Karnataka (1.93 lakhs) , Gujarat (1.71 lakhs) , Bihar (1.11 lakhs), Maharashtra (1.00 lakhs), and Rajasthan (0.6.7 lakhs). The other findings of the survey are: most of the bonded labourers, 86.6 percent of the total, come from the scheduled castes and scheduled tribes; twenty-five per cent of the bonded labourers are below the age of 20 years. Thirty per cent of bonded labour families send two or more of their family members into bondage about twenty per cent of bonded labourers have not taken any loan de jure a labourer is in bondage for six years on an average; in Bihar, Maharashtra and

Uttar Pradesh the duration of bondage is longer (above ten years) whereas it is shorter in Andhra Pradesh, Gujarat and Orissa (three to four years) fifty-five per cent of bonded labourers take loans for the purpose of domestic expenditure; forfeiting the right to seek alternative employment is one of the essential elements of bondage. The largest group of masters (5 per cent) comes from upper case Hindus whereas 15 per cent, belong to backward classes. Fifteen per cent of the masters belong to scheduled castes and 13, per cent to scheduled tribes fifty-one per cent of the masters employ two to five bonded labourers, 5.5 per cent employ six to ten bonded labourers, whereas 40 per cent of the masters keep only one bonded labourer.

Corrective Steps

Measures to abolish the barbaric practice of bonded labour have been initiated since the advent of the British rule and various international conventions held from time to time such as the Forced Labour Convention of 1930, the Universal Declaration of Human Rights, 1948, the Supplementary Convention on the Abolition of Slavery, the Slave Trade and Institutions and practices/similar to slavery adopted by the conference convened under the auspices of the United Nations in 1956, and the Abolition of Forced Labour Convention, 1957 have contributed to urge the government to take necessary steps to eliminate the menace of this crime against humanity by passing necessary legislations on the subject. The Constitution of India specifically provides for it in Article 23. After the adoption of the Constitution, State Governments had passed legislations on the subject like the Andhra Pradesh (Scheduled Tribes) Money lenders Regulation, 1960; Orissa Debt Bondage Abolition Rules, 1963; Lacchadives, Minicoy and Amindivi Islands (Debt Cancellation and Grant of loans) Regulation, 1964; Assam Rural Indebtedness Relief Act, 1975; V.P. Landless Agricultural Labour Debt Relief Act 1975; Orissa Dadan Labour Control and Regulation Act, 1975; Inter-state Migrant Workmen (Regulation of Employment and Conditions of Services and Miscellaneous Provisions) Act, 1979.

The Indian Penal Code (Section 371) also provides that "whoever unlawfully compels any person to labour against the will of that person shall be punished with imprisonment of either description which may extend to one year or fine or with both".

Serious efforts in the direction of statutory abolition of bonded labour throughout the country were made only after the announcement of the Twenty-point Programme in 1975 which unequivocally declared, "The practice of bonded labour is barbarous and will be abolished. All contracts or other arrangements under which services of such bonded labourers are secured, will be declared illegal." In pursuance of this declaration, the Bonded Labour System (Abolition) Ordinance, abolishing bonded labour with immediate effect, has promulgated on 4 October, 1975 which became the Bonded Labour System (Abolition) Act on 2 February 1976. The revised 20 Point Programme. 1986 stipulates: (i) full implementation of laws abolishing bonded labour and (ii) invol-vement of voluntary agencies in the programme of bonded labour.

The first implies (1) identification, (2) release, (3) action against offenders, (4) constitution and holding of regular meetings of the Vigilance Committees at the district and sub-divisional levels, (5) conferring of powers of Judicial Magistrates on Executive Magistrates under section 21 of the Bonded Labour System (Abolition) Act, 1976, and (6) maintenance of the registers etc. as prescribed under Rule 7 of the Bonded Labour System (Abolition) Rules, 1976.

The responsibilities for identification, release and rehabilitation of bonded tabourers rest with the State Governments who are the implementing authorities under the Bonded Labour System (Abolition) Act, 1976. The incidence of bonded labour system has been reported from 12 States viz., Andhra Pradesh, Bihar, Gujarat, Haryana, Karnataka, Kerala, Madhya Pradesh, Maharashtra, Orissa, Rajasthan, Tamil Nadu and Uttar Pradesh. According to the state Government all the bonded labourers in Kerala and Gujarat have already been rehabilitated and no further bonded labourers have been detected there. In Uttar Pradesh there was no backlog for rehabilitation of bonded labourers at the end of 1987-88. They had, however, identified 901 bonded labour by 30.11.88. Out of these, 417 had been rehabilitated. According to the latest reports of the State Governments, the total number of bonded labourers identified and freed as on 30.11.88 was 2,36,868 out of which 2,03,035 had been rehabilitated.

With a view to supplementing the efforts of the State Governments in rehabilitation of bonded labourers, the Ministry of Labour launched a Centrally Sponsored Scheme from 1978-79 under which the State Governments are provided central financial assistance of on a matching grant (50 : 50) basis for rehabilitation of bonded labourers. The Scheme originally envisaged provision of financial assistance upto a ceiling limit of Rs 4000 per bonded labourer which has since been enhanced to Rs 6,250 with effect from 1.2.1986. The rehabilitation scheme can be either land-based or animal husbandry based or skill/craft based depending upon the aptitude, skill and preference of the beneficiary. The land-based scheme comprises (i) allotment of land (ii) provision of back-up service and facilities such as plough, bullocks, seeds, fertilisers, etc. Animal husbandry based schemes involve supply of produc-tive assets and linkage with the market. The skill/crafts based schemes involve identification of skills/crafts, supply of raw material, working capital, sheds; implements and linkage with the market. For speeding up the pace of rehabilitation of bonded labourers, the State Governments have been allowed to delegate powers for sanction of rehabilitation schemes to the District Collectors/ Divisional Commissioners by setting up the Screening Committee at the District level. Prior to this, such power were vested with the State Governments. The State Governments have also been requested to set up a Monitoring and Review Committee at the State level under the chairmanship of the Chief Secretary or some other senior officer which will meet every quarter to monitor and review the progress of the programme of rehabilitation of bonded labour both in physical and financial terms and make suitable recommendations. The Director General (Labour Welfare), Ministry of Labour or his nominee is to be associated as a Member of the Committee.

Senior Officers from the Ministry of Labour visit different States to conduct on the spot review of the measures taken by the State Governments for identification, release and rehabilitation of bonded labourers. The deficiencies observed during these reviews are communicated to the respective State Governments for necessary corrective action. Based on such reviews, instructions and guidelines on the subject of bonded labourers are also issued to the State Governments for effective implementation of the programme.

As envisaged in the 20-Point Programme 1986-A New Plan Scheme "Grant-in-aid to Voluntary Agencies in the identification and rehabilitation of bonded labourers" has been launched since 30th October, 1987. Rs 1.00 crore and Rs 5.00 lakhs had been provided for the 7th Five Year Plan (1985-90) and Annual Plan (1988-89) respectively.

Under Agreement

Contract Labour (Regulation and Abolition) Act, 1970 was brought on the state book to regulate the employment of Contract Labour and to provide for its abolition in certain circumstances and matters connected there to. The Act provides for the regulation of conditions of work, payment of wages and other amenities relating to welfare and health of contract labour. The 'Appropriate Government' may, after consultation with the Central Board or as the case may be, a State Board, prohibit the employment of the contract labour in any process, operation of other work in any establishment as may be notified by it in the official Gazette having regard to the criteria laid down in the Act.

The term 'Appropriate Government' as defined in Section 2 (a) of the Act, has been amended on 28.1.86 through promulgation of the Contract Labour (Regulation and Abolition) Amendment Ordinance. 1986 which has since been replaced by an Act of Parliament (No. 14 of 1986) in the interest of healthy industrial relations and harmony in the implementation of the Act. With this amendment, the "Appropriate Government" in respect of an establishment under the Contract Labour (Regulation and Abolition) Act, 1970 would be the same as in the Industrial Disputes Act, 1947.

In pursuance of the recommendations of the Central Advisory Contract Labour Board, the Central Government has issued notifications prohibiting employment of contract labour in the following categories of work from the date indicated against each:

Sr. No.	Name of the Industry	Nature of Job/ operations	Date of abolition
(1)	(2)	(3)	(4)
1.	Coal Mines	(i) Raising or raising-cum selling of coal;	1.2.1975
		(ii) Coal loading and un-loading;	
		(iii) Coal loading and un-loading;	
		(iv) Overburden removal and earth cuting; and	
		(v) Driving of stone drifts and Miscellaneous stone cutting underground	
2.	Building	Sweeping, cleaning, dusting and watching of buildings owned or occupied by the establishments in respect of which the appropriate Government is the Central Government.	1.3.1977
		(i) Overburden removal;	
		(ii) Drilling and Blasting;	
3.	Iron Ore Mines	(i) Over-burden removal and	10.5.1980
		(ii) Drilling and blasting	
		(iii) Muck cleaning operations in crushing plants, screening plants and/or cover belts; and	28.5.1982
		(iv) Wagon levelling operations	
		(v) Float Ore operations.	10.5.1980
4.	Limestone, Dolomite and Manganese Mines.	(i) Overburden excavation and removal;	
		(ii) Drilling and blasting;	
5.	Coal Washeries	(i) Unloading of raw coal;	
		(ii) charging of magnetite; and	
		(iii) Plant cleaning including removal slippage, waste, muck cleaning, magnetite removal etc.	
6.	Chromite Mines	(i) Overburden removal;	
		(ii) Drilling and Blasting; and	
		(iii) Rasing of Ore; and	
		(iv) Transportation of overburden to dumps and ore to stocking sites	

Contd.

Sr. No.	Name of the Industry	Nature of Job/ operations	Date of abolition
(1)	(2)	(3)	(4)
7.	Magnetite Mines	(i) Over burden removal; (ii) Drilling and Blasting; (iii) Raising of Minerals	
8.	Mica Mines	(i) Raising of Mica; (ii) Drilling & Blasting (iii) Dewatering of mines; (iv) Muck removal; and (v) Processing of Mica.	
9.	Gypsum Mines	(i) Over burden removal; and (ii) Raising and stocking of Fire-clay;	
10.	Fire Clay Mines	(i) Loading and transportation; and (ii) Dewatering of mines.	
11.	Railways	Cleaning in catering establishments and pantry cars on railways.	

Provided that this notification shall not apply to the following categories:

(a) quarries in the North-east Coal field which can-only be worked for a few months every year due to heavy rainfall in the area; (b) quarries located by the side of the river in Pench valley and similar other patch deposits which can only be worked when the level of river has gone down during non-rainy season; (c) loading of coal when there is mechanical failure, failure of power or irregular supply of wagon by the railways; and (d) cutting of stone drifts/faults which cannot be detected in advance and are of short duration, say upto six months.

To safeguard the interests of the workmen who are recruited by contractors in one state for serving in an establishment situated in another state and to protect these workmen from the exploitation of contractors, the Inter-state Migrant Workmen (Regulation of Employment and Conditions of Services) Act, 1979 was enacted. This Act came into force with effect from the 2nd October, 1980. It ensures provisions of basic needs like housing, food, protective clothing and medical facilities, etc. for the workmen. The Act is to be implemented by the Central and State Governments in their respective spheres of jurisdiction.

Construction Sector

The Building and Construction Industry provides employment to about more than two million workers. Most of them are engaged by contractors and many of them are employed on casual basis. There is, however, no law governing the service conditions, safety and the health of the workers in the industry. The Building and other Construction Workers (Regulation of Employment and Conditions of Service) Bill, 1988 had since been introduced in the Rajya Sabha on 5th December, 88. The Bill inter-alia provides for the following matters, namely:

(i) to apply to every establishment which employs, or employed on any day of the preceding twelve months, fifty or more building workers in any building or other construction work; (ii) to empower the Central Government and the State Governments as the case may be to constitute Advisory Boards to advise on such matters arising out of the administration of the proposed legislation as may be referred to them. Such Advisory Boards shall consist, inter-alia of persons representing the employers, building workers, association of architects, engineers, accident insurance institutions and any other interest which in the opinion of the Government, ought to be represented on such Boards; (iii) to provide for the constitution of one or more expert committees consisting of persons especially qualified in building or other construction work for advising the Government for making rules under the proposed legislation; (iv) to provide for the registration of certain establishments, as defined in the proposed legislation, carrying on building or other construction work; (v) to enable the appropriate Government to fix hours for normal working day, day of rest, payment of wages for the day of rest, payment of overtime allowance and other welfare measures, such as facilities regarding drinking water, latrines and urinals, creches, first-aid and canteens in respect of building workers; (vi) to make adequate provisions in respect of building workers for their safety and health measures including appointments of safety committees and safety officers therefor; (vii) to empower the Central Government to frame model rules for safety measures; (viii) to provide for the appointment of appropriate inspecting staff including Director General of Inspection at the Central level and the Chief Inspector of Inspection of Building and Construction at the State level far ensuring effective implementation of the proposed legislation; (ix) to make special provisions regarding responsibility of employers to ensure compliance of the provisions of the proposed legislation and payment of wages in time to building workers; and (x) to provide for deterrent punishment for contravention of provisions of the proposed legislation.

Female Labour

Women and child labour are generally the most dis-advantaged and exploited sections of the labour force. The majority of women and child labour work in the unorganised sectors with low wages and at low levels of skills. Two separate cells-one for women labour and the other for the child labour have been set up in the Ministry of labour to pay special attention to the problems of women and child labour.

Women Labour : The Women's Cell is responsible for the formulation of policies relating to women labour that seek to remove the disadvantages under which women work, to strengthen their bargaining position to improve their wages and working conditions to enhance their skills and open up better employment opportunities for them. As part of this policy, the Ministry has passed certain laws for women workers, principal among them being the Equal Remuneration Act, 1976, which provides for payment of equal remuneration to men and women for the same work or work of similar nature and for prevention of discrimination on the grounds of sex against women in matters of employment and issues related thereto. A Committee has been set up at the Centre under the Act to advise the government for the purpose of providing increasing employment opportunities for women. Similar Committees have also been set up by the State Governments/Union Territories. The Central Government and most of the State Governments have also appointed authorities for hearing and deciding complaints and claims of the women workers under the Equal Remuneration Act. 1976.

***The Equal Remuneration (Amendment) Act, 1987* :** Remove certain ambiguities in the original Act and makes the penalties under the Act more stringent.

To improve their working conditions and increase their employment potential, the Women's Cell also gives financial assistance to voluntary agencies to take up action oriented projects. During 1988-89, following five projects had been funded:

(i) Organising Bidi workers in Indore City. The Project is being run by SEWA, Ahmedabad (ii) Training to domestic workers and running a placement service to find suitable employers at New Delhi; the project is being run by Nirmal Sewa Samiti, New Delhi; (iii) Skill training and organising of women construction labour at Chennai: the project is being run by the Tamil Nadu Construction workers Union, Chennai; (iv) Parivartan Programmes for the welfare of poor women in Mehrauli, New Delhi; the project is being run by the Centre for Social Research, New Delhi (v) Organising women workers through employment in Bihar; the project is being run by the Centre for Women's Development Studies, Bihar.

***Child Labour* :** Child labour though undesirable, persists in various employments on account of socio-economic compulsions. As such it is not possible to completely ban the employment of children in all occupations at present. The policy of the Government is to ban employment of children below the age of 14 years in factories, mines and other hazardous employments in accordance with the provisions of the Constitution and to regulate the working conditions of children in non-hazardous employments. The Child Labour (Prohibition and Regulation) Act 1986 passed in December 1986 sought to achieve this basic objective. The Labour Ministry finalised and notified in August; 1988, the rules framed under Section 18 (1) of the Act notification No. GSR 847 (E) dated the 10th August, 1988). In pursuance of Section 5 of the said Act, Government had set up a Child Labour Technical Advisory Committee to advise it as to what other occupations/processes could be added to the Schedule of prohibited employments. The

Committee, in its first report to the Government in August, 1988 had recommended the prohibition of the employment of children in the following occupations and processes:

Occupation : Employment in shops with temporary licences to sell crackers and fire-workers

Processes : Manufacture of slate pencils (including packing). Manufacture of products from agate. Manufacturing processes using toxic metals and substances such as Lead, Mercury" Manganese, chromium Cadmium, Benzene, Pesticides and Asbestos.

The Government has since accepted these recommendations of the Committee.

The Child Labour Cell of the Ministry is involved in the formulation, coordination and implementation of policies and programmes/schemes for improving the working conditions of children. During 1988-89, the Cell rendered financial assistance to seven voluntary organisations in the field of child labour for implementation of continuing as well as new projec's/programmes for the welfare of the working children, supplementary nutrition and health care and vocational/skill training. The projects financed by the Cell are:

(i) A pre-occupational training-cum-education and relief centre near Aurangabad (Maharashtra) for children working in rural and agricultural occupations. The project is run by the Institute of Rural Workers, Aurangabad.

(ii) A project to provide formal and non-formal education, health care and nutrition to urban children working as domestic servants as well as in automobile workshops, tea shops, pan shops, etc. in Kolkatta. These centres are ran by the Institute of Psychological and Educational Research, Kolkatta on Sundays and holidays.

(iii) An action project for the rehabilitation of child labour in Ahmedabad. The centres have been opened for training in handloom weaving, tailoring, electric wiring, etc. The project is being run by the Self-employed Women's Association, Ahmedabad.

(iv) The Jaya Rajendra Rag Pickers Project for the welfare of child labour in Bangalore. The project is run by the

Karnataka State Council for Child Welfare. The project gives non-formal education to the children and trains them in occupations which will earn them a proper income as adults. It also attempts to inculcate moral values in the children and wean them away from hazardous occupations.

(v) A centre for providing non-formal education, vocational training, health care, nutrition, etc. to the child labour withdrawn from the carpet weaving industry of Mirzapur-Bhadohi. The centre has been set up by the Saghan Kshetra Vikas Samiti, Sewapuri, Varanasi.

(vi) Organising non-formal education orientation camps in Hyderabad for children employed in rural occupations. The project has been taken up by the Shramik Vidyapeeth, Hyderabad.

(vii) A centre for working children in Ferozabad, Uttar Pradesh. This has been set up by the Indian Council for Child Welfare, New Delhi.

Keeping in view the fact that legislation alone would not be sufficient to tackle the problem of child labour, Government announced the National Policy on Child Labour in August, 1987 which inter-alia provided for taking up projects in areas of child labour concentration. A total of eight projects have so far been sanctioned under the project based plan of action. Of these, the following three projects were launched during 1988: (i) Project for the welfare of children working in the precious stone polishing industry in Jaipur, Rajasthan. (ii) Project for the welfare of children engaged in the slate pencil making industry in Mandsaur. (iii) Project for the Welfare of children working in the slate industry in Markapur, Andhra Pradesh.

The Project for the welfare of Children working in the match and firework industry in Sivakasi Tamil Nadu, which had been functioning since April 1986, i.e. prior to the formulation of the policy, has been suitably revised to make it conform to the basic objectives of the policy. In addition, four more projects for the welfare of children engaged in the lock and hardware industry in Aligarh, the brassware industry in Moradabad, the carpet-weaving industry in Mirzapur Bhadohi and the glass industry in Ferozabad all in Uttar Pradesh have been finalised and sanctioned by the Ministry.

No Organisation

The industrial development after the second World War had led to a phenomenal growth in the matter of workers employed in organised sector industries. They numbered 70.04 lakhs in 1980. The unorganised labour consists of those workers who work in unorganised or unregulated industries and have not been able to organise themselves in pursuit of common objectives because of such constraints as casual nature of their employments, ignorance and illiteracy, small size of establishments with low capital investment per person employed, scattered nature of establishments, and superior strength of the employer operating singly or in combination.

The actual number of unorganised labour is not available but they are estimated to be over 2 crores, over half (about 55%) of these workers are agricultural labourers working in the farms of other farmers; 17% in manufacturing (non-industry establishment and self-employed in house hold industry); 13% in services (personal services offered by small establishments and the self-employed outside the households or by individuals as employees of households); 1.5% in construction; and 2% in transport and communication. These different sectors of unorganised labour have some common characteristics:

(i) The earnings of workers in the unorganised sector are not only relatively lower than their counterparts in the organised sector but many a time are too low to provide the minimum subsistence level of living. In some cases, such as agricultural and construction, overall earnings of workers get further depressed due to the non-availability of work throughout the year.

(ii) They suffer from insecurity of job and employment on account of the intermittent nature of activity as in agriculture and construction, though they are employed most of the time on a regular basis in manufacturing and services but they can be dispensed with by their employers any time.

(iii) They are not in a position to benefit from certain kinds of facilities provided as part of general welfare activity by the government. For example, not being able to have residential accommodation in the relatively well served area in a town, they cannot take advantage of public utilities such as roads, electricity, water, schooling and hospital services, nor can they avail themselves of the subsidised housing schemes.

(iv) They in most areas, are not organised in Unions to protect their earnings and conditions of work and therefore are left to the vagaries of the labour market which generally operate against them.

(v) They are not covered by legislation in the field of labour as it is not applicable to the establishments in which they work. Consequently, their conditions of work do not provide for minimum safeguards in larger factories; they are not assured of regular and reasonable payment of wages and entitled to benefits such as medical care, compensation in case of accidents, injuries and death, bonus, paid leave and holidays and retirement benefits.

The unorganised labour thus suffers from serious disadvantages and though the Government is very much concerned to make labour welfare measures available to them, it feels certain difficulties in applying these measures for various reasons mainly for administrative ones: Firstly number of unorganised units is so numerous, and varied that it is unmanageable; Secondly it is feared that the majority of employers may not be able to survive and the workers may be deprived of even the kind of insecure and low paid employment that they are now able to get. Thirdly there are the problems of administrating certain welfare measures, particularly such of them as are based on a contributory insurance scheme, as the workers in certain activities such as agriculture and construction do not work round the year.

The significance of these difficulties cannot be undoubtedly minimised, yet the unorganised labour can be helped in more than one way, at least in some of the unregulated industries. The manufacturing sector in particular has an appreciable return on its capital and can afford labour welfare measures. And even if it is difficult to operate contribution based insurance scheme due to the incapacity of the employers and employees to contribute to the welfare funds, the welfare measures can be applied on the principle of social assistance as is being done in the case of social services for the society in general. Secondly workers in the unorganised sector can be recognised as a special target group for the implementation of programmes of welfare in the spheres of housing, education, health and other services. Thirdly it is true that certain benefits like bonus, retrenchment compensation and retirement benefits cannot be administered in the absence of regular employment with an employer but this should not deprive the unorganised labour of the amenities of housing and unemployment benefits. Fourthly, a large number of workers work for relatively long periods of time with the same employer in the manufacturing, trade and commerce and service establishments and even in an activity like construction (while it is true that workers have to change the place of work) in many cases a sizeable number of them continue with the same employer in the same town or city throughout their career. Therefore, in the case of such workers, who regularly work with the same employers even welfare measures based on the contributory insurance principle could be applied.

It is thus evident that welfare measures can be initiated at least in some of the sectors of unorganised labourers the basis of social insurance/social assistance with a separate administrative mechanism designed for their implementation. The Government of India and State Governments are committed to make welfare measures applicable to this exploited segment of labour and have introduced some of these as well as is discussed below:

Some states are extending welfare benefits of one kind or the other to unorganised labour. For example Haryana government had decided to insure all state farmers and farm labourers engaged in agriculture, dairy and farming operation against accidents. All eligible persons in the age group of 10 to 65 years would be covered under it and the Haryana Agricultural Marketing Board would pay Rs. 4.8 lakh per annum as premium to the Insurance company.

The scheme would cover death or disablement of any farmer or farm labourers while working on agricultural machinery, implements and equipments. Cases where death or disablement occurs due to the digging of tubewells, cane crushing operations, threshing and other agricultural operations are also covered. The scheme would also cover accidents that occur due to electricity shock, fire hazards and use of pesticides. In case of deaths a compensation of Rs 15,000 would be paid and in the case of two limbs or any other serious injury, the compensation of Rs 10,000 would be paid. Other compensations would be related to seriousness of physical injury on a graduated scale. The minimum payment would be Rs 1500 in case of severing of a finger.

Kerala government has decided to establish two welfare funds for construction workers and abkari workers in the state. The workers in the two sectors would receive old age pension, medical facilities, housing loans and assistance for death in harness.

Social Work in Villages

Government has been laying special emphasis on improving the social and economic conditions of the unorganised workers, particularly in the rural areas, through a number of measures.

The rates of minimum wages of agricultural workers in different States are given in the following Table:

Statement Showing Rates of Minimum Wage for Agricultural in Different States

Name of the State	*Date from which effective*	*Minimum wages per day*
Andhra Pradesh	9.2.87	Rs 8.50 to Rs 11.00
Arunachal Pradesh	1.9.86	Rs 15 to Rs 18 according to areas
Assam	1.7.88	Rs 19.00

Name of the State	*Date from which effective*	*Minimum wages per day*
Bihar	16.10.86	Rs 10 or 5 kg paddy or any other kind of grain of same value
Goa	1.7.86	Rs 12.00
Gujarat	5.2.86	Rs 11.00
Haryana	1.4.87	Rs 16.25 with meals of Rs 20.25 without meals
Himachal Pradesh	15.4.87	Rs 15.00
Jammu & Kashmir	7.7.84	Rs 10.50
Karnataka	21.7.88	Rs 12.00 to Rs 17.65 per day
Kerala	1.6.84	Rs 12 to 15.00
Madhya Pradesh	26.6.87	Rs 11.00
Maharashtra	1.5.88	Rs 12.00 to Rs. 20.00
Manipur	1.4.86	Rs 12 to Rs 13.40
Meghalaya	1.3.87	Rs 15.00
Mizoram	1.1.87	Rs 15.00
Nagaland	6.5.87	Rs 15.00
Orissa	15.7.86	Rs 10.00 Preliminary notification for Rs 11.00 issue
Punjab	1.4.87	Rs 18.48
Rajasthan	1.3.87	Rs 14.00
Sikkim	1.10.87	Rs 14.00
Tamil Nadu	5.4.83	Rs 8.00 to Rs 18.00
Tripura	8.8.86	Rs 12.00
Uttar Pradesh	28.5.87	Rs 11.50 to Rs 12.50
West Bengal	1.10.87	Rs 18.02

Minimum Wages : The objective of protecting the real wages of the workers in the unorganised sector is achieved through the fixation and timely revision of minimum wages as well as their enforcement through the Central and State Governments.

The minimum rates of wages in construction industry in the Central sphere have been revised with effect from 14.10.88 on the basis of increase in the consumer price index. Similarly, minimum wages in respect of 23 mining employments in the Central sphere have also been revised with effect from 25.10.88 on the basis of increase in the CPI Number. The present revision in the rates of wages is based on the twelve monthly average of consumer price index upto June, 1988, the average of which stood at 753. For the first time, special allowance or variable Dearness Allowance linked to the Consumer Price Index Number has also been introduced with a view to compensating the workers for increase in prices. The rate of Special Allowance will be adjusted every six months, in October, and April, on the basis of average of Consumer Price Index Number for preceding six months ending on 30th June, and 31st December respectively.

The rural unorganised labour constitutes the single largest segment of the work force. The effort should, therefore be to extend the socio-economic gains of development through a number of measures, such as, allotment of house sites and agricultural land, provision of employment on a regular basis, health and medical care, rural housing and drinking water supply, extension of rural credit and education. India has also ratified ILO convention No. 141 concerning rural workers organisation since August, 1977 and efforts have been made since then to identify different categories of rural labour so that they are brought into the mainstream of development. The Scheme for Organising Rural aims at motivating the rural workers to organise themselves and to give them knowledge about the laws enacted for their welfare. It was originally introduced in States by allocating 415 honorary-rural organisers, (HROs) during the year 1981-82. By the year 1985-86, the Scheme was extended to 14 States and Union Territory of Pondichery, and 1500 posts of HROs had been allocated to various states.

Under the Scheme, the concerned State Governments appoint Honorary Rural Organisers (HROs) at the Block level and each HRO is paid an honorarium of Rs 200 per month and a fixed conveyance allowance of Rs 50 per month. The expenditure involved is released to the States as Grant-in-aid.

National Commission on Rural Labour : The National Commission on Rural Labour has been set up by Government Resolution dated 11th August, 1987 for achieving a better understanding of all India as well as region specific problems of rural labour. The Commission consists of a full time Chairman, a full time Member Secretary and seven part-time Members. The term of the commission will be three years. The terms of reference of the Commission areas follows:

1. To study in a dynamic setting, the problems of identification, categorisation and quantification of rural labour, taking into account its economic, social and regional dimensions.
2. To study, in the context of changing traditional socio-economic framework, the economic social and working conditions of rural labour/and the disabilities including a lack of social security arising the reform.
3. To study the existing legislative and other provision intended to protect the interests of rural labour and to assess effectiveness of these measures as also that of the apartment administrative arrangements and delivery systems.
4. To study the formulation and implementation of land reform and other institutional reform measures having a bearing on rural labour, specially on its land dependent section.
5. To study the effects of the changes in the control and management of community property resources inclu-ding land forests and water on rural labour.
6. To study the phenomenon of migration, the various laws, administrative and recruitment practices relevant to migrant labour as also their particular disabilities.
7. To study in the context of the requirements of rural labour, issues relating to the planning process the various development plans and programmes and their implementations.
8. To study the social development measures in sectors such

as health family welfare, housing water supply education including training and the impact they have had on the quality of life of rural labour.

9. To study and report in particular on :

   (i) the efficacy of various legislative and other measures adopted so far with reference to share croppers and other types of tenants.

   (ii) the problems of bonded labour (including that of consumption loans) and the effect of legislative and other measures adopted for removing their bondage.

   (iii) supplemental plan for specific target groups\areas for employment creation; income generation and poverty alleviation.

   (iv) the investment pattern in the various plans, the choice of technologies and their effect on labour absorption,

   (v) factors impinging on the demand for rural labour, their effect on the bargaining power of rural labour and constraints on the organisation of rural labour.

   (vi) fixation of a minimum wage for rural labour as also the enforcement mechanism.

   (vii) the particular problems of women and children.

   (viii) arrangement for collecting data relevant to a study of the problems of rural labour, promoting research and dissemination of information.

   (ix) a comparative study of the experience in different regions of India and that of other countries.

The Commission will study the problems of rural labour and after studying the existing legislation and assessing the existing welfare measures would submit its recommendations to the Government.

In addition to holding discussions with state officials research institutes; voluntary agencies, etc. the Commission has been visiting rural areas to collect first hand information.

The Commission had since submitted its report to Shri P. V.

Narasimmah Rao, the former Prime Minister of India in August, 1991 and was examined by the government for appropriate action.

State Government's Role

All states/Union Territories have Departments of Labour to administer labour welfare under the charge of a Minister who is responsible to the State legislature. The Department is headed by Labour Commissioner of IAS rank. He is assisted by Additional, Joint Deputy and Assistant Labour Commissioner, Deputy Chief Inspector of Factories, Factory Inspectors, Medical Inspector of Factories, Labour-cum-conciliation Officers and other supporting officials. Commissioner for Workmen's compensation under the Workmen's Compensation Act 1923 and Registrars of Trade Unions Act, 1926 have also been appointed in most of the states. The Labour Commissioner also combines the functions of these officers as well.

Functions of the Department : The basic duty of the Labour Department is to maintain industrial peace, promote labour welfare and enforce labour laws. The Department emphasises timely intervention and early settlements between the workmen and employers as well as the awards given by the Industrial Tribunal and Labour Courts in respect of industrial disputes, so as to obviate the necessity or the possibility of the workmen adopting agitational approach. Besides the administration of central and state legislation, such as Workmen's Compensation Act, 1923, Factories Act, 1948, Indian, Boilers Act, 1923, Indian Trade Union Act, 1926, the Payment of Wages Act, 1936. The Minimum Wages Act, 1948, the Payment of Bonus Act, 1965, the Payment of Gratuity Act, 1972, and the Equal Remuneration Act, 1976 etc. the Department also looks after the implementation of settlements between the workmen and employers as well as the awards/orders given by the Industrial Tribunal and Labour Courts in respect of industrial disputes.

In some states, special machinery has been set up for the collection of labour statistics, while in others the above mentioned authorities are performing these duties as well. Competent authorities have also been appointed by various State Governments under the Minimum Wages Act, 1948 to ascertain from time to time the Consumer's Price Index Numbers applicable to persons covered by the scheduled employments, Labour departments in some states have Rural Wing and Labour Inspectors employed therein inspect agricultural farms to ensure that agricultural labour are paid wages according to the notified rates.

In some states Industrial Safety Councils-autonomous bodies on voluntary basis have been set up to develop safety consciousness amongst industrial workers and the employees. They organise safety programmes in different parts of the State to educate the workers in utilising various safety devices. The Council awards shields to factories showing improvement in safety standards and reduction of accidents.

The Labour Department also open Labour Welfare Centres where free training in sewing, knitting and embroidery on daily wages is imparted to female workers, and female dependents of male workers in the state. The Department also publishes Labour Gazettes/Labour News every month containing labour statistics and other important information of labour interest.

The key functionary in the Department is the Labour Welfare Officer whose functions are enumerated as follows:

Responsible Authority

The importance of labour officers in Indian industry had been realised as early as 1931, when the Royal Commission on Labour recommended the appointment of labour officers in order to protect the workers from the evils of jobbery and indebtedness, to act generally as a spokesman of labour and to promote amicable settlement between the workers and the management. The popular ministries in the states had forced employers to employ full time functionaries-Labour Officers in the factories. During the Second World War, these officers were generally entrusted with handing of welfare and labour administration and later on their functions came to include functions relating to welfare, personnel, and industrial relations and they began to be designated as Labour Welfare Officers, Legislative provisions for the appointment of welfare officers were made under section 49 of the Factories Act, 1948; and Section 58 of the Mines Act, 1952, whereby employers have a statutory obligation to appoint labour welfare officer in establishments with 500 or more workers. Section 18 of the

Plantations Labour act, 1951 also makes such a provision in plantations with 300 or more workers.

The National Commission on Labour has stated that Laws were made to ensure that the managements appointed a person exclusively to look after the welfare of their workers and help them in discharging their statutory obligation in respect of welfare measures.

Functions of Labour Welfare Officer : The Committee on Labour Welfare (1966) laid down the following duties of labour welfare officers, based on the Model Rules framed under the Factories Act of 1948 :

(i) Supervision of safety, health and welfare programme like housing, recreation, sanitation services as provided under the law: working of Joint Committees; grant of leave with wages; and red redressal of workers' grievances.

(ii) Counselling workers in personnel and family problems; helping them to adjust to their Work environment, and understand their rights and privileges.

(iii) Advising management in matters of formulating labour and welfare policies, apprenticeship training programmes; meeting Statutory obligations of workers; developing fringe benefits; and workers' education and use of communication media.

(iv) Establishing liasion with workers so that they may understand various limitations under which they work; appreciate the need of harmonious industrial relations if the plant; interpret company policies to workers and persuade workers to come to a settlement in case of disputes.

(v) Establishing liasion with management so that the latter may appreciate workers' viewpoint to various matters in the plant; Intervene on behalf of workers in matters under consideration of the management; help different department heads to meet their obligation under the Act; maintain harmonious industrial relations in the plant; and suggest measures for promoting general well-being of workers.

(vi) Working with management and worker to maintain harmonious industrial relations in the plant to arrange for prompt redressal of grievances and speedy settlement of disputes and to improve productivity and productive efficiency of the enterprise.

(vii) Working with outside public for securing proper enforcement of various Acts as applicable to the plant by establishing ccntact with factory inspectors, medical officers and other inspectors and other agencies in the community with a view to helping workers to make use of community services.

In short, the care of workers in all matters affecting their well-being at the place of work and outside puts a special responsibility on the welfare officer. He is primary concerned to ensure that social welfare services for industrial workers are administered in a satisfactory manner. In addition he acts as a staff functionary in matter of personnel management and industrial relations. Thus he serves as advisor counsellor, mediator and liasion man to both management and labour. Model rules framed under different Acts have given to the labour welfare officer a status equivalent to the head of a department and also enable him to function as a neutral person a kind of buffer between management and workers. For this purpose, the Model Rules provide protection to him against victimization by management.

Practice, however seems to vary from the norms set by the statues. In actual practice Labour Welfare Officers are often not given the role and status conferred on them by the statutes. Many employers tend to regard the statutory appointment of a labour welfare officer as an infringement of management prerogative. When they have perforced to employ one, they either render his functioning meaningless or burden him with many additional and peripheral duties. Such an approach helps poorly managed companies to avoid their responsibility and place the blame on the labour welfare officer if things go wrong. The legal protection afforded to the labour welfare officer makes him an outsider to the management group which blocks his promotion possibilities while formally retaining the position as a consequence labour welfare officers may not, in fact, be able to discharge the functions for which they were originally appointed to be effective it is desirable that the welfare officer should be part of the management team responsible to the management for efficient discharge of the welfare function in the plant. Sometimes a suggestion is made that the welfare officer should be appointed by and be fully answerable to the government, but this provision may result in his alienation from the management as there will be hardly any difference between them and the factory inspectorate staff.

A discussion of the labour welfare measures and the administrative machinery designed to implement them reflects the concern of the government for improving the lot of workers in appreciation of the role they have to play in economic development of the country. But these attempts on the part of the government leave much, to be desired. The state has enacted a plethora of labour laws-but these have not been implemented in letter and spirit for lack of adequate supervision. For example, the Minimum Wages Act has failed to achieve its objective due to institutional and economic reasons. There are great variations in welfare facilities as between state and state and from industry to industry and also as between the different units of the same industry. There must be some uniformity in welfare provisions and a definite minimum standard of welfare should be laid down. The industrial establishments continue to suffer from unhygienic and insanitary conditions, lack of security systems, and pollution control, devices which cause great health hazards to workers. Women workers are being ruthlessly exploited and discriminated in payment of equal wages with their male counterparts despite the legislation on this subject. Children present a pathetic figure as a result of their exploitation in agriculture, employment in establishments the unorganised labour have yet to be covered by the welfare measures available to the labour in organised sectors to rescue them from the ill-treatment by the employers. Bonded labour though prohibited by law remains to be identified; rescued and rehabilitated in some of the states. Labour welfare officers are not properly equipped with education and training enabling them to perform their duties consciously and effectively for the welfare of workers. They fail to act as maintenance "engineer" on human side due to the antagonism of the management. The welfare funds need to be augmented to provide maximum welfare services to workers in an industry in proportion to their number in it. The number of welfare centres in each state also needs to be increased and located near the working place to enable the workers and their families to make their maximum use. The participation of workers in the administration of welfare facilities in the form of various welfare committees is desirable to infuse among them sense of responsibility and removal of suspicions which they might entertain against the employers undertaking welfare measures.

As the welfare measures contribute to the health and efficiency of the workers, the employers in their own interest should discharge their obligation to their employees by providing them canteens, creches, recreational and other facilities in order to win them over and thus ensure optimum production and guarantee industrial peace. No doubt it is primarily the responsibility of the state to ensure the provision of various kinds of welfare measures to the workers for their health and safety through the implementation of different legislations, yet other agencies like the employers themselves and Trade Unions have also the obligation to contribute to their welfare by taking up the activities falling within their purview and sphere; Trade Unions no doubt, suffer from paucity of funds but they can easily apprise their members about their rights and duties and educate them against the evils of drinking, gambling, drug addiction and such other vices. It is unfortunate that increase in wages and extension of welfare measures have not been able to bring about significant improvement, in the conditions of workers and their problems of alcoholism, absenteeism, indebtedness and family disintegration have been on the increase. There is therefore the need of social workers to address themselves to the mitigation of these problems by interacting with the workers and their families. Lastly, the concept of labour participation in management to which all the political parties are committed requires to be implemented in all the industries to enable the labour to participate with the management in the formulation of policies, inter-alia, oriented towards their welfare and thereby to have a sense of satisfaction and ensure increase in production. In sum, labour welfare should be pursued more vigorously to realise its objectives which are enumerated in the following words of Prof. Kirkaldy :

> "The whole field of welfare is one in which much can be done to combat the sense of frustration of the industrial worker to relieve him of personal and family worries to improve his health to afford him a means of self-expression, to offer him some sphere in which he can excel all others, and to help to a wider conception of life. If within the field of welfare and particularly that part of which comprises sports and games a large measure of self-government, can be left to the workers; even in the management of facilities provided by the employer, a sense of responsibility; initiative and cooperation can be fostered and often among those whose daily task afford them the least opportunity or developing characteristics so essential to industrial enterprise and wise citizenship".

4

Deprived Groups

Two-thirds or more of the population of India are very backward, being illiterate and living in utter poverty. Their disadvantages derive from the fact that their status is ascribed to them by birth in certain castes, creeds and tribal groups. Their problems can be understood only in terms of the basic character of Indian society which consists of a multitude of closed status groups with unequal ranks, each with its own privileges and disabilities supported by traditional sanctions. Thus it must be recognized at the outset that the term class is not-appropriate since that term is associated with an economic category and indicates an open status group. By contrast, the backward classes in India form an aggregate of closed status groups; they belong to these groups by birth, not because of their individual economic characteristics.

There are three broad divisions among the backward classes: (a) the Scheduled Tribes (Girijans), (b) the Scheduled Castes (Harijans), and (c) the Other Backward Classes. The first two groups are listed in the Constitution while the third group is unlisted and loosely defined; it is the last homogeneous. As a result, the problem of the other backward classes is very complicated and very difficult to deal with. While it is possible to have an all-India list of the Scheduled Castes on the basis of untouchability and the Scheduled Tribes on the basis of their way of life, it is impossible to have any such list for the other backward classes.

The Constitutional Provisions. While the term 'backward classes' has not been defined by the Indian Constitution, the characteristics of backwardness are described here and there and also sometimes the categories are mentioned. Article 15(4) speaks of the socially and educationally backward. Article 16 (4) uses the term "backward class" and speaks of inadequate representation in services. Article 17 abolishes untouchability. Article 23 mentions forced labour. Article 45 mentions free and compulsory education. Article 46 mentions the weaker sections of the people and includes in that expression the Scheduled Castes and Scheduled Tribes. Article 340 empowers the state to investigate the condition of the backward classes and to help them by grants, etc. Thus, the Constitution has accepted the following elements of backwardness; illiteracy and lack of education, poverty, exploitation of labour, non-representation in services and untouchability. The main safeguards in the Constitution are:

1. Abolition of untouchability and forbidding of its practice in any form (Article 17);
2. Promotion of their educational and economic interests and their protection from social injustice and all forms of exploitation (Article 46);
3. Throwing open by law of Hindu religious institutions of a public character to all classes and sections of Hindus (Article 25b);
4. Removal of any disability, liability, restriction or condition with regard to access to shops, public restaurants, hotels and places of public entertainment or use of wells, tanks, bathing ghats, roads and places of public resort maintained wholly or partially out of state funds or dedicated to use of general public (Article 15 (2));
5. Curtailment by law in the interest of any scheduled tribes of general rights of all citizens to move freely, settle in and acquire property (Article 19 (5));

6. Forbidding or any denial of admission to educational institutions maintained by the State or receiving grant out of state funds (Article 29 (2));
7. Permitting the State to make reservation for backward classes in public services in case of inadequate representations and requiring the State to consider claims of the scheduled castes and scheduled tribes in the making of appointments to public services (Articles 16 and 335);
8. Special representation in the Lok Sabha and state legislative assembly to scheduled castes and tribes (Articles 330, 332 and 334);
9. Setting up of tribal advisory councils and separate departments in states and appointment of a special officer at Centre to promote their welfare and safeguard their interests (Articles 164 and 338 and Fifth Schedule);
10. Special provision for administration and control of scheduled and tribal areas (Article 244 and Fifth and Sixth Schedules), and
11. Prohibition of traffic in human beings and forced labour (Article 23).

In pursuance of decisions taken by the Cabinet, the government strengthened the office of the special officer. Under Article 338 of the Constitution by providing him two very senior officers i.e., equivalent to secretary to Government of India, one to look after issues involving scheduled castes and the other to take care of issues concerning scheduled tribes. A disciplinary mechanism has also been provided in the form of a secretary to be positioned in the Cabinet Secretariat to take action against defaulting government personnel violating the safeguards provided under the Constitution.

The Commission for Scheduled Castes and Scheduled Tribes renamed as National Commission for Scheduled Castes and Scheduled Tribes, will function as an advisory body on broad issues of policies and levels of development of scheduled castes and scheduled tribes. With this objective in view, the Commission may include experts in social anthropology, social work and other related social sciences. Its functions will be:

(a) to study the extent and ramifications of untouchability and social discrimination arising therefrom and effectiveness of present measures and to recommend further measures to be taken;

(b) to study socio-economic and other relevant circumstances leading to the commission of offence against persons belonging to scheduled castes and scheduled tribes and to recommend appropriate remedial measures to ensure prompt investigation of such offences;

(c) to take up studies on different aspects of development of scheduled castes and scheduled tribes with a view to ensuring integration of these groups with the mainstream of society in all aspects. These would include studies in socio-economic development, education, commerce, trade, art, literature, language, housing, communication, agriculture, forestry, horticulture, fisheries, rehabilitation, pollution and environment, and

(d) such other functions as may be entrusted to National Commission for Scheduled Castes and Scheduled Tribes in evolving general policies relating to any aspect of development of scheduled castes/scheduled tribes as may be thought proper by the Central Government.

The Commission shall comprise a chairman and not more than eleven other members. Terms and conditions of chairman and members shall be as determined by Government in each case, provided their term of office shall not normally exceed three years.

Area of Operation

For enlarging the scope and making the penal provision more stringent, the Untouchability (Offences) Act, 1955 had been comprehensively amended by the Untouchability (Offences) Amendment and Miscellaneous Provision Act, 1976 which came into force from 19 November 1976. With this amendment, name of the principal Act has been changed to Protection of Civil Rights Act, 1955. The Act provides for penalties for preventing a person, on the ground of untouchability, from enjoying the rights accruing out of abolition of untouchability. Enhanced penalties/punishments have been provided for subsequent offences.

Under the provision of Section 8 of the Representation of the People Act, 1951, a person who is convicted of an offence under the Act is disqualified from contesting elections of Parliament and state legislatures for a period of the six years commencing from the date of such conviction.

The PCR Act, 1955 is administered by the State Governments. Under a provision of Section 15A (4) of the Act, the Government also places every year, before each House of Parliament, an annual report on the working of the provisions of Section 15A of the Act.

In pursuance of the provisions made under Section 15A (2) of the Protection of Civil Rights Act, 1955, Central assistance is given to State Governments and union territory administrations. Provisions for legal aid to scheduled caste victims of the PCR Act cases have been made by 20 slates. Special cells/squads have been created by 19 states for initiating and exercising supervision over prosecution for contravention of the provisions of the PCR Act. Eighteen states have set up committees at various levels to make periodical review of the problems of untouchability and cases related to it and also suggest various measures for effective implementation of the PCR Act. Fifty two special courts/special mobile courts have been set up in untouchabitity/atrocity-prone districts of Andhra Pradesh, Bihar, Kamataka, Madhya Pradesh, Orissa,.Rajasthan and Tamil Nadu for expeditious disposal of such cases. Necessary guidelines and instructions are issued to states from time to time for effective implementation of the provisions of the PCR Act Matching Central assistance is provided to the states for implementation of the PCR Act. Liberation of scavengers by conversion of existing dry latrines has also been taken up under it. One hundred and sixteen towns in 16 states have so far been assisted under the scheme 'whole town approach' in selected towns with the conditions for providing alternative employment to liberated scavengers.

With a view to effectively dealing with crimes against scheduled castes and scheduled tribes and to tone up administrative machinery to tackle this vital issue, comprehensive guidelines containing precautionary, preventive, punitive and rehabilitative measures exist which states/UTs have to follow. Still these communities continue to be vulnerable and atrocities are committed against them in one form or the other. In order that scheduled castes and scheduled tribes are fully protected from atrocities, Government had enacted the Scheduled Castes and the Scheduled Tribes (Prevention of Atrocities) Act, 1989. The Act came into force from 30 January 1990. It specifies the offences which are considered as atrocities and provides for deterrent punishments for commission of the same. The Act also envisages preventive measures and states/UTs have to envolve schemes among other things, for economic and social rehabilitation of such victims.

Under Articles 330 and 332 of the Constitution, seats are reserved for scheduled castes and scheduled tribes in the Lok Sabha and state legislatures in proportion to their population. This concession initially was for a period of ten years from the commencement of the Constitution. Subsequently, this was extended through amendments up to 25 January 1990 then the Parliament had passed the Constitution (Sixty second Amendment) Bill, 1989 which seeks to extend the period of reservation of seats for S C/ST and representation of Anglo-Indians by nomination to selected bodies for another ten years beyond 26 January 1990. There is no reservation of seats in the Rajya Sabha and legislative councils. Table I gives details of their representation in the Lok Sabha and state legislative assemblies.

Article 335 of the Constitution provides that the claims of members of scheduled castes and scheduled tribes shall be taken into consideration, consistent with maintenance of efficiency of administration in making appointment to posts and services in connection with the affairs of the nation or the state. Article 16(4) permits reservation in favour of citizens of backward classes who may not be adequately represented in services. In pursuance of these provisions, Government has made reservations for scheduled castes and scheduled tribes in services under its control.

For scheduled castes, reservation is 15 per cent of the vacancies for which recruitment is made by open competition on all-India basis and 16.2 per cent of the vacancies to which recruitment is made on all-India basis other than by open competition. For scheduled tribes, reservation is 7.5 per cent in both cases. Reservation in direct recruitment to Group C and D posts which normally attract candidates from one locality or region, is fixed in proportion to the population of scheduled castes and tribes in respective states/UTs.

Reservation is also made at 15 per cent of the vacancies for scheduled castes and 7.5 per cent for scheduled tribes in promotions on the result of competitive examinations limited to departmental candidates in Group B, C and D and in promotion by selection in Group B, C and D and to the lowest rung of Group A in grades or services to which direct recruitment if any, does not exceed 7.5 per cent. Reservation has been provided for scheduled tribes in promotion on the basis of seniority subject to fitness in Group A, B, C and D posts in grades or services to which direct recruitment if any, does not exceed 7.5 per cent.

In promotion by selection within Group A to posts carrying a maximum salary of Rs 5,700 (revised scale 4500-5700) per month or less, scheduled castes and tribes officers who are senior enough to be in the zone of consideration for promotion and are within the number of vacancies for which the select list has to be drawn, are included in that list provided they are not considered unfit for promotion.

To facilitate their adequate representation, concessions such as : (i) relaxation of age limit, (ii) relaxation in the standards of suitability, (iii) selection provided they are not found unfit for the posts, (iv) relaxation of qualifications regarding experience in the case of direct recruitment only, wherever necessary and (v) inclusion of scientific and technical posts up to the lowest grade of Group A required for research in the scheme of reservations, have been provided for. Simultaneously, with notification to employment exchanges or advertisements in newspapers, vacancies and reservations for scheduled castes and scheduled tribes in Group C and D (Class III and IV) posts are announced over All India Radio in areas having a concentration of scheduled castes and scheduled tribes population and notified to voluntary associations of scheduled castes and scheduled tribes population, enlisted for this purpose and to Directors of SC/ST Welfare in the states and union territories. Vacancies filled through Union Public

Service Commission otherwise than through examination, are advertised on the first occasion as exclusively reserved for scheduled tribes/castes and are re-advertised if the first advertisement is infructuous. Dereservation of vacancies for direct recruitment in Group A, B, C and D has since been banned. If sufficient number of suitable SC/ST candidates are not available against the share of vacancies reserved for them, the shortfall will not be filled up by general category candidates and such vacancies will be kept unfilled till SC/ST candidates become available. Reservation for scheduled castes and scheduled tribes (including vacancies carried forward) is subject to the ceiling of 50 per cent of the total number of vacancies. This scheme of reservation is also being followed by public sector undertakings. Voluntary agencies which are in receipt of substantial grant-in-aid from Government, are also required, as a condition, to adopt certain specific features of the reservation scheme in their establishments.

To give effect to the reservations, model rosters of 40 points each have been prescribed for direct recruitment by open competition on all-India basis and other than open competition and promotions and 100-point roster for recruitment made on local and regional basis. If the vacancies in a service or cadre are too few for the purpose all isolated posts are grouped together in direct recruitment Annual statements are required to be submitted by recruiting authorities for scrutiny by Government. For ensuring implementation of special representation orders, liaison officers have been appointed in different Government ministries/ departments.

During the period from June to August 1989, a special drive was launched to fill up the huge backlog of vacancies for SC/ST in various Central ministries/departments and public sector undertakings. Another drive initiated in June 1990 is expected to be completed by October.

Position at State Level

State Governments have also framed rules under the powers given to them by item 41 of the State List of the Seventh Schedule to the Constitution for reservation of posts for these classes and have taken steps to increase their representation in state services.

Reservation in State Government services however is under the exclusive jurisdiction of State Governments.

Recognizing that the Indian society is made up of hundreds of millions of citizens who are utterly poor, illiterate and living in small, closed tribal and village societies, the Constitution has laid stress on social, economic and political justice along with equality of status and of opportunity in the preamble. While Articles 14 and 15 (1) and (2) emphasise equality of all citizens before law and prohibit discrimination on grounds of caste, creed, birth, etc., sub-clause (4) of Article 15 asserts that, these Constitutional provisions do not "prevent the State from making any special provision for the advancement of any socially and educationally backward classes of citizens or the Scheduled Castes and Scheduled Tribes." Thus the Constitution clearly recognized that mere legal equality in a society which practices social inequality cannot meet the ends of social justice. The Constitution recognized that it is necessary to take special steps to help the socially, educationally and economically backward classes to make use of the opportunities provided.

The tribal population of 39 million at the time of 1971 Census increased to 42 million with the Amendment Act of 1976 when the areas restriction within a state was removed. According to the 1981 Census, the tribal population further increased to 51.6 million. The majority of tribal population is concentrated in Eastern, Central and Western part of the country and about 25 per cent are dispersed in small pockets in the southern zone.

One pertinent question is: how have these people survived with their unchanging ways of life in a country which has had cities and civilization since three thousand ? B.C. Kosambi raises this question and answers it in his characteristic way, "The answer lies in the availability of food." Though the food gatherers lead a precarious life, the natural resources in the forests give the tribal people not only fish and game, but an abundance of fruits, nuts, vegetables, etc., so that on the whole they get a balanced diet. It must be conceded that the lack of proselytization in Hinduism is also one of the important reasons, as Hinduism allows for absorption and assimilation only through its caste system.

According to the Scheduled Tribe lists modification order 1956, there are 414 different tribes in the various States of India. In Madhya Pradesh alone there are nearly seven million tribal people belonging to the Oraon, the Munda, the Bhil, the Santhal, the Majhwar, the Kharwar, the Baiga, the Korwa, the Gond and the other tribes who practice shifting cultivation consisting of felling the trees on a hillside a little before the monsoon and setting them on fire. When the earth is covered over by a layer of ashes and when the rains fall, they scatter seeds and with an occasional shower of rain the seeds take root and grow. But the crops are scarce and are of an inferior quality. The soil becomes impoverished in the absence of ploughing and ; manuring. So they shift to another valley and cut the trees there. This process of agriculture, besides being inadequate, is very wasteful as it leads to deforestation and soil erosion and floods. So the forest laws prevent shifting cultivation. This leads to terrible hardship to the tribal people. Further, land alienation is the most important problem affecting these groups.

Many of the tribes are pastoral. The Todas furnish a classic example of the pastoral economy; their social and economic organizations are built around their buffaloes which form the economic as well as the religious basis of the life of the tribe.

Many of the tribes are good at handicrafts which include basket making, spinning and weaving. There are some functional classes among the Saore.. the Kond, and the Gond who devote themselves to metal working, cane working, pottery, weaving, and so on. The Korwar and the Agaria are well known iron-smelters, producing tools for local use.

Some of the tribal people like Santhals, the Kond, and the Gond from Bihar, Orissa and Madhya Pradesh have migrated in large numbers to Assam and work on tea plantations. The areas in Bihar, Madhya Pradesh and Bengal which are rich in coal, iron, etc., have led to the emergence of industrial labour. It is estimated that about half of the labourers in the manganese industry of Madhya Pradesh are tribal people. The Santhal and the Ho are prominent in the Bihar iron industry. Nearly the entire unskilled labour force of the Tata Iron and Steel Co. are tribals. There is both the inside "push" following economic hardship due to land alienation, indebtedness, and outside "pull" due to demand for labour in tea plantation and in industries. Thus, the tribesmen have been transplanted from the tribal life to the urban life and so are confronted by great difficulties in social adjustment.

The Anthropological Survey of India compiled data after a five year long project on the "People of India" to generate a brief descriptive profile of all communities in the country, and the impact of development process on them. The study identified 443 Scheduled Castes, 426 Scheduled Tribes and 1051 Backward Classes out of 4384 communities living in India.

The study reveals the strength and continuity of regional identities which go back to the prehistoric times, in terms of morphological and genetic characteristics of populations, language and literature, material culture, food habits, rituals, folk-lore, local forms of religion, fairs and festivals etc. These regional identities are primarily secular, according to the study.

The communities, no matter how ranked they are, share the regional space and ethos. This explains why about 80-90 per cent of the communities of India are within the boundaries of Indian states and union territories, which were recorganised on the basis of language. These are thus linguistic cultural and social identities, largely homogeneous.

Only about 10 per cent of communities are spread over more than one state or adjoining area of slates. They consist of traders, merchants, artisans minorities and so on.

There are few communities which do not consider themselves migrants. Every community recalls its migration in its folk-lore and history, set off by famines, wars, political considerations and sheer necessity.

The whole of India is a kurshetra and an Indian is a migrant par excellence. The immigrants accepted regional ethos. Their role in promoting the development of regional languages and literature, building economy is well known, the study emphasises.

Caste and Jati have now become rigid in their "political" role, but they have been dynamic entities when seen in the historical context, and in contemporaneous terms of a caste's perception of itself, its role, its relationship with others and with environment.

There has been a good deal of occupational mobility and change in spite of continuity. Segments of a community have moved away from traditional moorings or a section of a community has given up its traditional occupation, and or adopted a new technology.

Social Revolution

Almost all communities of India have felt the impact of change and development of market and technology. There is an all-pervasive sense of Indianness often elusive and indefinable but ever present. In the words of Jawaharlal Nehru, Indianness has been a matter of feeling, a dream, a vision, an emotion. In terms of prosaic anthropological concepts, it represents sharing of ethos and environment, a way of life and a world of rituals and fairs and festivals with their local meanings, of interaction in many ways, says the study.

We may now consider the changes brought about in the economic and social life of the tribal groups, as a result of cultural contacts. As Majumdar puts it, "Today most of these tribes have come in contact with advanced communities, have learnt traits of their neighbours, have borrowed patterns of their dress and developed an intricate material economy. Some of these tribes have progressed at a tremendous pace effecting in a few years changes which have taken centuries to achieve in other areas." These contacts have arisen in a number of ways. On the one hand are the itinerant vendors from the neighbouring villages and towns who have taken clothes and trinkets, metal utensils, patent medicines, etc., to the hills and the jungles; on the other, there are the administrative officers who have gone into these areas because of the forest laws and revenue laws. Next, there were Christian missionaries who wanted to convert them to Christianity in order to save their souls. All these contacts have been greatly increased because of the tremendous developments in transport and communication. In the recent years the existence of mineral resources in and around the primitive tracts have led to the establishment of mines and industries. Because of the forest laws many of the tribes had to give up jhum lands and had to migrate to work in the tea gardens of Assam and in the factories of the neighbouring areas. Many of the tribes have been prevented from quarrying stones, gravel, and ores without taking formal licence from the government. The governmental agencies as well as missionaries have started schools among these groups. As a result of all these cultural contacts there have been changes, in their food habits, dress, ways of living, etc.

As a result of these cultural contacts, the various tribes of India are now living at different cultural levels. Some of these tribal groups, however, continue to live even now in seclusion, comparatively uninfluenced by these cultural contacts. But some of the groups have adopted the Hindu customs because of their association with the village people. They have modified their tribal economy somewhat though they still retain their distinctive social organization. But the large majority of the tribal groups in India have now more or less settled down in the rural areas taking to agricultural and other allied occupations. Some of these groups have accepted the Hindu way of life and have formed themselves into castes who are either at the untouchable level or at the touchable level depending upon their way of life. Others have been convened to Christianity. It is estimated that about 98 per cent of the Indian Christians in Chotanagpur are recruited from the tribal groups.

As Saksena writes, "The problems arising out of culture contacts have been varying and also have a differential impact on the various sections of the tribal population. The major aim of tribal welfare programmes should be to solve the various problems arising out of uncontrolled, haphazard, and at times, disastrous culture contacts, to provide amenities of modern life and to create conditions of their systematic integration into the mainstream of Indian society."

However, there was a school of thought which favoured isolation. Hutton, who was a Commissioner for Census of 1931, gave a solution to the tribal problems of uncontrolled acculturation. He suggested the creation of self-governing tribal areas with free power of self-determination. Earlier Eiwin suggested the creation of "National Parks" where the tribal people could live safely without being victims of what Elwin calls an "over-hasty and unregulated process of belief and civilization." But later on Elwin discarded the idea of "a national park." Both Hutton and Elwin were severely criticized for recommending this policy of isolation which was looked upon as a proposal to create a museum or a zoo, instead of helping the tribal people to utilize the resources of modern knowledge and improve the conditions of their life.

Another school, particularly advocated by the social reformers and voluntary organizations, was one for assimilation. The Christian missionaries and some social reformers like Thakkar Bapa have recommended and have worked for the assimilation of these tribal groups either into Christianity or into Hinduism.

The third view, which is actively followed in the recent years, is that of integration. The policy of isolation was neither possible nor desirable; assimilation as advocated by some, would have meant imposition; therefore, the only approach that would make available to the tribes the benefit of modern advanced society and yet retain their separate identity is integration. The policy of integration aims at developing a creative adjustment between tribes and non-tribes of India leading to responsible partnership.

This policy of integration, as against isolation and assimilation, was laid down in five principles by Jawaharlal Nehru in 1957 in his foreword to Verrier Elwin's The Philosophy for NEFA. The tribal Pancha Sila as enunciated by him are as follows:

1. People should develop along the lines of their own genius and we should avoid imposing anything on them. We should try to encourage in every way their own traditional arts and culture.
2. Tribal rights in land and forests should be respected.
3. We should try to train and build up a team of their own people to the work of administration and development. Some technical personnel from outside will, no doubt, be needed especially in the beginning. But we should avoid introducing too many outsiders into tribal territory.
4. We should not over-administer these areas or overwhelm them with a multiplicity of schemes. We should rather work through and not in rivalry to their own social and cultural institutions.

5. We should judge results not by statistics or the amount of money spent but by the quality of human character that is evolved.

In accordance with the policy laid down under Article 46 of the Constitutional, the Ministry of Home Affairs and the Ministry of Community Development, set up 43 sub-multipurpose tribal blocks in the various states of India. When these blocks functioned for three years, a committee was setup in May 1959, with the anthropologist Verrier Elwin as the Chairman to examine the programmes of these blocks. They presented their report in March 1960. It dealt with the fundamentals on the approach to the tribals, staffing and training, the problem of land and agriculture, shifting cultivation, the problem of forests, the tribal culture and research, the techniques of block survey, the place of the non-official agencies, etc. The committee recommended that the staff should have intensive training at the Tata Institute or at the Ranchi Institute or other institutions before they are posted to the blocks. They recommended that the forest laws should be made simple, that they should be permitted to rake timber to build their houses, and the modification of the game rules, particularly special permission for their ceremonial hunts. They also recommended that forest extension officers should be appointed as a liaison between the tribal people and the forest officers and also to help them to form forest cooperatives. They recommended that the forest officers should also have training with respect to tribal life. They were eager that there should be a survey of existing arts and crafts and that steps should be taken to help them to utilize the local materials and use the local designs in their crafts. They emphasized that the traditional tribal councils should be encouraged.

By virtue of the power vested under Article 339 of the Constitution, the President appointed a Committee with Dhebar as Chairman in April 1960 to report on the administration of the scheduled areas, the formation of the tribal advisory council, the laws applicable to the scheduled areas, etc. The committee presented its report in October 1961. It agreed with the principle of integration of the tribals without disturbing the essential harmony of the group. The aim was integration without imposition and without disturbing the harmony in their lives. They emphasized that the tribal development blocks should concentrate on economic development, education, health and communication, so that by the end of the Fourth Plan, the tribal people living in the area should at least attain the stage comparable to the surrounding areas at the beginning of the plan. They emphasized the provision of land alienation and protection of the people against exploitation by the moneylenders. When land was required to start some modern industry, the land under cultivation should not be acquired when uncultivated land was available. They also emphasized that the principle of compensation, when necessary, should be land for land and house for house. When people are displaced, new colonies should be developed before they are asked to vacate their original land and homes.

Thus, the Elwin report of 1960 and Dhebar report of 1961 have emphasized and amplified the five fundamental principles enunciated by Nehru in 1957. From the beginning Tribal development has been based on a two-pronged approach, namely:

(a) promotion of development activities to raise their level of living; and

(b) protection of their interests through legal and administrative support.

The Tribal sub-plan concept was accepted during the Fifth Five-Year Plan period as the main instrument for the development of Tribals. The broad strategy of the Tribal sub-plan at present covers about 75 per cent of the scheduled tribe population in 17 states and 2 union territories. However, it does not cover the six states and union territories of Arunachal Pradesh, Meghalaya, Mizoram, Nagaland, Lakshadweep, and Dadra and Nagar Haveli, as the majority of the population of these states and union territories is tribal and their respective state plans take care of the needs of the tribal population.

The Tribal sub-plan is being implemented through financial resources drawn from: (a) state plan, (b) special Central assistance, (c) sectoral programmes of Central ministries/departments, and (d) institutional finance. As against an investment of Rs. 1,100 crore during Fifth Plan period, investment for Sixth Plan was of the order of Rs. 5,535 crore and during Seventh Plan it was expected to reach Rs. 10,500 crore. It is implemented through 191 integrated tribal development projects covering 303.41 lakh ST population, 268 MADA pockets with population of 45.82 lakh, 76 clusters of tribal concentration with 3.43 lakh and 74 primitive tribal groups with about 16.36 lakh population.

The Working Group on Development and Welfare of Scheduled Tribes for Eighth Five Year Plan has recommended new arrangements for quantification of funds under Tribal sub-plan.

Outlays for TSP in state plans will be earmarked separately and given to Tribal Development Department. These will be allocated to state sectoral departments looking to plans/schemes prepared by them for development of scheduled tribes.

Twenty-point Programme continues to focus greater attention on development of scheduled tribes. During Sixth Plan period (1980-85). 39.65 lakh families as against the target of 27.60 lakh were economically assisted to enable them to cross the poverty line. For Seventh Plan period (1985-90), 40 lakh tribal families were targetted to be provided economic assistance. In the first four years of Seventh Plan period 42.64 lakh families had been assisted.

Tribal research and training institutes have been functioning in Andhra Pradesh, Assam, Bihar, Gujarat, Kerala, Madhya Pradesh, Manipur, Maharashtra, Orissa, Rajasthan, Uttar Pradesh, Tamil Nadu and West Bengal. They play a useful role in formulation of Tribal sub-plan, project reports, monitoring and evaluation of programmes implemented for scheduled tribes and organising of training programmes for personnel.

For marketing of tribal produce especially minor forest produce and to eliminate private traders exploiting poor tribals, Tribal Cooperative Marketing Development Federation (TRIFED) has been set up. It has been registered under the Multi-State Cooperative Societies Act, 1984. It operates through state federations which are its constituent members. The Federation had gradually expanded its commercial operations to several items of tribal produce. From 1988-89 TRIFED has undertaken procurement of surplus agricultural produce in tribal areas as an agent of Food Corporation of India and it has also been appointed as procurement agency for coarse grains and oilseeds from tribal areas.

Seven marketing and service extension centres are being exclusively set up in tribal areas by Government for marketing tribal handicrafts. Assistance and support will also be provided in marketing of tribal handicrafts even in some centres located in non-tribal areas.

Fiscal Support

The Ministry of Welfare provides financial assistance on cent per cent basis to voluntary organisations of All India nature engaged in development of scheduled tribes. Grants are given to them for undertaking schemes, namely, running of Balwadis, creches, hostels, schools and training-cum-production centres. During 1988-89, 28 voluntary organisations were given financial assistance worth rupees one crore.

The tribal sub-Plan (TSP) strategy adopted comprises: (a) identification in a State of development blocks where tribal population is in a majority and their constitution into integrated tribal development projects (ITDPs) with a view to adopting therein an integrated and project-based approach for development; (b) earmarking of funds for the TSP and ensuring flow of funds from the Central and State Plan sectoral outlays and from financial institutions; and (c) creation of appropriate administrative structures in tribal areas and adoption of appropriate personnel policies. The TSP has, overall, a two-fold thrust, firstly, socio-economic development of tribal areas and secondly, that of the tribal families. These basic premises will continue to be operative in the Seventh Plan.

The majority of tribal areas have remained isolated and backward. With their low levels of training, skills and technology which have remained largely traditional, the natural resources of tribal areas have remained unexploited for the development of tribals. Tribal areas are, further, characterised by socio-economic exploitation by non-tribals. One of the major tasks in the Seventh Plan was to create an awareness of these factors among the tribals, and stringent anti-exploitative measures undertaken along-side socio-economic development programmes. Particular care needs to be taken of the small primitive tribal groups, some of which face extinction. One of the causes which has given rise to discontent among tribals is the loss of their lands, and remedial measures against this need to be given priority. Also, tribal families displaced as a result of location of projects like power, irrigation, industries, mining etc., in tribal areas will need to be properly rehabilitated.

The planning process in tribal areas has to be a judicious mix of beneficiary-oriented programmes, human resource development and infrastructure development the bias being towards the first two 30 lakh tribal families in TSP was to be assisted in the Seventh Plan to build up their economic base.

About 2 lakh tribal families of about 5,000 forest villages do not possess even now any rights to the land they cultivate. They have no access to development programmes. Without these forest villages being declared as revenue villages, the inhabitants cannot be the recipients of benefits flowing from development programmes.

Appropriate remedial measures are required to be taken up by the State. A policy for the rehabilitation of project displaced persons has to be formulated at the national level, prescribing the general policy for the rehabilitation of persons displaced by large-scale land acquisition for projects and the special measures to be taken in the interest of scheduled tribes in such cases. Among other things, the policy will have to enjoin that rehabilitation of displaced persons, particularly the tribals, will form an integral part of the investment costs of projects relating to industries, irrigation, power, mining and forestry and wild life, of more than a certain magnitude, whether taken up in the Government corporate, joint or private sectors.

Integration in administration in tribal areas at ITDP levels has been the aim, but there are several programmes operating in these project areas, like IRDP, DPAP, RLEGP and NREP, in respect of which the tribal area administration headed by the Project Administrator of the local ITDP has not been kept in the picture. This has had consequential effect on coordination.

The Fifth Schedule of the Constitution provides a legal and administrative framework for the Scheduled Areas. Even this schedule in not fully operational as yet and this lapse has to be rectified. Further, the design support of the Fifth Schedule will have to be meaningfully combined with the self-management thrust of the Sixth Schedule to lend emphasis to endogenous growth. Non-government voluntary organisations can make significant contributions by catalysing the involvement of and the active participation by, tribals, approaching the tribal problems from a closer perspective and taking up development programmes for primitive tribal groups in relatively inaccessible areas.

But this planned approach to the development of the tribal areas and the tribal people depends for its success on the vigour with which these programmes are implemented by the administrative authorities. It may be stated that the approach of the government to improve the life of the people belonging to the scheduled tribes is a fit illustration of the planned approach to social change.

How do the different Girijans look upon themselves? What is the sense of identity they possess and how do they think of their past and their future? These are very important questions which help us to understand the problems that confront them. Fortunately, we have a whole chapter devoted to this problem in a book written by the leaders of the tribal people from the various parts of the country. However, there is a limitation that the views expressed are by those who were all Christians. In spite of this, we get a glimpse here of how they look upon themselves and their problems. They clearly recognize that they could no longer hope to lead their life in isolation. They are aware that it is impossible in the present context of national development to live in isolation; they are aware that they have to throw in their lot with the nation as a whole.

But they are also conscious that they are a distinct group in the Indian nation like the other distinct groups constituting the nation. In this awareness they appear to be like the various linguistic minorities and the caste groups in India which seek multiple identities.

Thus, the political expediency has created in them the consciousness of belonging to one group, as it did among the Harijans, by the preparation of the two schedules and by setting apart special sums in the planned budgets for the development of the lot of these two sections of the Indian society.

Another important characteristic of the self-identification among the Girijans as well as the Harijans is that they are indigenous people, the original inhabitants of the areas. The former group is now conscious that they are Adivasis, the people who originally lived in that area. Similarly, the Harijans, when they describe themselves as Adikamatakas, Adiandhras, and so on, imply that they are the original linguistic groups living in the area. "This is of utmost significance for us. We have been in this land of ours with an ardent love which cannot be compared with love of it by others. . . and must also recognize our peculiar responsibility towards this land and its development." However, as we shall see presently, the latter part of the statement does not hold good in its entirety among some groups like Mizos and the Nagas of the North-East. It is this consciousness that was responsible for the intense grief they experienced when they were dispossessed of their land due to various laws on the one hand and the needs of the industrial development on the other, not to speak of land alienation because of indebtedness. As noted above, both the Elwin Committee and the Dhebar Committee have stressed the need for careful handling of these problems, particularly the problem of resettlement.

Yet another aspect of self-identity is the sense of group solidarity and the deep loyalty to the group. "Most of our customs and traditions manifest this loyalty." Clan endogamy, devotion to the clan chieftain, and the notion deep in his mind, "that he can develop according to his own particular genius only in his own tribal group and community" are all characteristic of the sense of group solidarity. The sense of this group solidarity is the fear of the other groups, the "fear and apprehension as a result of outside exploitation that we tribals would soon die out or at least that our tribes would become extinct by being absorbed into larger and more virile groups. We are afraid that we might lose our racial identity and forget our languages and cultures by adopting those of others."

Thus, we see that these thinkers, who belong to the various tribal groups and who are converted to Christianity, are eager to retain their group loyalty and tribal characteristics, though they are conscious that they have to participate in the economic, political, and social development of the nation as a whole. This is by no means, as seen above, peculiar to the tribal people in India. Since indèpendence, all the various groups in India are having this problem of retaining the small group identity while participating in and becoming members of die national group.

However, with the new forces making for national development, many of these old loyalties have to crumble. As far back as 1958, Majumdar wrote that as the tribes emerge into a new economy, the primitive attitude of life undergoes significant modification. The importance of the blood-bond or the kinship group is forced to the background, the communal economy of the clan is superseded by individual desire for gains and property, money assumes an importance it seldom had before, and the ties of reciprocity and mutuality of obligation are reoriented to suit the new conditions. Tribal customs and practices, which established social life, lose their value and the choice of the leader and of mate is guided by different considerations. The tribaJ elders are pushed to the background, the priests are required to satisfy a more exacting clientele. Individuality begins to assert itself and a desire for social equality manifests itself which reduces the status of the clan chief and sacerdotal head to impotence sometimes. New customs find favour with the people and new prescriptions for their old maladies gain popularity with astonishing quickness.

This is not a problem, however, peculiar to the tribal groups. It is common to the members of all the other groups like the Harijans groups, and the other caste groups and the various linguistic groups in India.

The essential problem is one of retaining the old group loyalty while becoming a member of the national group, the larger and the more inclusive group consisting of various other groups. If the old group loyalty gains the upper hand there will not only be social tensions between the different groups but there will also be resistance to the formation of the new identity as a member of the national group. However, there is also the influence of the new principle of individuality and a desire for social equality which will modify the outlook of the individual so that the national outlook can emerge along with the faith in individual endeavour, social equality and social justice. But all these are linked with economic development and occupational differentiation. Also, there is the influence of adult franchise and the general elections which help in the development of a new identity as a member of the nation.

The adult franchise and the general election once in five years have made the tribal groups to develop a desire ior autonomy, and has generated in them a spirit of assertiveness. The movements that have led to the national problem, the formation of the Hill State in Assam, and the Jharkand movement in Chotanagpur, are all significant expressions of this political awakening.

NEFA and other areas with large tribal population were administered by the British as "excluded areas"; the Governor of Assam was directly in charge of these areas. None of the Central or Provincial Acts could be applied to these areas unless the Governor so directed.

In the Indian Constitution, Pan Ten deals with "the scheduled and tribal areas" and the details of administration are given in the fifth and sixth schedules. The fifth schedule refers to the tribal areas in the various states of India and the sixth schedule refers to the tribal areas in the Assam State.

According to the fifth schedule, each state which has scheduled tribes living in it must establish a Tribes Advisory Council consisting of not more than twenty members of whom about three-fourth shall be the representatives of the Scheduled Tribes in the Legislative Assembly of the State, and other members of those tribes.

The sixth schedule refers to the tribal areas in Assam. These areas were divided into districts according to the groups: these districts were autonomous. It is also provided that when there are different tribes in a district, the Governor is empowered to divide the area into autonomous regions. Each district and each such region will have its own council of not more than twenty-four members, of whom not more than three-fourths shall be elected on adult suffrage.

Nagaland has been one of the most problem areas of the region because it is contiguous with Burma and close to Bangladesh as well as China. When the Japanese brought the Second World

War to this area, the Naga people were involved in protecting it from Japanese occupation. Right from the period of the First World War, the Nagas were recruited in the Indian Army and many of them had been well trained. Further the Nagas were practically untouched by both Hinduism and Buddhism through the centuries; however, during the nineteenth century Christian missions established themselves and converted most of the Nagas to Christianity. All these forces made the Naga people to develop a new concept of freedom. Besides, they appropriated vast quantities of arms left behind by the Japanese on the one hand and by the British and Indian forces on the other.

Thus, at the time of independence, the Naga public opinion was divided. The extremists led by Phizo stood for independence. But the moderates were in favour of working within the framework of the Indian Constitution.

In 1952, Phizo was able to unite the Nagas and make them boycott the general elections. He also started a civil disobedience movement and finally an armed revolt. But by 1957 there was a great change. The moderates who believed in the constitutional solution of the problem gained in strength and stood for the elections for the Assam Legislature. The Naga Convention was held in Kohima in August 1957. Nearly 2,000 delegates from the various tribes attended the Convention and decided that there should be a political settlement within the Constitution. The Third Naga Convention in 1959 agreed to the formation of a New State of Nagaland under the aegis of the External Affairs Ministry. The new State of Nagaland was formally inaugurated by the President of India in 1963. In the 1964 elections, more than three quarters of the electorate cast their votes to elect members of the State Assembly, in spite of the bitter opposition from the Naga extremists. As a result, the underground Nagas intensified their reign of terror and the Indian army had to be called in. In August 1964, there was a cease-fire as a result of the efforts of the Baptist churches. A peace commission was set-up to initiate talks between the underground Nagas and the Government of India. Since 1966, there have been several meetings between the Prime Minister of India and the extremist delegation. As a consequence, the peace commission was dissolved. In the 1969 elections most of the Naga people participated in the elections. After the election most of the underground Nagas have surrendered their arms and have announced that they would settle down as peaceful citizens in the State of Nagaland within the framework of the Indian Constitution.

Thus, the tribal people of the Naga area, who are turbulent and wanted independence, are gradually coming to accept the authority of the Naga State and to function as normal citizens of the Indian Union.

During the sixties there was great agitation among the people living in the other autonomous districts. The people of the Mizo groups became every turbulent.

The Government of India realized that the new aspirations in the various tribal groups had to be recognized. As a result the North-Eastern Areas (Reorganization) Act, 1971 was passed. In January 1972 Meghalaya State was formed and Arunachal Pradesh and Mizoram were made union territories. Thus there are now two states and two union territories in the region. Nagaland and Arunachal Pradesh have recognized English as the State language. The independent tribal groups in each state or union territory are now being coalesced into provincial groups and have entered the mainstream of the national life.

The Dalits

One of the earliest references to this group appears in the Chandogya Upanishad which uses the term "Chandala". The term referred to a degraded person who is ranked along with the dog and the pig. The earlier Buddhist Jatakas (second century B.C.) also speak of the Chandelas as a despised group living outside the village, who speak a special dialect and have their own hereditary occupation. The Dharmashastras declare the Chandela to be the progeny of a Brahmin woman and a Sudra man. Manu also declared that these people lived outside the village and that they were prohibited from entering the villages and towns in the day time.

These statements are confirmed by the observations of Alberuni, who wrote in about A.D, 1020. He noted the dom and the Chandela as the two groups who did the dirty work like cleaning the villages and who were distinguished by their occupations.

It can now be inferred that the Chandelas followed some degrading occupations, and that they lived outside the villages. But it is very difficult to imagine that persons born out of forbidden sex contacts were numerous enough to form a separate caste group, since they are to be found practically in all the villages of India. It is possible that because they were following occupations which were despised, they were characterized by the Dharma-shastras as equivalent to the despicable progeny of forbidden sex relations. In other words, these statements should not be taken in their literal sense as explaining the origin of these groups of people.

As Ghurye writes, "Ideas of purity, whether occupational or ceremonial, which are found to have been a factor in the genesis of caste are the very soul of the idea and practice of untouchability." Thus, because they were following occupations like scavenging, doing leather work, removing dead cattle from the village, and so on, they were looked upon as a profane group, contact with whom was defiling. So they were required to live in a separate colony outside the village. The practice of untouchability was at its worst in different parts of the Kerala State in the south-west corner of the country. As Aiyappan writes, "While the belief in human beings as carriers of graded degrees of ritual impurity is common to all Hindus, these manifestations are nowhere as hypertrophied as in Kerala. To avoid upper castes being polluted, the distance at which these castes had to remain, varied from about 30 feet to 150 feet.

According to Ambedkar, these groups persisted in practising Buddhism even after the bulk of the Hindus gave it up and so they were banished from the villages. This view also appears to be rather far-fetched.

In the opinion of the present writer, it looks as if these groups of people were declared untouchable and were made to live outside the villages for two reasons. First, they were following the lowest kinds of occupations like scavenging, leather work, removal of the carrion, etc., and second, they persisted in eating beef which was condemned as the most heinous crime by the caste Hindus. According to Vedic scholars, the upper castes also followed the practice of eating beef during the Vedic period. It is only during the period of the Dharmashastras that the eating of beef was totally condemned. But these groups appear to have persisted in the practice and so were condemned. "They are an integral pan of the village life," as Srinivas notes, "they perform certain essential tasks in agriculture, they are often village servants, messengers and sweepers, and they beat the drum at village festivals and remove the leaves on which people have dined at community dinners.

In dealing with the changes in the position of the Harijans which have taken place in the present century, we can briefly describe the activities of the following persons and their respective organizations: Sri Narayana Guru and S.N.D.P. Yogam in Kerala; Bhima Rao Ambedkar and the All-India Scheduled Caste Federation established by him; and Mahatma Gandhi and the Harijan Sevak Sangh.

Sri Narayana Guru (1854-1928) established the S.N.D.P. Yogam in 1902 with his gospel. "One caste, one religion, one God." This organization had two important programmes: one was to uplift the Ezhavas, a depressed caste group of Kerala; as part of the work of the Yogam, Narayana Guru started a number of schools and colleges throughout Kerala: secondly, he built a number of temples; he simplified rituals regarding worship, marriage and funerals. While S.N.D.P. Yogam was a secular organization with its branches throughout Kerala, he also established an order of Sanyasis to help the community regarding its religious and spiritual matters. For fifteen years he travelled widely and helped them to clean up their houses and streets and develop clean habits. He made them alter their diet and thus pointed the right road to reform and prosperity.By these two means—modern education on the one hand and Sanskritization on the other—Narayana Guru was able to transform the Ezhavas from an untouchable group in Kerala to a "backward caste" community within a short period of 30 years. The temple entry programmes undertaken by some of the Ezhava leaders, in association with the Nayar Service Society, finally led to the temple entry proclamation in 1936. Aiyappan writes that C.P. Ramaswamy lyer, the Dewan of the Travancore State, "felt the need for consolidating the Hindus and building up the unity of the Hindus of the State as a counterpoise against the growing power and influence of the Christians. The most discontented and at the same time the best organized among the Hindus caste were the Iravas. Nothing was dearer to the Izhavas of that generation than temple entry."

However, in recent years a new class trend has emerged among the Ezhavas. The middle class of this group supported the Congress Party, and their leader, R. Shanker, spearheaded the liberation struggle with Manath Padmanabhan of Nayar Service Society and caused the first Communist Government in Kerala to be dislodged in 1958. Shanker himself became the Deputy Chief Minister in 1962 and the Chief Minister of Kerala State in 1964. However, the lower classes among the Ezhavas were giving their solid support to the Communist Party. As Nayar writes, "The S.N.D.P. represents the Ezhava middle class which is numerically small and less influential than the Nair middle class. The vast majority of the Ezhavas have favoured the Communist Party. Thus there is a gulf between the Ezhava middle class and Ezhava lower class."

Another great Harijan leader Ambedkar (1891-1956) stayed in America for three years and took his Master's Degree and a Doctorate in Economics and returned to India in 1917 when the Franchise Committee was preparing its report for Montague, the Secretary, and Chelmsford the Viceroy. He met the Franchise Committee and made a strong plea for direct representation of the depressed class in the Bombay legislature in proportion to their population through a separate electorate.

He was a great leader of the Mahar Community in Maharashtra to which he belonged and he took many steps to reform the way of life of these people. He urged them to stop the dragging of dead cattle out of the village. He wanted them to give up eating carrion, alcoholic drinks, and begging. He wanted them to become literates and send their children to schools. Finally, he wanted them to dress well and have self-respect for themselves. Thus, one of his chief aims was to bring about a revolution in the way of life of the untouchables and in their aspirations for themselves and for their children.

He wrote in Mook Nayak (The Voice of The Dumb) which he started in 1920. "We are not yet ready to give an answer to the question of whether untouchables should have a temple of their own or attempt to enter the Hindu temple." But, on a few occasions Ambedkar made many attempts to forcibly enter the Hindu temple. The right to participate in the public Ganapathi festival was secured at least on one occasion. Ambedkar and his followers donned the sacred thread symbolizing rebirth. The abortive attempt to enter the temple at Amravati was followed in 1930 by large-scale Satyagraha at the Kalaram temple in Nasik. Ambedkar himself disbelieved in idol worship. So the programme of temple entry was more for social than for religious purposes. Thus, it looks as if in the period 1920-1930 he was in favour of the temple entry programme in order to establish the rights of the untouchables. But after 1930 he gave up these attempts and concentrated his attention on the improvement of the educational standard of the community and their political status.

In the same period there is the evidence that his approach to the political problem underwent a drastic change. "The demand for General Electorates for adult franchise before the Simon Commission in 1928 gave way to the insistence on separate electorate at the Round Table Conference in 1930, probably in the light of Muslim minorities demand." At the First Round Table Conference he emphasized that the untouchables constitute a distinct group and cannot be looked upon as the members of the Hindu community. So he wanted a separate electorate to be established for the untouchables.

In May 1920, an All-India Conference of the untouchables was held at Nagpur. It was presided over by the Maharaja of Kolhapur. At the end of this conference Ambedkar made an attempt to consolidate the forces of the depressed classes, by arranging an intercaste dinner. Among the Mahars alone, the community to which Ambedkar belonged, there were 18 sub-castes without interdining and inter-marriage. Ambedkar found that it was very difficult to get the various sub-castes of the Mahars and the sub-castes of the other castes of the depressed classes to join together at a dinner. Thus, Ambedkar was faced with two problems, to consolidate all the depressed classes as one group and to get all the Hindus, the Savarna, and the Avarna together so that the Avarna Hindus have their rightful place in the Hindu society.

Before proceeding further, we may briefly describe the great Harijan movement started by Mahatma Gandhi (1869-1948). The Indian National Congress devoted all its efforts to the political problems up to 1917. It was in 1917 that the Congress adopted a resolution urging "the necessity of justice and righteousness of removing of disability imposed by customs on the untouchables."

Though Gandhi arrived in India in 1915 from South Africa, he did not start his public life immediately. At the behest of Gokhale he went round the country for one year studying the condition of the people in the various parts. It was during 1917-18 that he plunged himself in the three great movements Champaran Satyagraha, Kaira Satyagraha, and Ahmedabad mill strike ,which not only made him the undisputed leader in India but also changed the very character of the Indian National Congress. These movements transformed the Indian National Congress into a mass organization. In 1920, Gandhi wrote: "Untouchabilily cannot be given a secondary place in the programme. Without the removal of the taint, Swaraj is a meaningless term." Thus from 1920 onwards, the Indian National Congress under the leadership of Mahatma Gandhi became committed to the removal of untouchability. In December 1921, the Congress at its session in Ahmedabad resolved to start a voluntary organization throughout the country and signed a pledge. Item five of the pledge read, "As a Hindu I believe in the justice and necessity of removing the evil of untouchability and shall on all possible occasions seek personal contact with and endeavour to render service to the submerged classes."

The next most important event is the Vykom Satyagraha which was started in 1924 in Kerala to throw open the temple streets to the untouchables. But the people as well as the Government were strongly against this movement. The Government of Travancore State put up barricades and prohibited the untouchables from entering the streets near the temple. In 1925, Gandhi visited Travancore State and informed the Government that this act of theirs "was lending itself to the view that they were supporting the conservatism of the Hindus of Travancore with their own physical forces." In April 1925, Gandhi wrote in Young India," "For the opening of the roads is not the final but the first step in the ladder of reform. Temples, public wells and public schools must be open to the untouchables equally with caste Hindus." In response to this appeal, the Travancore Government removed the barricades but the opposition of the caste Hindus went on unabated. The problem now was to change the public opinion. At this point satyagraha was suspended. However, as Aiyappan writes, "The Vykom satyagraha, though it had failed to produce any effect on the Travancore Government or the upper caste in Kerala, made untouchability a problem of national importance."

Another notable event was the conviction of an untouchable, Murugesha, in 1926 when he entered a temple to offer his prayers. He was discovered, arrested, and convicted on the charge of defiling the temple. Gandhi was greatly moved by this incident and he wrote in Young India: "It is simply fanatical obstinacy to persist in persecuting men in the sacred name of religion. Its persecutors who are knowingly defiling their own religion by keeping out of public temples men who are at least as honourable as they claim to be themselves, and are willing to abide by all the ceremonial rules."

On 2 March 1930, ten days before Gandhi's Dandi March, Ambedkar launched a big temple entry movement at Nasik before the Kalaram temple. A huge band of 15,000 volunteers, including 500 women, was brought there to offer satyagraba. The police, anticipating violence, closed the gates of the temple and guarded them. A public meeting was convened to solve the problem peacefully. But the orthodox section was strongly against the temple entry. The Nasik satyagraha brought great resentment among the people against the depressed classes and it went on until 1935.

But after the Simon Commission report in May 1930 and probably due to the Nasik satyagraha which provoked the caste Hindus to punish the Harijans throughout the district, Ambedkar reconsidered his position and demanded separate electorate with greater conviction.

Ambedkar also denounced the civil disobedience movement set afoot by Gandhi and asserted that this would lead to revolution.

He traced the differences between revolution and a real social change. According to Ambedkar, a revolution is merely transference of political power from one parly to another party. Real social change will occur if the revolution is accompanied by a redistribution of power among the forces operating in the society.

The British Government was confronted with a new situation when the Simon Commission report was rejected for different reasons by the various political panics in India. So they convened the First Round Table Conference in London in November 1930 with Indian representatives. But the Indian National Congress was out of the picture since all the leaders were in prison. Still, the conference was convened and Ambedkar attended the conference. At the conference Ambedkar spoke about the loathsome condition of the untouchables in India and said, "150 years of British rule did not alter even a little the position of the untouchables. They were prevented from drawing water from the wells, from entering into temples, etc., by the caste Hindu society. The Government itself prevented their recruitment in the police and the military services on the ground that they were untouchables." This strong denunciation by Ambedkar brought the position of the untouchables into focus. Ambedkar prepared a declaration of fundamental rights safeguarding culture, religion, and economic rights of the depressed classes and submitted it to the minorities sub-committee. He demanded the abolition of untouch-ability and the establishment of equal citizenship. He also demanded separate electorates for the depressed classes.

The Gandhi-Irwin Pact was signed in March 1931, and, consequently, the civil disobedience movement was called off. All the political prisoners were released. The Congress organized the Karachi Session in the last week of March 1931. A little before this session Gandhi had declared during his stay in Bombay that he would fight for the temple entry after freedom was won. This directive was clearcut and expressive.

The discrimination and the humiliations suffered by the depressed classes can be judged by the criteria adopted to identify them. In the Census of 1931 the Census Commissioner J.H. Hutton identified the following disabilities:

1. Whether the caste or class in question can be served by Brahmins or not.

2. Whether the caste or class in question can be served by the barbers, water-carriers, tailors, etc., who serve the caste Hindus.
3. Whether the caste in question pollutes a high-caste Hindu by contact or proximity.
4. Whether the caste or class in question is one from whose hands a caste Hindu can take water,
5. Whether the caste or class in question is debarred from using public conveniences, such as roads, ferries, wells or schools.
6. Whether the caste or class in question is debarred from the use of Hindu temples.
7. Whether in ordinary social intercourse a well-educated member of the caste or class in question will be treated as an equal by the high-caste men of the same educational qualifications.
8. Whether the caste or class in question is merely depressed on account of its own ignorance, illiteracy or poverty and but for that, would be subject to no social disability.
9. Whether it is depressed on account of the occupation followed, and whether, but for that occupation it would be subject to no social disability.

At the Karachi Session, the Congress adopted the fundamental rights resolution. Section 4 declared, "All the citizens are equal before law irrespective of caste, creed or sex." Section 6 declared, "At citizen have equal rights and duties in regard to wells, tanks, roads, schools and places of public resort maintained out of the State or local funds or dedicated by private persons for the use of the general public." Section 10 declared universal adult suffrage. Thus, in March 1931, the Congress finally liquidated the social institution of untouchability as far as it was concerned.

At about this time, the Government of Bombay announced that members from the depressed classes would be recruited for the police department. This was an important result of Ambedkar's efforts to get a just treatment for the depressed classes.

On 14 August 1931, Ambedkar met Gandhi. They discussed

at length the problem of untouchability. Ambedkar wanted Gandhi to make the removal of untouchability as a pre-condition for a person to become a member of the Congress as it had done with regard to wearing of the Khadder. He also informed him of the way in which the President of the District Congress Committee in Nasik opposed the temple entry. Gandhi was startled when Ambedkar told him that he had no homeland because he was treated worse than a cat or a dog by the Hindus. When he asked Gandhi about his opinion on the political rights of the depressed classes Gandhi said, "The political separation of the untouchables and the Hindus would be suicidal to the nation." Thus, there was no bridge between the two leaders on this point.

Ambedkar and Gandhi left India to attend the Second Round Table Conference in London. At the Minorities Committee Gandhi declared, "We do not want the untouchables to be classified as a separate class. Sikhs may remain such in perpetuity, so may Muslims and Christians. Will the untouchables remain untouchables in perpetuity? I would rather feel that Hinduism died than that untouchability lived .... I will resist it with my life."

As members of the Round Table Conference were unable to agree to any solution of the minorities problem and communal representation including the political status of the untouchables, Prime Minister Ramsay MacDonald made it clear that the British Government would be forced to give its own award. He got the members to sign a requisition authorizing him to settle the communal problem and to pledge themselves to accept his decision.

Thus, the Second Round Table Conference clearly brought out the conflict between the views of Ambedkar and Gandhi.

On 14 August the British Prime Minister announced the communal award according to which the depressed classes were granted separate seats in the provincial assemblies and they were given the right of double vote in which they could elect their own representative and also vote in the general constituencies.

Earlier, in January 1932, Gandhi was arrested and sent to Yervada Jail. Even in the jail he was fighting against separate electorate for Harijans. Early in March 1932, he wrote to the British Cabinet from the jail that he would resist with his life the separation of the untouchables from the Hindu community.

When the award was announced he declared his resolution of fast-unto-death from 20 September. Madan Mohan Malaviya and other Hindu leaders decided to hold a conference in Bombay on 19 September 1932 to resolve the deadlock and save Gandhi's life. Malaviya wired to Ambedkar to participate in the conference.

On the eve of the conference, Ambedkar issued a statement asserting "there have been many Mahatmas in India whose sole object was to remove untouchability and to elevate and absorb the depressed classes but every one of them has failed in his mission. Mahatmas have come and Mahatmas have gone but the untouchables have remained as untouchables."

The declaration of fast-unto-death opened the eyes of the whole country towards this problem of the untouchables. The conference tried to evolve various solutions.

A deputation waited on the fasting Gandhi at the jail on 21 September. Ambedkar demanded 197 seats as against 71 given by the award. Finally, the number of reserved seats was settled at 148. This is the famous Poona Pact. Immediately, it was transmitted to London and the British Government announced its acceptance. The Hindu Maha Sabha also ratified it at its meeting in Delhi. Gandhi broke his fast on 26 September 1932, but he announced that he would resume his fast-unlo-death if the movement for the removal of untouchability was not achieved within a measurable period. It was at this time that the Harijan Sevak Sangh was formed and the conference at Bombay pledged that the right to use the public roads, wells, etc., would be given statutory recognition when the Swaraj Parliament met, in case such a legislation was not passed earlier.

This pledge was reiterated by Gandhi in December 1932 when he expressed, "There could be no rest, therefore for me or for those who by word of mouth or show of hand, willingly endorsed the resolution, until untouchability becomes a thing of the past,"

However, Ambedkar warned his people not to get lost in the temple entry and inter-dining. He wanted them to solve their economic problems because the temple entry would not give them economic security. In his letter to Thakkar Bapa he said, "The salvation of the depressed class will come only when the caste

Hindu is made to think and is forced to feel that he must alter his ways. I want a revolution in the mentality of the caste Hindus." He asserted that such a social revolution will come only when the Anti-untouchability League, of which Thakkar Bapa was the Joint Secretary, launched a campaign all over the country to secure for the depressed classes enjoyment of their civil rights such as taking water from the village wells, admission of the children in village schools, etc. However, such a civil campaign, according to Ambedkar, needed an army of workers in the rural parts. He wrote, "It is true that this programme involves social disturbances, and a violent struggle. But I do not think it could be avoided." He pointed out, "The direct action in respect of Chowder Tank in Nahed, the Kalaram temple at Nasik, and the Guruvayur temple in Malabar have done in a few days what million days of preaching by reformers would never have done." For this task he wanted the League to engage full-time workers from the depressed classes themselves.

Gandhi started his Harijan in 1933. In his message Ambedkar wrote, "The outcaste is a by-product of the caste system .... Nothing can emancipate the outcaste except the destruction of the caste system." However, Gandhi wrote that though many educated Hindus held such a view he was not able to share it.

In order to redeem the pledge of the removal of untouchability it was necessary to pass new laws. Rajagopalachari said: "It has often pointed out by eminent jurists that British Court and British Law in India, by enforcing the established usages and customs of the Hindus, prevented natural growth and evolution of the Hindu customs." The case of Murugeshan noted above illustrates the point. Even though the large majority was in favour of the temple entry of the depressed classes, one or two dissentients could move the courts to uphold the custom. According to Rajagopalachari, by this means the courts actually enforced untouchability. So the most important thing was the ena tment of a law forbidding the practice of untouchability.

On 1 November 1932, the Madras Legislative Council passed a resolution unanimously that the Government should recognize the public sentiment and bring forward legislation to enable trustees to throw open temples to all Hindus. On 1 December 1932,

Subbarayan, a former Chief Minister of Madras State, moved a Bill outlining procedure to enable the trustees to ascertain the will of the people regarding temple entry. Within a few days, Ranga lyer moved a Bill in the Delhi Assembly on the lines of the November 1932 resolution of the Madras Council. According to law, in all social matters the Governor-General had to give his assent for moving the Bills either in the Central or in the Provincial legislatures. In January 1933, the Governor-General announced that he was not in favour of the two Madras Bills as they affected many devotees who live outside Madras State but who come to those temples. He, however, gave permission to Ranga lyer to move the Bill in the Central Assembly. Immediately, Ranga lyer presented another Bill on the lines of Subbarayan's Bill to ascertain public opinion. The Governor-General accorded his permission to move this Bill also.

Thus we see the tremendous obstacles put by British Courts and the British administration to remove untouchability even when the people were in favour of it.

On the other hand, in February 1933, Ambedkar gave his famous statement on temple entry Bills and looked upon them as an affront to the depressed classes since these Bills left the problem of temple entry to the option of the people rather than enforcing it by law. Thus, Ambedkar was keen on a political approach to the problem rather than a mere social reform approach.

The Anti-untouchability League was now renamed the Harijan Sevak Sangh. Ambedkar was a member of the League, but now he severed his connection because the Harijan Sevak Sangh, by its constitution, excluded the depressed class leaders and workers from its executive. However, the Harijan movement launched by Gandhi gained strength throughout the country. Gandhi went on an all-India tour to collect huge sums of money for this programme.

Another very important incident took place in 1935 in Kavita, a small village in Gujarat. The Harijan workers in that village tried to get the Harijan children admitted to the village school. But the Savamas of the village were against it. Gandhi, in the Harijan of October 1935, wrote: "The Kavita Savamas had not recognized the time spirit." The Harijan workers offered to help the Harijans to leave Kavita so that they could settle down in another place, but they refused to leave their homes. Ambedkar was provoked by this incident and by the method adopt, by the Harijan workers to solve the problem. He attacked Gandhi that he wanted the Harijans to leave the village rather than launch cases against Savarnas. However, the Harijans succeeded a little later in sending their children to the school because of the boldness of a Rajput living in that village. He visited the Harijan locality frequently and gave them moral support. As a result of this, the Savarnas changed their attitude and allowed the Harijan children to be admitted to the school. The instance also had a repercussion in the surrounding villages, and the Harijan children were admitted to the schools in practically the whole area.

This incident brought out several features of the situation. Because of their up bringing and their prejudice, the Savarnas of the village were unable to tolerate the idea of their own children studying along with Harijan children in the school. For them Harijan children were more "Harijans" rather than "children". On the other side, the local Harijans were unable to revolt against the Savarnas again because of their upbringing and also because they constituted a minority in the village. Even when the Harijan workers offered to take them to another village where they could send their children to the school, me Harijans refused to leave their homeland. This is again a very typical reaction that they would rather put up with the humiliation than be uprooted. Finally, the incident shows how the determined efforts of a few Savarnas brought about a change in favour of social justice.

The whole problem is typical of the village situation not only in 1935 but even today, more than 49 years after the incident. The alternatives are whether to wait for a social change among the Savarnas or to force them to change through law and risk social tension in the village.

For the first time in the Government of India Act, 1935, the Scheduled Castes were defined as "such castes, races or tribes or parts of or groups within castes, races or tribes, being castes, races, tribes parts or groups which appear to His Majesty in Council to correspond to the classes of persons formerly known as 'the depressed classes', as His Majesty in Council may specify." According to the Indian Statutory Commission, 1930 the population of untouchables varied from 8 per cent to 26.5 per cent in different Provinces of British India.

As noted earlier one unique step was taken by the ruler of Travancore by the Temple Entry Proclamation in 1936 in one of the most orthodox states of India, at the instance of the Dewan, Ramaswamy Iyer. However, this gesture did not influence the rulers of the other states even in Kerala.

Swift changes took place in the political situation at this time because the Congress Party resolved to participate in the 1937 elections. All the Congress candidates had pledged themselves to the removal of un touch ability. In 1938, the removal of the Civil Disabilities Act was passed by the Madras legislature which provided that no Harijan shall be disabled from any social or public amenity. In the same year, it also passed the Malabar Temple Entry Act which threw open the temples in Malabar.

In July 1939, at the instance of the workers of the Harijan Sevak Sangh and the Congress leaders, the temple at Madurai was opened to the Harijans. This event was followed by the opening of temples in the other districts of Tamil Nadu. However, the orthodox sections filed civil and criminal suits. The Congress Government at Madras felt it necessary to condone the technical breach of law and it published an Indemnity Bill for protecting the participants. Within a few months, in the same year, a temple entry Authorization and Indemnity Act, 1939, was passed by the Madras legislature authorizing the trustees to throw the temple open if in their opinion worshippers are not opposed to such an innovation.

Thus, Gandhi's fast and the Poona agreement had released tremendous forces throughout the country which led to the removal of the disability of the Harijans.

The Congress Governments in the states had to resign in 1939 as the Viceroy declared that India was a participant in the Second World War without consulting the legislatures. Because the war effort was not quite successful, the Viceroy appointed a number of Indians to the Executive Council in 1942. Ambedkar was invited to take up the Labour portfolio. This event was received with great satisfaction by the public as well as by the Press in India. It was a matter of great significance that a person belonging to the untouchable caste was appointed a Central Minister. Before assuming office, Ambedkar attended the All-India Depressed Class Conference in Nagpur in July 1942. More than 7,000 delegates from all over India attended the conference. At the conference Ambedkar declared, "It is a matter of immense satisfaction that untouchables have made great strides all along on all sides." He went on and said that they have now acquired political consciousness. They had also made considerable progress in education and secured a foot-hold in the public services. He also expressed great satisfaction that a large number of women were attending the conference. "My final word of advice is to educate, agitate and organize; have faith in yourself. It is a battle for the reclamation of human personality." The conference announced the formation of the All-India Scheduled Caste Federation and passed a resolution urging separate electorate.

The 1937 elections clearly showed that the majority of the Harijan leaders throughout the country were with the Indian National Congress.

When elections were held in 1946 for the Constituent Assembly in the various provincial legislatures, Ambedkar found that the legislators in Bombay would not support him. They elected only the Congress Harijans. He was able to get into the Constituent Assembly only with the help of the Scheduled Caste representatives and ihe Muslim League from the Bengal Assembly. Later on, the Congress Harijan leader, Jagjivan Ram from Bihar, was nominated to the interim ministry by the Congress, and Jogendranan Mandal, a member of the Scheduled Caste Federation, was nominated as the Muslim League representative in the interim ministry. Thus, neither the Congress nor the League was able to invite at this time Ambedkar who had hardly any followers among the elected Harijan leaders.

The Congress redeemed its pledge to the Harijans by declaring in the third session of the Constituent Assembly in April 1947 that "untouchability in any form is abolished and imposition of any disability on that account shall be an offence," The declaration was hailed not only by the Indian press throughout the country but also by the world press.

But the most dramatic event was that the Prime Minister, Nehru, invited Ambedkar to be the Law Minister in the First Cabinet of Independent India. Even more significant was the appointment of Ambedkar as the Chairman of the Drafting Committee to draft the Indian Constitution.

Article 17 of the Constitution abolished untouchability. As a result of this the Harijan enjoys the same legal rights as any other citizen. Further, adult franchise has given them political power. The various political parties in India seek their support. It is often asserted that the Congress has been able to get considerable majorities in various slates and in the Centre because of the solid support of the Harijans. In 1955, the Untouchability (Offences) Act was passed fixing penalties for infractions. Thus, after long struggle by Gandhi and the Congress on the one hand, and by Ambedkar and the organizations started by him on the other, the legal disabilities of Harijans were removed. Equality before law was assured.

But the great problem is the removal of social disabilities. These are not automatically removed with the removal of legal disabilities. Legislation is necessary but not enough. Realizing this the Constitution-makers laid down under Article 46 that "the State shall promote with special care the educational and economic institutions of the weaker section of the people, in particular of scheduled castes and scheduled tribes and shall protect them from social injustice and all forms of exploitation." Further, Article 338 of the Constitution empowers the President of India to appoint a Commission to study the conditions of the scheduled castes and scheduled tribes and submit an annual report to the President.

There has been a great change in the position of the Harijans with the spread of education among them and with the consciousness of their rights according to the Constitution. It is inevitable that this new awareness among these people should generate tension between the Savarna Hindus and the Avama Hindus.

The caste Hindus, became enraged when the Harijans claimed the new rights given to them by the Constitution. They accept the Constitution but they also want that the old customs should continue. This is particularly so among the people in the villages where the vast majority of the Harijans live and work.

There have been a number of attempts, right from the days of Gandhi to reinterpret the ancient social values to incorporate the modern social values. As an example, we could give the new meaning given by the great philosopher Radhakrishnan to the ancient word dharma. He interpreted the old definition of Dharma. Dharanaath Dharma, which means that which holds the society together, that which consolidated the society, and that which brings people together. On the basis of this, he enunciated a test by means of which one could judge the value of the social institutions. He said, "Does this institution make for social coherence or integration, or does it make for social confusion and its disintegration?" Judged by this test, the institution of untouchability must be regarded as opposed to dharma, as something which is adharma, something which is not in consonance with dharma.

However, the social legislation does not help the discriminated individual particularly in the rural areas where caste feelings are strong. As a matter of fact, a good deal of work has been done in the rural areas by way of exclusive and segregated welfare work like putting up special wells, special quarters, special schools, and so on. But such segregated welfare work, though it may help the Harijans to some extent, does not remove social inequality; on the other hand it perpetuates it.

Though such problems do not exist in the urban areas, still there is considerable discrimination. The educated middle-class Harijans are made to suffer because of their caste. Harold Issacs has given many illustrations of the subtle ways in which untouchability is practised in the urban areas. One of the chief difficulties of the middle class Harijans in the urban area is to secure houses. The house owner not only wants to know the ability of the prospective tenant to pay the rent regularly, he also wants to know his caste.

Basic Issues

The main problem is that all the welfare programmes are now rendered on the basis of the caste. As Shaw writes, "Further, all concessions and privileges are admissible to a member of an untouchable community only if he is a member of the scheduled caste duly notified and only if he could produce an authentic certificate to that effect. Thus, caste is officially recognised as a feature of comprehensive social welfare policy of the Republic of India." Though through education a person could improve his class status, easte status pursues him and his children. This is the paradox that is arising on account of the welfare policy of the Government which insists on caste as a basis for the promotion of the welfare of his family. As Issacs writes, "The need to be identified and labelled in order to be helped, relentlessly pursues the individual all the way through school and later into the world."

Secondly, there is the problem of endogamy which is an essential feature of the various castes irrespective of whether they are Savama castes or Avarna castes. Every caste insists upon the boy or the girl marrying within the caste. Further, the caste system is at once rigid and flexible. It is flexible because even if a man marries outside his caste and there is rejection by the caste people in the initial stages on both sides, generally the families ultimately reconcile themselves, and, as noted above, the couple is not rejected from the family. They continue to enjoy membership and the privileges and affections of their families; so will their children. Generally, the children of the intercaste marriages are accepted as members of the caste to which the father belongs. Thus, this practice of endogamy among all the various castes including the lowest of the low—the bhangis—is a great obstacle for the abolition of the caste system in actual practice.

Finally, there is the problem of hierarchy. The members of the Harijan castes follow the hierarchical principle among themselves as rigidly as those of the higher castes. For example, all the various castes follow these rules of hierarchy not only with respect to endogamy but also with respect to interdining and even untouchability. The higher caste Harijan will practice untouchability towards lower caste Harijan.

Thus, apart from all other considerations, these three considerations based on caste, endogamy, and hierarchy are very important to understand why the constitutional abolition of caste has not resulted in the social abolition of castes.

The whole of Indian society was shocked by speech made by the Jagatguru Shankaracharya of Puri at the second Hindu World Conference inaugurated at Patna on 29 March 1969. He asserted that untouchability was supported by the tenets of Hindu religion. Even as he was speaking there were many interruptions. On 1 April 1969, the Jagatguru reiterated that the Hindu religion accepted that some people are born untouchables. While it was impossible for him to go back upon what the sastra held, the Jagatguru said that as a citizen he would not violate the law of the land.

It is very interesting to note that this statement was made by the Jagatguru in the Gandhi Birth Centenary year and nearly twenty years after the Constitution abolished untouchability. When one reads the proceedings of this second World Hindu Conference, according to the press reports, it is likely that the Jagatguru was provoked to make the statement in response to the inaugural address by Karan Singh, the Union Minister, who said that Hinduism like all the other religions in the world, must face the challenge of the changing times and readjust itself to the requirements of the new age of science. Karan Singh is also reported to have said that while the basic concepts of Hinduism remain the same, the social order of Hinduism needed thorough revitalization. He also pointed out that while many old religions and cultures have faded, Hinduism is surviving because it could march with the times. He pointed out the necessity for the removal of the practice of untouchability. Probably, it is this emphasis to adjust the values of religion, particularly with respect to the social order, to the needs of the times, that must have provoked the Jagatguru to justify the practice of untouchabilily on the basis of sastras. However, during the twenties and later during the thirties when Gandhi challenged the religious leaders to give him the authority of the ancient Indian texts for the practice of untouchability, they were not able to substantiate it. It was more a custom rather than a practice based on the religious texts. This is why not only the Hindus, but the Muslims, Christians, Parsis, Jews and other religious groups also practice untouchability. This has nothing to do with the religious tenets of these latter groups.

In Parliament on 2 April 1969, many speakers demanded the

immediate arrest and prosecution of the Jagatguru. The Home Minister Chavan, and later on the Law Minister Govinda Menon, condemned the speech of the Jagatguru and said that they would take up the matter with the Bihar Government which had to deal with the problem. In the various newspapers of the country, letters were written to the editors, condemning the outlook of the Jagatguru. Many attacked the Government for its weakness. This is a very significant indication of the great change in the attitude of the intelligentsia and the parliamentarians.

In 1964, the Government appointed a Committee on Untouchability headed by Elayaperumal. The Committee presented its report to the Lok Sabha in April 1969. The Committee has reported that untouchability is still rampant all over the country. The extreme economic and educational backwardness of these communities was stressed.

The report has given several instances of the practice of untouchability in rural as well as urban areas in various states. There have been many cases of murder. Particularly, the murder of a Harijan by the Hindus in a village in Andhra Pradesh in 1967, shocked the whole country. The Minister of State in his statement to the Rajya Sabha in April 1969 quoted several cases of murder and torture. In particular, he gave the case of the caste Hindus employed in the Lignite Corporation in Neyveli of Tamil Nadu who beat up two Harijans for riding bicycles and fined them Rs. 200.

The Committee also found that many Police Officers in the districts were not aware of the 1956 Act and had no knowledge of the provisions of this Act. So one could understand how helpless the poor Harijans are in getting the police to protect their rights according to this Act.

The Elayaperumal Committee has suggested several measures to eradicate untouchability. One of the suggestion is that the Government of India should frame a social policy resolution in order to break the hold of the caste system. One wonders whether such a resolution will have any effect. It might be as effective as all the provisions right from the Charter Act of 1833 and the proclamation of Queen Victoria in 1857.

Another suggestion of the Committee is the abolition of the hereditary priesthood confined to the Brahmins in the Hindu society. According to the present practice, only particular sects of Brahmins are appointed as priests (poojaris) in the temples and are permitted to function as family priests (purohits). These people not only belong to certain families but are well versed in the temple and family rituals. The suggestion of the Committee is along the lines of the practice adopted since many decades by the Dravida Kazhagam and Dravida Munnetra Kazhagam parties in Tamil Nadu. They not only condemned this practice of appointing Brahmin poojaris and purohits but they also started a scheme lo train non-Brahmin youth in the practice of ritualism. The Committee has taken up this model and have recommended that the criteria for appointing people as poojaris in temple should be the acquisition of knowledge and training rather than caste.

In the middle of April 1969, the Union Minister of Law and Social Welfare in his budget speech indicated in the Lok Sabha that the Constitution would shortly be amended to further extend the period of reservation of seats for the scheduled castes and scheduled tribes in Parliament and in the State Legislatures. The Minister pointed out that even after twenty years, the disabilities of these groups have not been removed and so the Government is now taking steps to extend the reservation for another period of ten years up to 1980. It must be recognized that the presumption of the Constitution was too optimistic on the basis of the social trend. It failed to assess the deep-seated prejudices, particularly in rural India containing 80 per cent of the population. It may be noted that the Constitution was amended in the latter pan of 1969 and now the concessions are extended up to 1980.

The Minister pointed out that the number of scheduled castes employed, excluding sweepers, had gone up from 2,20,000 in 1960 to 3,00,000 in 1968. He also drew the attention of the House to the efforts of the Government in setting up institutions in Allahabad in the North and Madras in the South to give special training to the candidates from the scheduled castes and the scheduled tribes who desire to take competitive examinations for the higher levels of administrative services. He reported that in the first competitive examination for the Indian Foreign Service, ten out of the fifty persons qualified belonged to the scheduled castes and scheduled tribes.

While the efforts of the government have not succeeded in removing disabilities of the scheduled castes, there is considerable achievement in the field of education.

A three-pronged strategy has been involved to speed up the development of scheduled castes: (a) special component plans of the Central ministries and State Governments, (b) special Central assistance to the special component plans for the scheduled castes of the states, and (c) scheduled caste development corporations in the states.

Special Component Plans (SCPs) envisage identification of schemes under general sector of development which would be of benefit to scheduled castes, quantification of funds from all divisible programmes under each sector and determination of specific targets as to the number of families which are to be benefited from these programmes under each sector. Overall objective is to assist scheduled caste families to substantially improve their income. Provision of basic services and facilities and access to opportunities for social and educational development are also to be brought into special component plans.

Central ministries/departments have also begun to formulate special component plans for scheduled castes. So far only 10 Central ministries/ departments have formulated such plans.

Government provides Special Central Assistance (SCA) to state special component plans for scheduled castes. Special Central assistance is an additive to State Plan and programmes for scheduled castes and it does not follow the systematic pattern for special schemes. It is meant for the totality of state efforts for development of scheduled castes. The additionality, according to states, from the assistance is to be used by them only for income-generating economic development schemes in conjunction with outlays in their special component plans so as to assist economic advancement of the maximum possible number of scheduled caste families living below the poverty line. Assistance is apportioned among State Governments and union territory administrations taking into account factors like scheduled caste population, backwardness of states and efforts of State Governments. Special Central assistance has helped in motivating State Governments to put in larger outlays in their special component plans

With a view to effectively tackling operational aspects involved in implementation of economic programmes for scheduled castes, particularly in mobilisation of institutional credit for income-generating schemes, Government decided in 1978-79 the establishment of scheduled caste development corporations (SCDCs) in states which have significant population of scheduled castes. At present, 21 such corporations are functioning in the country. The corporations were envisaged as an interface between SC families and financial institutions in respect of bankable schemes of economic development They were also required to function as guarantors and promoters and to act as a catalyst by providing missing inputs by way of contributing seed money or margin money loans to scheduled castes entrepreneurs. Margin money loans are intended to help in a number of ways. By sharing the loan burden with financial institutions, the corporations help in demonstrating the involvement inducing banks to come forward with loans for schemes for scheduled castes in a big way.

While there is a large number of financial institutions to finance the ventures of those who can afford to start industries, business, etc., there are no institutions which can support poor SC families living below the poverty line. This responsibility has been entrusted to SC development corporations,

Under this scheme, Government is participating in the share capital investment of these corporations at the rate of 49 per cent as against 51 per cent investment by State Governments. Share capital is intended to be used towards margin money loans. The scheme was amplified in July 1981 to include assistance for promotional activities and staff for monitoring, evaluation, technical and recovery wings. Grant-in-aid for promotional activities is subject to a maximum of one per cent and for staff for monitoring and evaluation subject to three per cent of Centre's cumulative share capital contribution to a corporation. Central grant for those purposes can be availed of by State Governments, provided matching share is also contributed by them.

Movement for Emancipation

The backward class movement, started in the early part of the twentieth century. When schools and colleges were giving courses in secular subjects through the medium of English, only the castes and classes with the tradition of education utilized the opportunity to educate themselves. As a result only the members of these castes and classes could get the jobs in the government services and increase their prestige. This further increased the cultural, social and economic distance between them and the lower castes. This made the lower castes to realize that they were now here in this situation. They wanted a share in the new opportunities. As Srinivas (1966) himself puts it, the lower castes realized that mere Sanskritization was not enough. It did not provide them the avenue for social mobility and obtain well-paid and prestigious jobs in the administrative services. So they desired to get themselves educated through the English medium in order to qualify themselves for the new jobs in administration and the new professions like law, medicine, engineering, etc. "It is no accident that the movement was strongest in peninsular India where only one caste, the Brahmins enjoyed a preponderance in higher education, the professions, and government employment. It is also the area where a wide social and cultural gulf obtained between the Brahmins and others" (Srinivas, 1966).

The characteristic feature of this movement is that it is caste based. It has already been noted that caste organizations had been started in the various parts of the country to press their claims for new designations according to the varna categorization in order to improve their social position in the hierarchy. These organizations now made education of the children and youth an important part of their programme.

However, it was soon realized that the qualified youth could not get admission in the professional courses and in the postgraduate courses because admission was based on marks in the high school and college examinations. Here they were at a handicap since the boys from the homes with education as a tradition were able to score high marks. Another complication arose as a result of the fact that the teachers and examiners were from the forward castes. This gave rise to the fear that they were being discriminated against on the basis of caste. A similar situation arose when they competed for jobs in the government services. Here also the appointing authorities at the lower levels were mostly Brahmins, With not very high marks and with the prevalence of nepotism, the young men from the lower castes found themselves at a disadvantage. This led to anti-Brahmin feelings both among the leaders of the various lower castes and the frustrated youth.

The partition of Bengal in 1905 led not only to the intensification of nationalism and the desire for freedom, but also to the rise of communalism, castism, linguism and regionalism. The Minto-Morley Reforms of 1909 conceded separate electorates to Muslims, Sikhs, Indian Christians, Anglo-Indians and Europeans. Valentine Chirol, in his book "Indian Unrest" published in 1910, asserted that Brahminism and Western education constituted serious threat to the continuance of the British rule in India. During the World War I, the expectation of transfer of more power to Indians after the war made the non-Brahmin leaders of the composite Madras Presidency to fear that Brahmins will become more powerful. So they wanted that there should be communal representation. There were similar sentiments in Bombay and Bengal Presidencies also.

This led to the movement becoming political. The non-Brahmin leaders of the old Composite State of Madras formed the South Indian Liberal Federation in 1916 to advance, and protect the interests of the non-Brahmins. The Federation later on called itself the Justice Party. It started newspapers in English and other languages to educate and put forward the case of the Non-Brahmins. In the same way many weeklies were started in the various Indian languages by caste organizations in different parts of India (Ghurye, 1969).

The movement spread to the neighbouring Mysore State. In 1918, finding that the postgraduate classes and the government jobs were monopolized by the Brahmins, the government appointed the Miller Committee to recommend how the backward classes could be helped to secure better representation. In its report, the Committee recommended that all communities, except the Brahmins, the Europeans and the Anglo-Indians,. short fee included in.Then the Secretary of State for India, Montague visited India in 1917-18, the Justice Party, representing the Non-Brahmins in the

South was outspokenly against the Brahmin community. The Montague-Chelmsford reforms published in July 1918 adopted the principle of diarchy. In the provinces, the executive consisted of two sections, one section nominated by the Crown and the other section made up of ministers from the majority party in the legislature. In the Madras State, the Justice Party automatically secured the majority of seats since the Non-Brahmins constituted about 97 per cent of the population. The elected ministers were in charge of education and local self-government. The Justice Party now utilized its political power to apply the principle of reservation for admission to the postgraduate and professional courses and for recruitment to the jobs in the government. The Miller Committee of Mysore State also made similar recommendations.

Thus, the aim of the Backward class movement at this stage was to limit the Brahmin monopoly in the two fields of education and appointment to government posts. However, this was by no means a mass movement. "The opposition of Brahmin dominance did not come from the low and the oppressed castes but from the leaders of the powerful, rural dominant castes such as the Kammas and Reddis of the Telugu country, the Vellalas of the Tamil country, and the Nayar of Kerala" (Srinivas, 1966). These were high caste groups with a social position next to the Brahmins. They included not only the Hindus but also the Muslims, Christians and other communities. Incidentally it may be noted that most of the Muslims and Christians are converts to those religions from the lowest castes; their conversion to these religions does not enable them to overcome their social disabilities, particularly in the villages and in the city slums. This is the important reason why the term used to describe these groups is "Backward classes" and not "Backward castes". Further the term Backward class is very old; it has been in usage since 1917 when the Indian National Congress resolution emphasised "the necessity of justice and rightness of removing all disabilities imposed by custom upon the depressed classes;" it was also used by the Franchise Committee in 1918.

The great controversy of the fifties, regarding the steps of uplift the backward classes so that they can enter the mainstream of social and economic life of the society, has centred around the determination of (a) the unit, and (b) the criteria. As regards the unit, the nationalist elite and the localist Brahmin elite are in favour of the logical democratic unit of the individual as the basis, while the localist non-Brahmin and minority community elite are in favour of the caste as the basis. With respect to the criterion again the nationalist elite and localist Brahmin elite are in favour of income being the criterion because it is a universal criterion, while the localist non-Brahmin elite are in favour of caste as the sole criterion.

The nationalist elite are afraid that if caste is taken as a basis to determine who should get the concessions regarding opportunities for higher education and government jobs, the society will be fragmented. The localist Brahmin elite are against caste being a criterion since their opportunities for education and for appointment will be narrowed by the concessions given to the powerful and numerous lower castes.

The localist non-Brahmin elite are afraid that if the universalistic economic criterion is used, their opportunity will be limited by the large number of well-qualified but poor Brahmins who will enter the competition and walk away with the concessions.

Thus, the real conflict is between the localist Brahmin elite and the localist non-Brahmin elite. By the large, the nationalist Brahmin elite are universalistic and egalitarian in their outlook. But the localist Brahmin elite are particularistic and caste-oriented in their daily lives but universalistic in their outlook. This is the threat of universalism perceived by the localist non-Brahmin elite; they feel that in the name of universalism and egalitarianism the localist Brahmin elite want to perpetuate inequalities and exploit the situation lo consolidate their own position and leave the vast majority in illiteracy and poverty so that the traditional cultural gap is perpetuated. This is why they are in favour of caste being the criterion to provide relief.

There is no doubt that since caste is particularistic the utilization of the caste criterion perpetuates the fragmentation of the Indian society. Experience in the last quarter of a century has clearly shown that the number of groups in the list increases rather than decrease with the time. Concessions create a vested interest in backwardness. No group wants to forgo the concessions; it is because no group as a whole can truly say that all its members have now become 'forward', that no section of the group needs special concessions. It is true that some sections of the scheduled castes and scheduled tribes are now as 'forward' as any 'forward' section. But it is also true that large majorities of these groups are yet very backward. So when the leaders of these groups put forward the case in the Parliament, their arguments are neither untrue nor unjust. The basic fact which every citizen of India has to acknowledge is that two-thirds or more of the citizens of India are steeped in illiteracy and suffer utter poverty. Even the most advanced group in India, the Parsis, created a trust many decades ago to provide houses and pensions lo the poor among them so that they do not go round begging. It is a normal social phenomenon that about five to ten per cent of any group in any nation will need social welfare services,

On the other hand, one of the glaring realities is that it is the more advanced and politically well-organized sections of the backward classes who manage to get all the benefits and they are the most vocal in their professions for the welfare of the backward sections of their caste or group. It is also well known thai these sections of the caste make full use of the backwardness of their group to consolidate their own political power and to recruit well educated and well employed sons-in-law to their families.

It is because of this social reality that the constitution provided for the uplift of the backward classes .

The Backward Class Commission was appointed in 1953 with Kaka Kalelkar as the chairman. The Commission was appointed according to the Article 340 of the Constitution. The Commission was asked to determine the criteria to be adopted to provide concessions to "socially and educationally backward classes" besides the scheduled castes and scheduled tribes. The Commission was also asked to prepare a list of such classes. Inaugurating the Commission, the late Prime Minister Nehru said that he disliked the term "backward classes" since ninety per cent of the people were poor and backward.

At the very outset, the Commission found that while the various groups came forward to represent their condition as castes, no statistical information was available in this respect since the census of 1951 had not collected such information. This is one of the basic contradictions in the social life of the country. Caste is a social fact among the Hindus as well as such minority creedal groups like Muslims and Christians, even though the latter do not theoretically recognize such differences. According to the terms of reference the Commission had to "prepare a list of such classes". Since caste is a social fact such lists may be presumed to be made in terms of caste. But the Constitution does not recognize caste, except the scheduled castes. The collection of caste-wise figures according to caste given up because they were presumed to perpetuate caste-distinctions, but caste-wise figures are necessary to provide them relief on the model of scheduled castes. This is the anomaly.

One of the first recommendations of the Commission was that the 1961 census should provide caste-wise figures so that "before the disease of caste is destroyed all facts about it have to be noted and classified in a scientific manner as in a clinical record" (p. 11). But the formidable difficulties in this regard were also noted. Can the census officer force a citizen to give information which he is not prepared to volunteer or one who refuses to accept his caste label and looks upon himself as being just an Indian? Can he be prevented from giving his caste according to his own concept, which may vary from state to state? This contingency will mean that the same caste group will have different varna labels or even different/ labels according to the aspirations of the local groups. What about the converts to Islam or Christianity or Buddhism? They may give their preconversion jati names. There is also the problem of caste label with respect to the children of intercaste marriages. The Commission also pointed out the anomaly which arose when some scheduled caste persons called themselves "Harijans" but found that they were not eligible for scholarships, etc., since the term "Harijan" is not in the authorized list. On account of all these complications, the Chairman in his covering letter to the President declared "Thus, the confusion and anarchy of opinion about all communal matters is going to make the work of the next census well nigh impossible." He further declared, "this was a rude shock and it drove me to the conclusion that the remedies we suggested were worse than the evil we were out to combat," In effect, while the Commission recommended census on caste basis the Chairman ruled it out (p. XVIII).

The Commission also recommended that certain sections of the Muslims, Christians, Sikhs should be included among the "Other Backward classes" (pp. 27-29).

As regards causes for backwardness, the Commission has concluded "A variety of causes—social, environmental, economic and political—have operated both openly and in a subtle form for centuries to create the present colossal problem of backwardness. Economic backwardness is the result and not the cause of many social evils." With respect to criteria of backwardness the Commission recommended for general guidance: (1) Low social position in the traditional caste hierarchy; (2) lack of education in the major section of the caste or community; (3) inadequate or no representation in government service; and (4) inadequate representation in the field of trade, commerce and industry (p. 46).

The Commission prepared a list of about 2400 castes on the basis of the position of the caste in social hierarchy, percentage of literacy and its representation in government service and in industries, etc., taking as a basis the lists of Other Backward classes published by the Education Ministry and by the State Governments and also the representations made by several groups. The Commission also revised the lists of Scheduled Castes and Scheduled Tribes on the basis of the new information available,

The Commission noted that the great majority of the backward classes are ignorant, illiterate, and poor. They are easily exploited by several classes of persons like the traders, the moneylenders.

It has also noted that the rigours of caste system prevail and untouchability is being still practised in a pronounced manner in the rural areas. This has led to the formation of caste groups or combines in order to secure redress of their grievances; some of the representatives of the backward classes pleaded that though this trend is not healthy, it is inevitable to protect themselves. Another discrimination being practised in the rural areas is to prevent admission of their boys and girls to schools. Unless these social inequalities are removed, they cannot have a fair deal. The Commission also noted that the administrative system itself, which has to implement the constitutional provisions, is tainted by casteism; this is one of the reasons why the backward classes have no confidence in securing a fair deal even from the administration. The Commission warns that unless this is immidietly remedied there would be class conflicts which would affect national solidarity (p. 101).

The Commissions also draws pointed attention to the contradiction between the theory and practice of Hinduism. While in theory Hinduism recognizes the concept of universality in practice it follows the Laws of Manu which perpetuate the fourfold division of the social order and the superiority of the Brahmin class. The Commission asserted, "Perhaps in theory no other religion elevated the concept of the equality of man to such a high philosophical level as the Vedic theory that the individual soul is the manifestation of the One Eternal Soul. Yet in practical life no other religion in the world has been more guilty of maintaining invidious distinctions between man and man" (p. 102). Thus there is no code of social justice. Hinduism "was not opposed to the perpetuation of a social order based on the privileges of the strong, the shrewd, the organized and the cunning...the minority ruled the majority and always claimed moral superiority. Religion and mythology were utilized to support the claims of the ruling minority" (p. 103). By contrast, the reform movements and the freedom struggle emphasised social equality and social justice. This is now embodied in the Constitution. It is on this basis that adult franchise was introduced. As a result the exploited backward classes are not prepared to submit any longer to the old social order of inequality. The Commission notes "A complete revolution in the social outlook of the people is necessary for rendering social justice to all the backward people" (p.104). The Commission, however, realises that poverty, ignorance and illiteracy make this task very difficult. To overcome these age-old prejudices, the Commission recommends that "Organizations consisting of persons drawn from different communities and pledged solely to social service must be set-up all over the country for this purpose. The members of such organizations must themselves firmly believe in the ideal of equality and work it out in their own lives. By their personal conduct as well as by their work they must impress on the people the need for eradication of caste prejudices." It is also pointed out mat at present there are no institutions devoted solely to the cause of removal of social inequalities or for the promotion of inter-communal harmony (p. 105).

Dealing with the problems of educational backwardness, the Commission noted that the only general figures available are the literacy rates which show a very slow progress. "The problem of education in most of the States is chiefly the problem of the backward classes, for it is they who are extremely backward in education" (p. 109). Even when special scholarships and other amenities are provided the children of these classes do not study. "The essential stage of education, viz., elementary education is not yet made free and compulsory throughout the country...The Directive Principles of State Policy under Article 45 of the Constitution have not yet been implemented" (p. 110). It is needless to point out that the position remains the same in 1975, nearly twenty years since the publication of the report. While recommending liberal budget provision to give scholarships to the students of the backward classes, the Commission recommends that 70 per cent of the seats in professional colleges should be reserved for them and in making selections preference should be given to those coming from the most backward classes which are indicated in the lists drawn up (p. 125).

With respect to representation in government and local body services the Commission recommended the reservation of 25 per cent of the Class I vacancies, one-third of the Class II vacancies and 40 per cent of the Classes III and IV for the Other Backward Classes (p. 142); this percentage has to be over and above that which has already been conceded to the scheduled castes and tribes.

However, in his covering letter, the chairman rejected the remedies formulated by the Commission on caste basis in view of the facts noted earlier regarding the difficulties of obtaining census figures on the basis of caste and in view of the fact that there are backward castes among the Muslims and Christians also. Instead he recommended the children from "Families whose income is less than Rs 800 a year do need special help irrespective of the community to which they belong," care being taken to see that the "forward communities", "do not carry away all state help and leave the extremely backward communities unattended to" (p. VIII). As regards reservation in services he laid down "In this matter one clear principle must be accepted and observed. Reservations, if contemplated, must not exceed 49 per cent, whatever the total population of all the "Reserved" communities be, as far as classes III and IV are concerned. In the case of Classes I and II he recommended that "the backward classes will stand to gain, both morally and materially if they do not demand a reservation percentage in vacancies .... They should demand greatest facilities for training and education in order to fit themselves for the highest jobs, as speedily as possible" (p. IX).

According to the terms of reference the Commission was asked to consider whether any sections of the people, in addition to the scheduled castes and the scheduled tribes should be treated as socially and educationally backward classes. Thus the words specifically used are classes and sections and not castes and yet, as explained in the body of the report the words 'sections and classes' can in the present context mean nothing but castes, and no other interpretation is feasible. But casteism affects the solidarity of the nation. This is the basic dilemma; unless castes are noted remedial measures cannot be implemented; if remedies are on caste basis, the solidarity of the nation will be seriously affected. It must be fully recognized that the backwardness of this large section of the people is based on their birth; they are treated as inferiors on account of their birth in a caste. There are many restraints on them particularly in the rural areas where eighty per cent of the people live and where social relations are based solely on the basis of caste. Even in the urban areas they are handicapped because of their dress, appearance and speech which reveal their poverty as well as illiteracy. In other words, their backwardness is due to their social handicaps.

The Janata Party mentioned in its manifesto of 1977 that it would implement the recommendations of the Kalelkar Report but did not do so for 21 months and suddenly in December, 1978 announced its decision to appoint the Second Backward Classes Commission with B.P. Mandal as its Chairman. The commission was required to present their report to the President not later than 31.12.1980.

A summary of recommendations of the commission is given below:

Reservation for SCs and STs is in proportion to their population, i.e., 22.5%. But as there is a legal obligation to keep reservations under Articles 15(4) and 16(4) of the Constitution below 50%, the Commission recommends a reservation of 27% for OBCs. This reservation should apply to all Government services as well as technical and professional institutions, both in the Centre and the States.

Special educational facilities designed at upgrading the cultural environment of the students should be created in a phased manner in selected areas containing high concentration of OBCs. Special emphasis should be placed on vocational training. Separate coaching facilities should be provided in technical and professional institutions to OBC students to enable them to catch up with students from open quota.

Special programmes for upgrading the skills of village artisans should be prepared and subsidised loans from financial institutions granted to them for setting up small scale industries. To promote the participation of OBCs in the industrial and business life of the country, a separate network of financial and technical institutions should be created by all State Governments.

Under the existing scheme of production-relations, Backward Classes comprising mainly small land holders, tenants, agricultural labour, village artisans, etc., are heavily dependent on the rich peasantry for their sustenance. In view of this, OBCs continue to remain in mental and material bondage of the dominant castes and classes. Unless these production-relations are radically altered through structural changes and progressive land reforms implemented rigorously all over the country, OBCs will never become truly independent. In view of this, highest priority should be given to radical land reforms by all the States.

At present no Central assistance is available to any State for implementing any welfare measures for Other backward Classes. Several State Governments expressed their helplessness in undertaking more purposeful development programmes for backward classes in view of lack of resources. It is, therefore, recommended that welfare programmes specially designed for

OBCs should be financed by the Central Government in the same manner and to the same extent as done in the case of SCs and STs.

The Mandal Commission's Report was laid before the Parliament on April 30, 1982. The Government stated that after obtaining the views of the State Governments on various recommendations contained in the Report the Government would formulate its views.

Sh. R. Venkataraman, then a Cabinet Minister, said in Parliament on 11.8.82, "If the Government of India accepts the Mandal Commission's Report and identifies 3743 castes as backward classes, and the States want different kinds of castes to be treated as backward classes, there would be utter confusion....There will always be applications to the centre to modify the list and to the States to modify the list".

Instead of the Mandal Commission's Report being discussed in Parliament, and the V.P. Singh Government clearly spelling out which of the recommendations of the Commission have been accepted and which rejected, a bureaucratic memorandum signed by a Jt. Secretary to the Government in the Department of Personnel & Training was issued, inter alia, containing the following:

1. In a multiple undulating society, like ours, early achievement of the objective of social justice as enshrined in the Constitution is a must. The Second Backward Classes Commission called the Mandal Commission was established by the then Government with this purpose in view, which submitted its report to the Government of India on 31.12.1980.
2. Government have carefully considered the report and recommendations of the Commission in the present context regarding the benefits to be extended to the socially and educationally backward classes as opined by the Commission and are of the clear view that at the outset certain weightage has to be provided to such classes in the services of the Union and their Public Undertakings. Accordingly orders are issued as follows:

   (i) 27% of the vacancies in civil posts and services under the Government of India shall be reserved for SEBC.

(ii) The aforesaid reservation shall apply to vacancies to be filled by direct recruitment. Detailed instructions relating to the procedure to be followed for enforcing reservation will be issued separately.

(iii) Candidates belonging to SEBC recruited on the basis of merit in an open competition on the same standards prescribed for the general candidates shall not be adjusted against the reservation quota of 27%.

(iv) The SEBC would comprise in the first phase the castes and communities which are common to both the list in the report of the Mandal Commission and the State Governments lists. A list of such castes/communities is being issued separately,

(v) The aforesaid reservation shall take effect from 7.8.1990, However, this will not apply to vacancies where the recruitment process has already been initiated prior to the issue of these orders.

3. Similar instructions in respect of public sector undertakings and financial institutions including public sector banks will be issued by the Department of Public Enterprises and Ministry of Finance respectively.

The Mandal Commission's Report and the announcement of V.P. Singh that the Report has been accepted and will be implemented created a national controversy, violent agitations and student immolations in different parts of the country.

Professor B.K. Roy Burman who was associated with the Mandal Commission as Chairman of Research Planning Team and Technical Sub-Committee and also as the member of the Expert Committee, has questioned the findings of the report and also the basis of its recommendations. He, inter alia, stated that the report is without any scientific basis. It exaggerates the number of other backward classes. It ignores every suggestion that the experts associated with it made. The experts were used and were not consulted on the basis for ultimate finding.

1. The experts did not want caste to be the basis.
2. It is not known whether the findings were based on the survey or personal impression or plain imagination.

3. Not caste but occupation or a mix of the two appeared satisfactory to the experts.
4. A pilot survey in Birbhum revealed startling results.
5. A spectrum for various types of weightages given by experts were dumped.
6. A spectrum of weightages for literacy given by the experts was not adopted. "The system the panel adopted is unscientific. It multiplies the number of backward classes."
7. Mr. Mandal wanted caste to be the sole criterion.
8. The experts did not know whether their survey design were being used, They were not consulted.
9. The experts wanted 152 tables to be used which Shri Mandal reduced to just thirty-one.
10. The social scientists were not shown the processed data.
11. The data had to be shown to the experts. But it was overruled.
12. Complaint was made to the Home Minister who said that he himself had not seen the data. He was helpless,
13. Projection on the basis of 1931 data was unscientific as so much social mobility had taken place since then, (emphasis added). (Indian Express, Aug. 31,1990).

Mounting a scathing attack on the very structure of the recommendations of the Mandal Commission, Prof. Burman stated at a Press conference on September 19, 1990 that the Government should forthwith release all information about the data-base as processed by the Mandal Commission.

Prof. Burman while answering a question said that if proper procedures were made use of, not more than 20 per cent of the recommended OECs come within the domain of the protection in jobs. "I stand for reservations for economically vulnerable sections of society particularly from the OBCs," he said. (Hindustan Times, 20th September, 1990).

Prof. M.N. Srinivas, an eminent sociologist, said that he had nothing to do with the report. He attended a one-day seminar conducted by the Commission in Delhi and later when some members of the commission had called on him in Bangalore he offered them a cup of coffee.

In an interview to a weekly he said:

1. The policy of reservation has extracted a big price—the level of corruption and inefficiency is very high, incompetent people will have acquired jobs on the basis of reservation.
2. "The biggest crime is, of course, the reservation of jobs on the basis of caste, in schools and universities. Setting aside a professor's post and then filling the vacancy in an arbitrary fashion, because the right applicant of a particular caste is not available, is not in the interests of the students, the education system and the country.
3. Is it fair for the first generation school-goers from poor and backward classes to be taught by unqualified, unsuitable teachers, merely because the latter belongs to which is eligible for reservation? While seeking to do justice to one individual, one is condemning the students to perdition.
4. "With the reservation system, we are fast moving away from the egalitarian society which our Constitution had enshrined." (emphasis added) (Indian Express, 1.9.1990)

Prof. M.N. Srinivas in an article in the Times of India asserted that caste-based reservation results in the establishment of oligopolies among elites in OBCs. The addition of an economic criterion is not of much help either. The division of OBCs into less and more backward is better, but even here large castes benefit at the expense of small ones. In short group-based criteria, paradoxically, benefit only individuals, not entire groups. And such individuals are frequently cut off from their social bases, except when they are politicians.

Clearly, the way out is to opt for objective criteria applicable to individuals and not hereditary or other groups. That way the poor from every category are helped. Criteria such as parental income, levels of education, occupation (manual or non-manual, unskilled or skilled), place of residence (rural or urban), and asset structure can be used to determine the level of backwardness of a person. With the computer facilities available in the country it is possible to provide every eligible school goer with a card profiling his backwardness.

Nearly 25 years ago I wrote two articles in The Statesman arguing that numerous castes had developed a vested interesting backwardness and that the solution to this lay in developing "neutral indices" to determine the backwardness of individuals. Needless to say, no one took the slightest notice of them.

Why did the framers of the Constitution use the terms "scheduled castes" and "scheduled tribes" in one case and "socially and educationally backward classes" in another? If they had desired that the benefits had to go to backward castes surely they would have said so plainly. Sociologically speaking, "class" and "caste" are distinct if not opposed terms. How then did "backward classes" come to be interpreted as "backward castes."

There is a puzzle if not a problem demanding an explanation. (To equate "backward classes" with "backward castes" and then to assert that the introduction of reservation on economic grounds alone is to indulge not in "double speak" but "treble speak").

Social and educational backwardness are best tackled by anti-poverty programmes. Backwardness is due in large measure to poverty and the many ills that go with it. Malnutrition affects productivity, illiteracy is inseparable from ignorance and superstition. The lack of access to shelter, clothing and hygiene and sanitation makes people backward. There is such a thing as a "culture of poverty".

Reservations go to a small number of the better-off members of the castes concerned. Anti-poverty programmes benefit large numbers of the poor everywhere, and so offer the best route to tackle backwardness. Most important, they do not further deepen the many cleavages already present in society.

The case of the scheduled castes is qualitatively different. They have been oppressed and exploited by all the others, and subjected to shameful discrimination. The constitutional provision for them and the scheduled tribes, who have long been isolated from the mainstream, needs to be respected. But even here care should be taken to see that the benefits go to really poor, and that there is a time limit to reservation.

Caste is a terribly divisive institution. Given that literacy is 36 per cent and 70 per cent of the people live in rural areas, caste still has a lot of clout. During the last 43 years, it has been used successfully in mobilising people during elections. Reservations have further strengthened the institution. It is high time we started thinking about where such policies are leading us. We need statesmanship and not political gimmickry which has the potential for destroying the cumulative achievements of 150 years of nationalist struggle. (Times of India, September 18, 1990)

Writing in The Hindustan Times, Pran Chopra an eminent Journalist, inter alia, stated that even if the Constitution were amended it would not immediately undo a basic feature of the Indian scene which Dr. Ambedkar summed up very pithily in the Constituent Assembly. "What is called backward classes are nothing but a collection of certain castes." Any large group identified as economically backward identifies itself very quickly in terms of caste, a position upheld by many court judgements though backwardness identified only on caste basis has been rejected by them as a criterion for reservations. The disabilities imposed by castes are the commonest cause of poverty, and the benefits of economic upliftment often assume the contours of caste, as happened in 1960s and 1970s in the case of the agrarian and tenurial reforms introduced in the 1950s. These reforms were a purely economic concept but became a primary cause of the rise of the backward castes, which in turn powered the rise of the Janata Party/Janata Dal and its commitment ever since the late 1970s to reservations for the backward classes.

In fact reservations without reference to caste would be unjustified. The only clear case for them is that they are an indispensable part of a package of measures of stepped up assistance to poverty groups to enable them to overcome the contemporary legacy of the social injustices which the caste system has heaped upon them throughout history. Poverty which is specific to individuals and families may be relieved by measures specifically targeted to them. The poverty of areas may be relieved by area development (although that will only perpetuate caste-based inequalities in these areas if unaccompanied by measures aimed at these specific inequalities).

But the poverty of large and dispersed groups, arising from centuries old disabilities related to caste, are only amenable to measures which recognise the role of caste, though they must also recognise the changes which have occurred over time in status and economic relations either between individual castes or between individuals/families within a caste, for otherwise they would only create a new injustice in trying to remedy an ancient one.

Positive discrimination in their favour on grounds of social justice is as just for many among the backward classes as it is for the Scheduled Castes and Tribes. It is also strong on constitutional, legal, democratic and parliamentary grounds, being enshrined in the Constitution, upheld by courts, undoubtedly backed by the electoral process, and unveiled in Parliament in the last Address by the President. Thus endorsed by all the basic forums of our political system, it cannot be sacrificed to street agitations.

But while reservations are an essential measure, they are not sufficient by themselves and must be accompanied by other measures for upgrading the competence of the beneficiaries. Similarly, while a comprehensive package for the backward classes is necessary, it is not enough unless accompanied by a comprehensive attack on general poverty along a wide front. The stages by which the Report should be implemented must also be considered more systematically than they have been so far. Democracy is an evolutionary process, not a revolutionary one. and phasing a reform, howsoever desirable, is a characteristic part of it. There should be a systematic dialogue on these issues.

But it is very likely that despite every effort to reach a consensus, there will be some resistance to this major measure of social change. If so, the resistance, and the turbulence that it may cause, must be accepted, as the price of change. A dialogue can mitigate the price but cannot remove it. (Hindustan Times, October 1, 1990)

N.A. Palkhiwala, an eminent Jurist writing in the Indian Express (August 29, 1990) slated that perhaps there is no other country which has such a genius for creating torture and tribulations for itself as modern India—the inheritor of the age-old practice of self-flagellation.

Physicists describe the relationship of oxygen to fire as "necessary but not sufficient". Casteism and its prophet Mandal, are necessary and sufficient to ignite an unprecedented national conflagration. His report will create two nations nearly balanced numerically—and never the twin shall meet.

The avowed decision of the Indian Government to implement "without any dilution" the Mandal report (which had been wisely kept in cold storage for more than a decade), is a Himalayan blunder. Since people are convinced that the Government listens only to the language of violent agitation, there has been an explosion of violent mass revolt in several states. It will gather momentum in the days to come; with unforeseen consequences for the integrity and unity of India.

The Mandal report suffers from five fatal flaws:

(a) It contemplates rich and rigid reservations for employment under the state in its infinite variety, and in business undertakings and educational institutions—where merit would be unable to find a berth. The sub-standard has to replace the standard, and the reins of power are to pass from meritocracy to mediocrity.

(b) It enjoins reservations based exclusively on caste, as if a poor Brahmin or a rich Dalit is a contradiction in terms. It firmly ignores the stark reality that there are no backward castes but only backward individuals. Economic backwardness or the opposite is treated as wholly irrelevant.

(c) Not only employment but even promotions are to be reserved for the privileged (euphemistically called 'backward') castes. That would be disastrous enough for the civil administration, but far worse for the military. Our armed forces are the pride of the nation—the only institution which we have not devalued and degraded. What kind of an Army, Navy and Air Force shall we have, when field marshals and generals, admirals and air commodores, have secured their promotions on caste considerations? This raises the most momentous of all issues—the security of the stale.

(d) The only known solvent of casteism is change in the national consciousness : harmony among, and social intermingling of, the anachronistic castes. Petrified and ossified for centuries, casteism should be the dust on the shelf of Indian history. Instead, the Mandal report emphatically ensures a fresh lease of life to the canker of casteism for a long, indefinite future.

(e) The progress of India has been from casteism to egalitarianism. It has been from feudalism to freedom; and equality is the very heart of a free republic. There never was, and never will be, a free democracy without equality of all citizens. The foundation of a true republic, the source of its inspiration, the criterion for its citizenship, the hope for its welfare—all lie in the incandescent ideal of equality. (It is the exact opposite of what prevails in totalitarian states where you enjoy privileges as card-holding members of the ruling party.) The bedrock of the Mandal report is discrimination in reserve; it is discrimination against merit and calibre.

Like the expanding universe, the list of backward castes is ever expanding. The Mandal report has listed 3,743 (from 2,399 in an earlier report) backward castes. Many more are already waiting in the wings to receive recognition.

The challenge to land reforms legislation could be staved off by inserting an item in the Ninth Schedule to the Constitution which insulates the law from judicial invalidation on the ground that it violates the fundamental rights. But implementation of the Mandal report would go against the basic structure of the Constitution. Therefore, any constitutional amendment to avoid judicial scrutiny would itself be unconstitutional and void. Our thoughtless action—to achieve the thoughtful object of doing justice to the "backward" castes—can be allowed to prevail only by scrapping the noble Constitution and promulgating a backward Constitution for a backward nation. (Indian Express, 29.8.90).

Prosperous Groups

Some of the castes included among the Other Backward classes are very powerful in the economic, social and political fields though large proportions of their members are not as well educated as the advanced castes; nor are they well represented in the government jobs. Being powerful landowners and the traditional village headmen they are very powerful in the political field at the local, district and state levels. Among them are the Vokkaligas and Lingayats of Karnataka State, Reddis and Kammas of Andhra Pradesh, Nayars and Ezhavas of Kerala State, Vellalas and recently Nadars of Tamil Nadu. Some of them are high caste groups, immediately below the Brahmins in status and with a relatively high English education. The members of these castes have been able to utilize the funds provided by the Central and State Governments for the award of backward class scholarships, the funds allotted for agricultural development and have also been successful in securing jobs of prestige in the governmant offices and are powerful in the legislatures and in the formation of the State Cabinets.

One of the big problems facing the society is the fact that these dominant castes have developed a vested interest in remaining backward as this enables them to enjoy the benefits of education and employment. They resist all attempts to take them out of the "other backward class" lists, since they are now fairly well-advanced and since the funds and opportunities available should be utilized for the benefit of the castes which are more backward. This is one of the reasons why the various Commissions try to develop criteria to distinguish between the "backward castes" and the "more backward castes." But, these caste groups do not want to give up the advantages; it is a fact that though some members are quite forward, the majority of them are yet poor and illiterate; they would like these sections of their castes to get the benefits. Also they are eager to retain these advantages for their own benefit. No one wants to lose what one has.

As a result new tensions are being generated between these "powerful backward castes" and the "weak backward castes" as well as the scheduled castes. There are now signs of these two latter groups joining their forces to fight, what may be called, the "advanced backward castes". Thus it may be said that a "new backward classes movement" is now emerging. While the first phase (roughly from 1916 to 1969) saw the struggle of the non-Brahmins against the well-entrenched Brahmins and the attempts to dislodge them, the second phase now being witnessed is the struggle of the "more backward non-Brahmins" against the "more advanced non-Brahmins." These sections now desire that the advantages should accrue to them since they stand in greater need than the more advanced sections. There is a new awareness in them. Probably one of the important reasons for the rise of this new awareness among those belonging to these sections is the realization that in the rural areas the dominant castes are keeping them in subjection. A new polarization is emerging between the advanced section of the Indians, which includes the upper castes and the backward sections which includes the lower castes, the Muslims, the Christians and other minorities. This polarization was in evidence in Karnataka State towards the end of 1973 when the advanced sections joined together and condemned one of the Harijan ministers who was outspoken against exploitation of the backward groups by the forward groups; the other sections joined together in supporting him. Another evidence of this was the convening of the Backward Class Conference in Bangalore in which representatives from these sections from all the four Southern States participated.

This is a manifestation of the new desire in these sections for education and social mobility; in other words, a new desire to give up their traditional way of life and the poverty and illiteracy associated with it.

Justice for All

The composite Madras State as well as the old Mysore State had framed rules regarding the admission to medical and other colleges. For example, Madras State had allotted six out of fourteen seats to Non-Brahmin Hindus, two to Backward Hindus, two to Harijans, two to Brahmins, one to a Christian and one to a Muslim Admission was according to this fixed ratio for three decades ever since the Justice Party formed the Government. When a case was filed against this after the Constitution was adopted, the Supreme Court declared it unconstitutional in 1951. This resulted in the first Constitutional amendment to Article 15 and the framing of sub-clause of Article 15 which enables the State to make special provision for the advancement of the "socially and educationally backward classes" of citizens. There were similar rules in the

Mysore Stale and the Mysore High Court declared that such allotments violated Article 15(4) of the Constitution. This led to the appointment of a Committee in 1960 in Mysore State to lay down the criteria for the classification of backward classes. This Committee recommended thai caste should be a criterion and that the backwardness of the caste should be determined by (a) the number of high school students per thousand of its population and (b) its representation in government service. On the basis of these criteria, the Committee classified the Lingayats as a "forward" caste and this immediately led to an agitation by the Lingayats. As a result in 1962 the Mysore Government drew up a list of 81 "backward classes" and 135 "more backward classes" and provided for the reservation of 68 per cent of the seats in professional colleges for these and the scheduled castes and tribes. The Supreme Court struck down this order in 1963 and declared it a "fraud on the Constitution". The court held that classification of backward classes on the sole basis of caste was not in accordance with Article 15(4). The Court also held that the reservation was excessive since reservation of 68 per cent of the seats weakened the fundamental rule of equality of opportunity.

A reference to some of the important decisions of the Supreme Court on the scope and interpretation of Article 15(4), 16(4), 29(2), and Part XVI of the Constitution of India would throw some light on the difficulties involved in the resolution of the "reservation issue".

In the case of M.R. Balaji v State of Mysore (AIR 1963 SC 649) the Supreme Court, inter alia, held that Article 15(4) was added by the Constitution (First Amendment) Act, 1951. The object of this amendment was to bring Articles 15 and 29 in line with Art. 16(4). Article 15(4) has to be read as a proviso or an exception to Arts. 15(1) and 29(2). If an order is justified by the provisions of Article 15(4) its validity cannot be impeached on the ground that it violates Art. 15(1) or Art. 29(2). The fundamental rights guaranteed by the said two provisions do not affect the validity of the special provision which it is permissible to make under Art. 15(4).

Article 15(4) provides that nothing in this Article or in Cl. (2) of Art. 29 shall prevent the State from making any special provision for the advancement of any socially and educationally Backward Classes of citizens or for the Scheduled Castes and the Scheduled Tribes. This Article was added by the Constitution (First Amendment) Act, 1951. The object of this amendment was to bring Arts. 15 and 29 in line with Art. 16 (4).

The fundamental rights guaranteed by Arts. 15(1) and 29(2) were not controlled by any exception, and that since there was no provision under Art. 15 corresponding to Art. 16 (4), the order of the Madras government in the case of Champakam Dorairajan (AER 1951 SC 226) could not be sustained fixing the admissions in the stated proportions by reference to the communities of the candidates. When this impugned order was struck down by the Madras High Court the same was confirmed by the Supreme Court in appeal.

Thus, there is no doubt that Art. 15(4) has to be read as a proviso or an exception to Arts. 15(1) and 29(2). In other words, if the impugned order is justified by the provisions of Art. 15(4), its validity cannot be impeached on the ground that it violates Art. 15(1) or Art. 29(2). The fundamental rights guaranteed by the said two provisions do not affect the validity of the special provision.

Article 15(4) authorises the State to make a special provision for the advancement of any socially and educationally backward classes of citizens, as distinguished from he Scheduled Castes and Scheduled Tribes. No doubt, special p revision can be made for both categories of citizens, but in specifying the categories, the first category is distinguished from the second. Sub-clauses (24) and (25) of Art. 366 define Scheduled Castes and Scheduled Tribes respectively, but there is no clause defining socially and educationally backward classes of citizens, and so, in determining the question as to whether a particular provision has been validly made under Art. 15(4) or not, the first question which falls to be determined is whether the State has validly determined who should be included in these Backward Classes. It seems fairly clear that the Backward classes of citizens for whom special provision is authorised to be made are, by Art. 15(4) itself, treated as being similar to the Scheduled Castes and Scheduled Tribes. Scheduled Castes and Scheduled Tribes which have been defined were known to be backward and the Constitution-makers felt no doubt that special provision had to be made for their advancement. It was realised that in the Indian Society there were other classes of citizens who were equally, or may be somewhat less, backward than the Scheduled Castes and Tribes and it was thought that some special provisions ought to be made even for them. Article 341 provides for the issue of public notification specifying the castes, races or tribes which shall, for the purposes of this Constitution, be deemed to be Scheduled Castes either in the State or the Union territory as the case may be. Similarly Art. 342 makes a provision for the issue of public notification, in respect of Scheduled Tribes. Under Art. 338(3), it is provided that references to the Scheduled Castes and Scheduled Tribes shall be construed as including references to such other Backward Classes as the President may, on receipt of the report of a commission appointed under Article 340(1), by order, specify and also to the Anglo-Indian community. It would thus by seen that this provision contemplates that some Backward Classes may be the Presidential order be included in Scheduled Castes and Tribes. That helps to being out the point that the Backward Classes for whose improvement special provision is contemplated by Art. 15(4) are in the matter of their backwardness comparable to Scheduled Castes and Scheduled Tribes.

In considering the scope and extent of the expression "backward classes" under Art. 15(4), it is necessary to remember that the concept of backwardness is not intended to be relative in the sense that any classes who are backward in relation to the most advanaced classes of the society should be included in it. If such relative tests were to be applied by reason of the most advanced classes, there would be several layers or strata of backward classes and each one of them may claim to be included under Art 15(4). The backwardness under Art. 15(4) must be social and educauonal. It is not either social or educational, but it is both social and educational; and that takes us to the question as to how social and educauonal backwardness has to be determined.

Let us take the question of social backwardness first. By what test should it be decided whether a particular class is socially backward or not? The group of citizens to whom Art. 15(4) applies are described as 'classes of citizens', not as castes of citizens. A class, according to the dictionary meaning, shows division of society according to status, rank or caste. In the Hindu social structure, caste unfortunately plays an important part in determining the status of the citizen. Though according to sociologists and vedic scholars, the caste system may have originally begun on occupational or functional basis, in course of time, it became rigid and inflexible. The history of the growth of caste system shows that its original functional and occupational basis was later over-burdened with considerations of purity based on ritual concepts, and that led to its ramifications which introduced inflexibility and rigidity. This artificial growth inevitably tended to create a feeling of superiority and inferiority, and to foster narrow caste loyalties. Therefore, in dealing with the question as to whether any class of citizens is socially backward or not, it may not be irrelevant to consider the caste of the said group of citizens. In this connection it is, however, necessary to bear in mind that the special provision is contemplated for classes of citizens and not for individual citizens as such, and so, though the caste of the group of citizens may be relevant, its importance should not be exaggerated. If the classification of backward classes of citizens was based solely on the caste of the citizen, it may not always be logical and may perhaps contain the vice of perpetuating the castes themselves.

Besides, if the caste of the group of citizens was made the sole basis for determining the social backwardness of the said group, that test would inevitably break down in relation to many sections of Indian society which do not recognise castes in the conventional sense known to Hindu society. How is one going to decide whether Muslims, Christians or Jains, or even Lingayats are socially backward or not? The test of castes would be inapplicable to those groups but that would hardly justify the exclusion of these groups in toto from the operation of Art. 15(4). It is not unlikely that in some States some Muslims or Christians or Jains forming groups may be socially backward. That is why though castes in relation to Hindus may be a relevant factor to consider in determining the social backwardness of groups or classes of citizens, it cannot be made the sole or the dominant test in that behalf. Social backwardness is on the ultimate analysis the result of poverty to a very large extent. The classes of citizens who are deplorably poor automatically become socially backward. They do not enjoy a status in society and have, therefore, to be content to take a backward seat. It is true that social backwardness which results from poverty is likely to be aggravated by considerations of caste to which the poor citizens may belong, but that only shows the relevance of both caste and poverty in determining the backwardness of citizens.

The occupations of citizens may also contribute to make classes of citizens socially backward. There are some occupations which are treated as inferior according to conventional beliefs and classes of citizens who follow these occupations are apt to become socially backward. The place of habitation also plays not a minor part in determining the backwardness of a community of persons. In a sense, the problem of social backwardness is the problem of Rural India and in that behalf, classes of citizens occupying a socially backward position in rural area fall within the purview of Art. 15(4) The problem of determining who are socially backward classes is undoughtedly very complex. Sociological, social and economic considerations come into play in solving the problem, and evolving proper criteria for determining which classes are socially backward is obviously a very difficult task; it will need an elaborate investigation and collection of data and examining the said data in a rational and scientific way. That is the function of the State which purports to act under Art. 15(4).

The Supreme Court was not satisfied that the state was justified in making the view that communities or castes whose average of student population was the same as, or just below, the State average, should be treated as educationally backward classes of citizens. If the test has to be applied by a reference to the Slate average of student population, the legitimate view to lake would be that the classes of citizens whose average is well or substantially below the State average can be treated as educationally backward. The Supreme Court do not purpose to lay down any hard and fast rule; it is for the State to consider the matter and decide it in a manner which is consistent with the requirements of Art. 15(4).

In this connection, it is necessary to add that the sub-classification made by the order between Backward Classes and More Backward Classes does not appear to be justified under

Article 15(4). Article 15(4) authorises special provision being made for the really backward classes. In introducing two categories of Backward Classes what the impugned order, in substance purports to do is to devise measures for the benefit of all the classes of citizens who are less advanced compared to the most advanced classes in the State, and that, in our opinion, is not the scope of Art. 15(4). The result of the method adopted by the impugned order is that nearly 90 per cent of the population of the State is treated as backward, and that illustrates how the order in fact divides the population of the State into most advanced and the rest, and puts the latter into two categories of Backward and More Backward. The classification of the two categories, therefore, is not warranted by Art. 15(4).

Article 15(4) authorises the State to make any special provision for the advancement of the Backward Classes of citizens or for the Scheduled Castes and Scheduled Tribes.

Art. 46 which contains a directive principle, provides that the State shall promote with special care the educational and economic interests of the weaker sections of the people, and, in particular, of the Scheduled Castes and the Scheduled Tribes, and shall protect them from social injustice and all forms of exploitation. There can be no doubt that the object of making a special provision for the advancement of the castes or communities, there specified, is to carry out the directive principle enshrined in Art. 46. It is obvious that unless the educational and economic interests of the weaker sections of the people are promoted quickly and liberally, the ideal of establishing social and economic equality will not be attained, and so, there can be no doubt that Art. 15(4) authorises the State to take adequate steps to achieve the object which it has in view. No one can dispute the proposition that political freedom and even fundamental rights can have very little meaning or significance for the Backward Classes and the Scheduled Castes and Scheduled Tribes unless the backwardness and inequality from which they suffer are immediately redressed.

When Art. 16(4) refers to the special provision for the advancement of certain classes or scheduled castes or scheduled tribes, it must not be ignored that the provision which is authorized to be made is a special provision; it is not a provision which is exclusive in character, so that in looking after the advancement of those classes, the State would be justified in ignoring altogether the advancement of the rest of the society. It is because the interest of the society at large would be served by promoting the advancement of the weaker elements in the society that Art. 15(4) authorises special provision to be made. But if a provision which is in the nature of an exception completely excludes the rest of the society, that clearly is outside the scope of Art. 15(4). It would be extremely unreasonable to assume that in enacting Art. 15(4) the Constitution intended to provide that where the advancement of the Backward Classes or the Scheduled Castes and Tribes was concerned, the fundamental rights of the citizens constituting the rest of the society were to be completely and absolutely ignored.

In this connection, it is necessary to remember that the reservation made by the impugned order is in regard to admission in the seats of higher education in the State. It is well-known that as a result of the awakening caused by political freedom, all classes of citizens are showing a growing desire to give their children higher university education and so, the Universities are called upon to face the challenge of this growing demand. While it is necessary that the demand for higher education which is thus increasing from year to year must be adequately met and properly channelised, we cannot overlook the fact that in meeting that demand standards of higher education in Universities must not be lowered. The large demand for education may be met by starting larger number of educational institutions, vocational schools and polytechnics. But, it would be against the national interest to exclude from the portals of our Universities qualified and competent students on the ground that all the seats in the Universities are reserved for weaker elements in society. As has been observed by the University Education Commission, "he indeed must be blind who does not see that mightly as are the political changes, far deeper are the fundamental questions which will be decided by what happens in the Universities" (p. 32).

Therefore in considering the question about the propriety of the reservation made by the impugned order, we cannot lose sight of the fact that the reservation is made in respect of higher university education. The demand for technicians, scientists, doctors, economists, engineers and experts for the further economic advancement of the country is so great that it would cause grave prejudice to national interests if considerations of merit are completely excluded by wholesale reservation of seat in all technical, Medical or Engineering colleges or institutions of that kind. Therefore, considerations of national interest and the interests of the community or society as a whole cannot be ignored in determining the question as to whether the special provision contemplated by Art. 15(4) can be special provision which excludes the rest of the society altogether. In this connection, it would be relevant to mention that the University Education Commission which considered the problem of the assistance to backward communities, has observed that the percentage of reservation shall not exceed a third of the total number of seats, and it has added that the principle of reservation may be adopted for a period of ten years (p. 53).

The Backward Classes Commission observed that the representatives of the upper classes did not complain about any lack of efficiency in the offices recruited by reservation (p.135). This opinion, however, is plainly inconsistent with what is bound to be the inevitable consequence of reservation in higher university education. If admission to professional and technical colleges is unduly liberalised, it would be idle to contend thai the quality of our graduates will not suffer. That is not to say that reservation should not be adopted; reservation should and must be adopted to advance the prospects of the weaker sections of society, but in providing for special measures in that behalf care should be taken not to exclude admission to higher educational centres to deserving and qualified candidates of other communities. A special provision contemplated by Art. 15(4) like reservation of posts and appointments contemplated by Art. 16(4) must be within reasonable limits. The interests of weaker sections of society which are a first charge on the States and the Centre have to be adjusted with the interests of the community as a whole. The adjustment of these competing claims is undoubtedly a difficult matter, but if under the guise of making a special provision, a State reserves practically all the seats available in all the colleges, that clearly would be subverting the object of Art. 15(4). In this matter again, we are reluctant to say definitely what would be a proper provision to make. Speaking generally and in a broad way, a special provision should be less than 50 per cent: how much less than 50 per cent would depend upon the relevant prevailing circumstances in each case. In this particular case it is remarkable that when the State issued its order on July 10, 1961, it emphatically expressed its opinion that the reservation of 68 per cent recommended by the Nagan Gowda Committee would not be in the larger interests of the State. What happened between July 10, 1961, and July 31, 1962 does not appear on the record. But the State changed its mind and adopted the recommendation of the Committee ignoring its earlier decision that the said recommendation was contrary to the larger interests of the State. In our opinion, when the State makes a special provision for the advancement of the weaker sections of society specified in Art. 15(4) it has to approach its task objectively and in a rational manner. Undoubtedly, it has to take reasonable and even generous steps to help the advancement of weaker elements; the extent of the problem must be weighed, the requirements of the community at large must be borne in mind and a formula must be evolved which would strike a reasonable balance between the several relevant considerations. Therefore, we are satisfied that the reservation of 68 per cent directed by the impugned order is plainly inconsistent with Art. 15(4).

When it is said about an executive action that it is a fraud on the Constitution it does not necessarily mean that the action is actuated by malafides. An executive action which is patently and plainly outside the limits of the constitutional authority conferred on the State in that behalf is struck down as being ultra vires the State's authority. If, on the other hand, the executive action does not patently or overtly transgress the authority conferred on it by the Constitution, but the transgression is covert or latent, the said action is struck down as being a fraud on the relevant constitutional power. It is in this connection that courts often consider the substance of the matter and not its form and in ascertaining the substance of the matter, the appearance or the cloak, or the veil of the executive action is carefully scrutinized and if it appears that notwithstanding the appearance, the cloak or the veil of the executive action, in substance and in truth the constitutional power has been transgressed, the impugned action is struck down as a fraud on the Constitution. We have already noticed that the impugned order in the present case has categorised the Backward Classes on the sole basis of caste which, in our opinion, is not permitted by Art. 15(4); and we have also held that the reservation of 68 per cent made by the impugned order is plainly inconsistent with the concept of the special provision authorised by Art. 15(4). Therefore, it follows that the impugned order is a fraud on the Constitutional power conferred on the State by Art. 15(4).

In this connection, it may be relevant to refer to Maharashtra in exercising its powers under Art. 15(4) is a proper method to adopt. It appears that the Maharashtra Government has decided to afford financial assistance, and make monetary grants to students seeking higher education where it is shown that the annual income of their families is below a prescribed minimum. If any State adopts such a measure, it may afford relief to and assist the advancement of the Backward Classes in the State, because backwardness, social and educational, is ultimately and primarily due to poverty. An attempt can also be made to start newer and more educational institutions, polytechnics, vocational institutions and even rural Universities and thereby create more opportunities for higher education. This dual attack on the problem posed by the weakness of backward communities can claim to proceed on a rational, broad and scientific approach which is consistent with, and true to, the noble ideal of a secular welfare democratic State set up by the Constitution of this country. Such an approach can be supplemented, if necessary by providing special provision by way of reservation to aid the Backward classes and Scheduled castes and Tribes. It may well be that there may be other ways and means of achieving the same result. In our country where social and economic conditions differ from State to State, it would be idle to expect absolute uniformity of approach; but in taking executive action to implement the policy of Art. 15(4), it is necessary for the States to remember that the policy which is intended to be implemented is the policy which has been declared by Art 46 and the preamble of the Constitution. It is for the attainment of social and economic justice that Art. 15(4) authorises the making of special provisions for the advancement of the communities there contemplated even if such provisions may be inconsistent with the fundamental rights guaranteed under Art. 15 or 29(2). The context, therefore, requires that the executive action taken by the State must be based on an objective approach free from all extraneous pressures. The said action is intended to do social and economic justice and must be taken in a manner that justice is and should be done.

It would be relevant to add that the provisions of Art. 15(4) are similar to those of Art. 16(4) which fell to be considered in the case of General Manager, Southern Railway v. Rangachari, AIR 1962 SC 36. In that case, the majority decision of the Supreme Court held that the power of reservation which is conferred on the State under Art. 16(4) can be exercised by the State in a proper case not only by providing for reservation of appointments, but also by providing for reservation of selections posts. This conclusion was reached on the basis that it served to give effect to the intention of the Constitution-makers to make adequate safeguards for the advancement of Backward Classes and to secure their adequate representation in the Services. The judgment shows that the only point which was raised for the decision of this Court in that case was whether the reservation made was outside Art. 16(4) and that posed the bare question about the construction of Art. 16(4). The propriety, the reasonableness or the wisdom of the impugned order was not questioned because it was not the respondent's case that if the order was justified under Art. 16(4), it was a fraud on the Constitution. Even so, it was pointed out in the judgment that the efficiency of administration is of such a paramount importance that it would be unwise and impermissible to make any reservation at the cost of efficiency of administration; that, it was stated, was undoubtedly the effect of Art. 335. Therefore, what is true in regard to Art. 15(4) is equally true in regard to Art. 16(4). There can be no doubt that the Constitution-makers assumed, as they were entitled to, that while making adequate reservation under Art. 16(4), care would be taken not to provide for unreasonable, excessive or extravagant reservation, for that would, by eliminating general competition in a large field and by creating wide-spread dissatisfaction amongst the employees, materially affect efficiency. Therefore, like the special provision improperly made under Art.

15(4), reservation made under Art. 16(4) beyond the permissible and legitimate limits would be liable to be challenged as a fraud on the Constitution. In this connection, it is necessary to emphasise that Art. 15(4) like Art. 16(4) is an enabling provision; it does not impose an obligation but merely leaves it to the discretion of the appropriate Government to take suitable action if necessary.

In the case of Chitralekha v State of Mysore (AIR 1964 SC 1823) the Supreme Court, inter alia, observed that the two principles stand out prominently namely, (i) the caste of a group of citizens may be a relevant circumstance in ascertaining their social backwardness; and (ii) though it is a relevant factor to determine the social backwardness of a class of citizens, it cannot be the sole or dominant test in that behalf. While the Supreme Court said that caste is only a relevant circumstance and that it cannot be the dominant test in ascertaining the backwardness of a class of citizens, the High Court said that it was an important basis in determining the class of backward Hindus and that the Government should have adopted caste as one of the tests. As the said observations made by the High Court may lead to some confusion in the mind of the authority concerned who may be entrusted with the duty of prescribing the rules for ascertaining the backwardness of classes of citizens within the meaning of An. 15(4) of the Constitution, the Supreme Court would hasten to make it clear that caste is only a relevant circumstance in ascertaining the backwardness of a class and there is nothing in the judgment of the Supreme Court which precludes the authority concerned from determining the social backwardness of a group of citizens if it can do so without reference to caste. While the Supreme Court has not excluded caste from ascertaining the backwardness of a class of citizens, it has not made it one of the compelling circumstances affording a basis for the ascertainment of backwardness of a class. To put it differently, the authority concerned may take caste into consideration in ascertaining the backwardness of a group of persons; but, if it does not, its order will not be bad on that account, if it can ascertain the backwardness of a group of persons on the basis of other relevant criteria.

The Constitution of India promises justice, social, economic and political; and equality of status and of opportunity, among others. Under Art. 46, one of the Articles in Part IV headed "Directive Principles of State Policy," the State shall promote with special care the educational and economic interests of the weaker sections of the people, and in particular, of the Scheduled Castes and the Scheduled Tribes, and shall protect them from social injustice and all forms of exploitation. Under Art. 341, "The President may with respect to any State or Union territory, and where it is a State after consultation with the Governor thereof by public notification specify the castes, races or tribes or parts of or groups within castes, races or tribes which shall for the purpose of this Constitution be deemed to be Scheduled Castes in relation to that State or Union territory, as the case may be."

Under Art. 342, in the same manner, the President may specify the tribes or tribal communities as Scheduled Tribes. Article 15(4) says:

"Nothing in this Article or in clause (2) of Art. 29 shall prevent the State from making any special provision for the advancement of any socially and educationally Backward Classes of citizens or for the Scheduled Castes and the Scheduled Tribes."

These provisions form a group of Articles which have relevance in making of a special provision for the advancement of any socially and educationally Backward Classes of citizens in the matter of admissions to Colleges.

These provisions recognize the factual existence of backward classes in our country brought about by historical reasons and make a sincere attempt to promote the welfare of the weaker sections thereof. They shall be so construed as to effectuate the said policy but not to give weightage to progressive sections of our society under the false colour of caste to which they happen to belong. The important factor to be noticed in Art. 15(4) is that it does not speak of castes, but only speaks of classes. If the makers of the Constitution intended to take castes also as units of social and educational backwardness, they would have said so as they have said in the case of the Scheduled Castes and the Scheduled Tribes. Though it may be suggested that the wider expression "classes" is used in Cl. (4) of Art. 15 as there are communities without castes, if the intention was to equate classes with castes, nothing prevented the makers of the Constitution to use the expression "Backward Classes or castes". The juxtaposition of the expression "Backward Classes" and "Scheduled Castes" in Art. 15(4) also leads to a reasonable inference that the expression "classes" is not synonymous with castes. It may be that for ascertaining whether a particular citizen or a group of citizens belong to a backward class or not, his or their caste may have some relevance, but it cannot be either the sole or the dominant criterion for ascertaining the class to which he or they belong.

This interpretation will carry out the intention of the Constitution, expressed in the aforesaid Articles. It helps the really Backward Classes instead of promoting the interests of individuals or groups who, they belong to a particular caste a majority whereof is socially and educationally backward, really belong to a class which is socially and educationally advanced. To illustrate, take a caste in a State which is numerically the largest therein. It may be that though a majority of the people in that caste are socially and educationally backward, and effective minority may be socially and educationally far more advanced than another small sub-caste the total number of which is far less than the said minority. If we interpret the expression "classes" as "castes", the object of the Constitution will be frustrated and the people who do not deserve any adventitious aid may get it to the exclusion of those who really deserve. This anomaly will not arise if, without equating caste with class, caste is taken as only one of the considerations to ascertain whether a person belongs to a backward class or not. On the other hand, if the entire sub-caste, by and large, is backward, it may be included in the Scheduled Castes by following the appropriate procedure laid down by the Constitution.

The laying down of criteria for ascertainment of social and educational backwardness of a class is a complex problem depending upon many circumstances which may vary from State to State and even from place to place in a State. But what we intend to emphasize is that under no circumstance a "class" can be equated to a "caste" though the caste of an individual or a group of individuals may be considered along with other relevant factors in putting him in a particular class. We would also like to make it clear that if in a given situation caste is excluded in ascertaining a class within the meaning of An. 15(4) of the Constitution, it does not vitiate the classification if it satisfied other tests,

In the case of C.A. Rajendran v. U.O.I. (AIR 1968 SC 507), the Supreme Court observed that under Art. 16 of the Constitution, there shall be equality of opportunity for all citizens in matters relating to employment or appointment to any office under the State or promotion from one office to a higher office thereunder. Article 14, 15 and 16 form part of the same constitutional code of guarantees and supplement each other. It follows therefore that there can be a reasonable classification of the employees for the purpose of appointment and promotion. To put it differently, the equality of opportunity guaranteed by Art. 16(1) means equality as between members of the same class of employees, and not equality between members of separate, independent classes.

Clause (4) of Art. 16 does not cover the entire field covered by Cls. (1) and (2) of that Article. The only matter which Cl. (4) covers is a provision for the reservation of appointments in favour of a backward class of citizens. It is well settled that CI.(4) of Art. 16 is an exception clause and is not an independent provision and it has to be strictly construed. It is also apparent that the language of Art. 16(4) has to be interpreted in the context and background of Art. 335 of the Constitution. In other words, in making a provision for reservation of appointments or posts the Government has to take into consideration not only the claims of the members of the backward classes but also the maintenance of efficiency of administration which is a matter of paramount importance AIR 1962 SC 36 and AIR 1963 SC 649 Foil.

Art. 16(4) does not confer any right and there is no constitutional duly imposed on the Government to make a reservation for Scheduled Castes and Scheduled Tribes, either at the initial stage of recruitment or at the stage of promotion. In other words, Art. 16(4) is an enabling provision and confers a discretionary power on the State of make a reservation of appointments in favour of backward class of citizens which, in its opinion, is not adequately represented in services of the State.

In the case of State of A.P. v. P. Sagar (AIR 1968 SC 1879) the Supreme Court, inter alia, held that the expression "class" in Art. 15(4) means a homo geneous section of the people grouped together because of certain likenesses or common trails and who are identifiable by some common attributes such as status, rank, occupation, residence in a locality, race, religion and the like. In determining whether a particular section forms a class, caste cannot be excluded altogether. But in the determination of a class a test solely based upon the caste or community cannot also be accepted. The Parliament has by enacting Cl. (4) attempted to balance as against the right of equality of citizens the special necessities of the weaker sections of the people by allowing a provision to be made for their advancement. In order that effect may be given to Cl. (4), it must appear that the beneficiaries of the special provision are classes which are backward socially and educationally and they are other than the Scheduled Castes and Scheduled Tribes, and that the provision made is for their advancement. Reservation may be adopted to advance the interests of weaker sections of society, but in doing so, care must be taken to see that deserving and qualified candidates are not excluded from admission to higher educational institutions. The criterion for determining the backwardness must not be based solely on religion, race, caste, sex, or place of birth, and the backwardness being social and educational must be similar to the backwardness from which the Scheduled Castes and the Scheduled Tribes suffer.

In the case of State of Kerala vs. N.M. Thomas (AIR 1976 SC 490) Justice V.R. Krishna lyer, inter alia, held that a case which turns the focus on the political philosophy pervading the Constitution and affects a large human segment submerged below the line of ancient social penury, naturally prompts me to write a separate opinion substantially concurring with that of the learned Chief Justice. Silence is not always golden.

Law, including constitutional law, can no longer 'go it alone' but must be illumined in the interpretative process by sociology and allied fields of knowledge. Indeed, the term 'constitutional law' symbolizes an intersection of law and politics, wherein issues of political power are acted on by persons trained in the legal tradition, working in judicial institutions, following the procedures of law, thinking as lawyers think." So much so, a wider perspective is needed to resolve issues of constitutional law. May be, one cannot agree with the view of an eminent jurist and former Chief

Justice of India; 'the judiciary as a whole is not interested in the policy underlying a legislative measure' (Mr. Hidayalullah, 'Democracy in India and the Judicial Process', 1965, p. 70). Moreover, the Indian Constitution is a great social document, almost revolutionary in its aim of transforming a medieval, hierarchical society into a modern, egalitarian democracy. Its provisions can be comprehended only by a spacious, social-science approach, not by pedantic, traditional legalism. Here we are called upon to delimit the amplitude and decode the implications of Art. 16(1) in the context of certain special concessions relating to employment, under the Kerala State (the appellant), given to Scheduled Castes and Scheduled Tribes (for short, hereinafter referred to as harijans) whose social lot and economic indigence are an Indian reality recognized by many Articles of the Constitution. An overview of the decided cases suggests the need to reinterpret the dynamic import of the 'equality clauses' and to stress again, beyond reasonable doubt, that the paramount law, which is organic and regulates our nation's growing life, must take in its sweep "eithics , economics, politics and sociology'. Equally pertinent to the issue mooted before us is the lament of Friedman:

"It would be tragic if the law were so petrified as to be unable to respond to the unending challenge of evolutionary or revolutionary changes in society."

The main assumptions which Friedman makes are:

> "first, the law is, in Holmes' phrase, not a 'brooding omnipotence in the sky', but a flexible instrument of social order, dependent on the political values of the society which it purports to regulate...."

Naturally surges the interrogation, what are the challenges of changing values to which the guarantee of equality must respond and how? To pose the problem with particular reference to our case, does the impugned rule violate the constitutional creed of equal opportunity in Art. 16 by resort to a suspect classification or revivify it by making the less equal more equal by a legitimate differentiation? Chief Justice Marshall's classic statement in McCulloch v. Maryland, (1816-19) 17 US (4 Wheat) 316, 421 quoted in (1966) 384 US 650 followed by Justice Brennan in Kazenbach v. Morgan, (1966) 384 US 641 remains a beacon light:

> "Let the end be legitimate, let it be within the scope of the constitution, and all means which are appropriate, which are plainly adapted to that end, which are not prohibited, but consist with the letter and spirit of the constitution, are constitutional."

Back now to the rule of exemption and its vires. Frankly, here the respondents who have passed the 'test' are stalled in their promotion because of the new rule of harijan exemption. As individuals, their rights vis a vis their harijan brethren are regarded unequally. In a strictly competitive context or narrowly performance-oriented standard, Rule 33AA discriminates between a harijan and a non-harijan. The question is whether a perceptive sensitivity sees on 'equal opportunity a critical distinction between distribution according to 'merit' of individuals and distribution according to 'need' of depressed groups subject to broad efficiency criteria.

Factual contexts dictate State action. The differential impact of a law on a class will influence judicial evaluation of the reasonableness of a classification and its relation to a purpose which is permissible. Courts, however, adopt a policy of restrained review where the situation is complex and is intertwined with social, historical and other substantially human factors. Judicial difference—not abdication—is best expressed by Justice Holmes in his dissent in Louisville Gas & Elec. Co. v. Coleman, (1927) 277 US 32:

> "But when it is seen that a line or a point there must be, and that there is no mathematical and logical way of fixing it precisely, the decision of the legislature must be accepted unless we can say that it is very wide of any reasonable mark."

In Buck v. Bell, (1926) 274 US 200 at p. 208 Holmes J. observed:

> "The law does all that is needed when it does all that it can, indicates a policy, applies it to all within the lines, and seeks to bring within the lines all similarly situated so far and so fast as its means allow."

Given a legitimate over-riding purpose for selectivity the Court passes, leaving it to the law-maker the intricate manner of implementation. Faced with a suspect classification based on a quasi-caste differentia and apparently injuring administrative quality, the Court turns activist. Conceptual equilibrium between these two lines is the correct guideline.

The operational technique may vary with time and circumstance but the goal and ambit must be constitutionally sanctioned. In the instant case, the State has taken a certain step to advance the economic interests of harijans. What—if we break down the rule into its components—have Government done? Have they transgressed the rights under Art. 16(1) & (2)? If they have, the Court, as constitutional invigilator interdicts, after making permissible presumptions in favour of State actions and importing the liberal spirit of effective equality into the mandate of Arts. 14 and 16. Otherwise, the hammer does not fall.

Why was this second 'holiday' under rule 13AA to harijans granted? The hapless circumstance which compelled this course was, according to the State, the need to help this class, acting within the constitutional bounds, to avert mass reversion to lower posts, without abandoning insistence on passing "tests." The Note to Rule 13AA is explanatory. The State viewed this disturbing situation with concern, and having regard to their backward condition, made R. 13AA which conferred power on Government to grant further spells of grace time to get through these tests. Simultaneously, a period within which two opportunities for passing tests would be available was afforded by a G.O. issued under Rule 13AA. The consequence was their immediate reversion was averted and the promotion prospects of the non-harijan writ petitioners who were test-qualified, stood postponed. This grievance of theirs drove them to the High Court where the rule of temporary exemption from passing tests for promotional eligibilty in favour of harijans was held ultra vires Arts. 16 (1) and 335.

Let us proceed to assess the constitutional merit of the State's ex facie 'unequal' service rule favouring in-service harijan employees in a realist socio-legal perspective. But before that, some memorable facts must be stated. The Father of the Nation adopted, as his fighting faith, the uplift of the bhangi and his assimilation, on equal footing, into Hindu society, and the Constitution, whose principal architect was himself a militant manor, made social justice a founding faith and built into it humanist provisions to lift the level of the lowly scheduled castes and tribes to make democracy viable and equal for all. Studies in social anthropology tell us how cultural and material suppression has, over the ages, crippled their personality, and current demography says that nearly every fifth Indian is a harijan and his social milieu is steeped in squalor. The conscience of the Constitution found adequate expression on this theme in Dr. Ambedkar's words of caution and premonition in the Constituent Assembly:

"We must begin by acknowledging first that there is complete absence of two things in Indian society. One of these is equality. On the social plane, we have in India a society based on privilege of graded inequality which means elevation for some and degradation of others. On the economic plane, we have a society in which there are some who have immense wealth as against the many who are living in abject poverty. On the 26th of January, 1950, we are going to enter into a life of contradictions. In politics we will have equality and in social and economic life we will have inequality. We must remove this contradiction at the earliest possible moment, or else those who suffer from inequality will blow up the structure of political democracy which this Assembly has so laboriously built up." (Vol. II, pp. 184-187).

Judges may differ in constitutional construction but, without peril of distorting the substance, cannot discard the activism of the equal justice concept in the setting of deep concern for the weaker sections of the community. What I endeavour to emphasize, as I will elaborate later, is that equal justice is an aspect of social justice, the salvation of the very weak and down trodden, and the methodolgy for levelling them up to a real, not formal, equality, being the accent.

The Kerala State, the appellant, has statistically shown the yawning gap between what number of posts in Government service harijans are entitled to, population-ratio-wise, and the actual number of posts occupied by them. Their 'official' fate is no less ominous elsewhere in India and would have been poorer on the competitive market method of selection unaided by 'reservation'. The case for social equality and economic balance, in terms of employment under the State, cries for more energised administrative effort and a Government that fails to repair this depressed lot, fools the public on harijan welfare. Indeed, an aware mass of humanity, denied justice, for generations, will not take it lying down too long but may explode into Dalit Panthers, as did the Black Panthers in another country,—a theme on which Sri Gajen-dragadkar, a former Chief Justice of India, has laid disturbing stress in two Memorial Lectures delivered recently, Jurists must listen to real life and, theory aparts, must be alert enough to read the writing on the wall! where the rule of law bars the doors of collective justice, the crushed class will seek hope in the streets. The architects of our Constitution were not unfamiliar with direct action where basic justice was long withheld and conceived of 'equal opportunity' as inclusive of equalising opportunity. Only a clinical study of organic law will yield correct diagnostic results.

Social engineering—which is Law in action—must adopt new strategies to liquidate encrusted group injustices or surrender society to traumatic tensions. Equilibrium, in human terms, emerges from release of the handicapped and the primitive from persistent social disadvantage, by determined creative and canny legal manoeuvres of the State, not by hortative declaration of arid equality. To discriminate positively in favour of the weak may sometimes be promotion of genuine equality before the law as Anthony Lester argued in his talk in the B.B.C. in 1970 in the series: 'What is wrong with the Law." 'One law for the Lion and Ox is oppression', Or, indeed, as was said of another age by Anatole France, "The law in its majestic equality forbids the rich as well as the poor to sleep under bridges, to beg in the streets and to steal bread.'" Re-distributive justice to harijan humanity insists on effective reforms designed to produce equal partnership of the erstwhile 'lowliest and the lost', by State action, informed by short-run and long-run sociologically potent perspective planning and implementation. An uneven socio-economic landscape hardly gives the joy of equal opportunity and development or draw forth their best from man-power resources now wallowing in the low visibility areas of discontented life.

The domination of a class generates, after a long night of sleep or stupor of the domited, an angry awakening and protestant resistance and this conflict between thesis, i.e. the status quo, and anti-thesis i.e., the hunger for happy equality, propels new forces of synthesis i.e., an equitable constitutional order or just society. Our founding fathers, possessed of spiritual insight and influenced by the materialist interpretation of history, forestalled such social pressures and pre-empted such economic upsurges and gave us a trinity of commitments—justice: social, economic and political. The 'equality Articles' are part of this scheme. My proposition is, given two alternative understandings of the relevant sub-Articles (Arts. 16 (1) and (2)), the Court must so interpret the language as to remove that ugly 'inferiority' complex which has done genetic damage to Indian polity and thereby suppress the malady and advance the remedy, informed by sociology and social anthropology. My touchstone is that functional democracy postulates participation by all sections of the people and fair representation in administration is an index of such participation.

Justice Brennan, in a somewhat different social milieu, uttered words which may not be lost on us.

"Lincoln said this Nation was 'conceived in liberty and dedicated to the proposition that all men are created equal'. The Founders dream of a society where all men are free and equal has not been easy to realize. The degree of liberty and equality that exists today has been the product of unceasing struggle and sacrifice. Much remains to be done—so much that the very institutions of our society have come under challenge. Hence, today, as in Lincoln's time, a man may ask 'whether (this) nation or any nation so conceived and so dedicated can long endure'. It cannot endure if the Nation falls short on the guarantees of liberty, justice, and equality embodied in our founding documents. But it also cannot endure if our precious heritage of ordered liberty be allowed to be ripped apart amid the sound and fury of our time. It cannot endure if in individual cases the claims of social peace and order on the one side and of personal liberty on the other cannot be mutually resolved in the forum designated by the Constitution. If that resolution cannot be reached by judicial trial in a court of law, it will be reached elsewhere and by other means, and there will be grave danger that liberty, equality, and the order essential to both will be lost."

A word of sociological caution. In the light of experience, here and elsewhere, the danger of 'reservation', it seems to me, is three-fold. Its benefits by and large, are snatched away by the top creamy layer of the 'backward' caste or class, thus keeping the weakest among the weak always weak and leaving the fortunate layers to consume the whole cake. Secondly, this claim is over-played extravagantly in democracy by large and vocal groups whose burden of backwardness has been substantially lightened by the march of time and measures of better education and more opportunities of employment, but wish to wear the 'weaker section' label as a means to score over their near-equals formally categorised as the upper brackets. Lastly, a lasting solution to the problem comes only from improvement of social environment, added educational facilities and cross-fertilisation of castes by intercaste and interclass marriages sponsored as a massive State programme, and this solution is calculatedly hidden from view by the higher 'backward' groups with a vested interest in the plums of backwardism. But social science research, not judicial impressionism, will alone tell the whole truth and a constant process of objective re-evaluation of progress registered by the 'under-dog' categories is essential lest a once deserving 'reservation' should be degraded into reverse discrimination. Innovations in adminis-trative strategy to help the really untouched, most backward classes also emerge from such socio-legal studies and audit exercises, if dispassionately made. In fact, research conducted by the A.N. Sinha Institute of Social Studies, Patna, has revealed a dual society among harijans, a tiny elite gobbling up the benefits and the darker layers sleeping distances away.

The core conclusion is that every step needed to achieve in action actual, equal, partnership for the harijans, alone amounts to social justice—not enshrinement of great rights in Part III and good goals in Part IV. Otherwise, the solemn undertakings in Articles 14 to 16 read with Arts. 46 and 335 may be reduced to a 'teasing illusion or promise of unreality'. A clear vision of the true intendment of these provisions demands a deep understanding of the Indian spiritual-secular idea that divinity dwells in all and that ancient environmental pollution and social placement, which the State must extripate, account for the current socio-economic backwardness of the blacked-out human areas described euphemistically as Scheduled Castes and Scheduled Tribes. The roots of our constitutional ideas—at least some of them—can be traced to our ancient culture. The noble Upanishadic behest of collective acquisition of cultural strength is involved in and must evolve out of 'equality' if we are true to the subtle substance of our finer heritage.

The Directive Principles of State Policy, fundamental in the governance of the country, enjoin on the State the promotion "with special care the educational and economic interest of the weaker sections of the people, and, in particular, of the Scheduled Castes and the Scheduled Tribes,... and protect them from social injustice."

To neglect this obligation is to play truant with Art. 46. Undoubtedly economic interests of a group—as also social justice to it—are tied up with its place in the services under the State. Our history, unlike that of some other countries, has found a zealous pursuit of government jobs as a mark of share in State power and economic position. Moreover, the biggest—and expanding, with considerable State undertakings,—employer is Government, Central and State, so much so appointments in the public services matter increasingly in the prosperity of backward segments. The Scheduled Castes and Scheduled Tribes have earned special mention in Art. 46 and other 'weaker sections' in this context, means not every 'backward class' but those dismally depressed categories comparable economically and educationally to Scheduled Castes and Scheduled Tribes. To widen the vent is to vitiate the equal treatment which belongs to all citizens, many of whom are below the poverty line. Realism reveals that politically powerful castes may try to break into equality, using the masterkey of backwardness but, leaving aside Art. 16(4), the ramparts of Art. 16(1) and (2) will resist such oblique infiltration.

The Constitution itself makes a super-classification between harijans and others, grounded on the fundamental disparity in our society and the imperative social urgency of raising the former's sunken status. Apart from reservation of seats in the Legislatures for harijans, which is a deliberate departure, taking note of their utter backwardness (Arts. 330 and 332), a special officer to investigate and report to the President upon the working of special constitutional safeguards made to protect harijans has to be appointed under Art. 338. Gross inadequacy of representation in public services is obviously one subject for investigation and report. Art. 335 reads:

"335. Claims of Scheduled Castes and Scheduled Tribes to services and posts.— The claims of the members of the Scheduled Castes and the Scheduled Tribes shall be taken into consideration, consistently with the maintenance of efficiency of administration, in the making of appointments to services and posts in connection with the affairs of the Union or of a State."

This provision directs pointedly to (a) the claims of—not compassion towards—harijans to be given special consideration in the making of appointments to public services; and (b) lest this extra-attention should run riot and ruin administrative efficiency, a caution is uttered that maintenance of efficiency in administration should not suffer mayhem.

Now one may deduce from these and other like Articles, unaided by authority, certain clear conclusions of great relevance to the present case: (1) The Constitution itself demarcates harijans from others. (2) This is based on the stark backwardness of this bottom layer of the community. (3) The differentiation has been made to cover specifically the area of appointments to posts under the State. (4) The twin objects, blended into one, are the claims of harijans to be considered in such posts and the maintenance of administrative efficiency. (5) The State has been obligated to promote the economic interests of harijans and like backward classes, Arts. 46 and 335 being a testament and Arts. 14 to 16 being the tool-kit, if one may put it that way. To blink at this panchsheel is to be unjust to the Constitution.

The controlling distinction between two visions of the mood and message of the supreme law, the Constitution, being the dynamic and the static, the sociological and the formal. It is unexceptional to say that any insightful construction must opt for the former methodology and also seek a good fellowship among the various provisions, conventionally called 'harmonious construction.' In an elevating and organic instrument, antagonisms cannot exist. If that be the lodestar to help interpret the supreme lex we have to discover a note of unison in Art. 16(1), (2) and (4) as well as Arts. 46 and 335, the background tune being one of the profound effort first to equalise and then to march together without class-creed distinction. The social engineering know-how of our Constitution, viz., levelling up the groups buried under the debris by a generous consideration and thereafter enforcing strict equality among all—this two-tier process operating symbiotically, is the life of the law and the key to the 'equal opportunity' mechanism. Equally emphatic is the grave concern shown for a casteless and classless society—not in magic instant but through a careful striving—and for the standards of performance of the Administration, noted from Curzon's days for drowsiness.

Efficiency means, in terms of good government, not marks in examinations only, but responsible and responsive service to the people. A chaotic genius is a grave danger in public administration. The inputs of efficiency include a sense of belonging and of accountability which springs in the bosom of the bureaucracy (not pejoratively used) if its composition takes in also the weaker segments of We, the people of India. No other understanding can reconcile the claim of the radical Present and the hangover of the unjust Past.

Now to the precedential guidelines. I am alive to the correctly reluctant attitude of this Court to depart from precedent lest an unstable and uncertain situation be created. Khanna J. has rightly emphasized this great need but also quoted Brandeis and Cardozo JJ. (per Khanna J. in Maganlal v, Munic. Corporation; (1975) 1 SCR 1 at pages 26 and 28 = (AIR 1974 SC 2009 at pages 2042, 2043):

"As observed by Cardozo:

'.........But I am ready to concede that the rule of adherence to precedent, though it ought not to be abandoned, ought to be in some degree relaxed. I think that when a rule, after it has been duly tested by experience, has been found to be inconsistent with the sense of justice or with the social welfare, there should be less hesitation in frank avowal and full abandonment. We have had to do this sometimes in the field of constitutional law.'

Anyway, here no case is being overruled because no case has said Scheduled Castes and Tribes are a caste nor that advancement of sunken sections of society consistently with administrative efficiency cannot be a rational object linked with outrageous backwardness of a class as the intelligible differentia within an official cadre.

Keshavananda Bharati, AIR 1973 SC 1461 has clinched the issue of primacy as between Part III and Part IV of the Constitution. The unanimous ruling there is that the Court must wisely read the collective Directive Principles of Part IV into the individual fundamental rights of Part III, neither Part being superior to the other. Since the days of Dorairajan, 1951 SCR 525 = (AIR 1951 SC 226) judicial opinion has hesitatingly tilted in favour of Part HI but in Keshavananda Bharati the supplementary theory, treating both Parts as fundamental, gained supremacy. Khanna J. spoke with a profound sense of depth at p. 1878:

"The Directive Principles embody a commitment which was imposed by the Constitution makers on the State to bring about economic and social regeneration of the teeming millions who are steeped in poverty, ignorance and social backwardness. They incorporate a pledge to the coming generations of what the State would strive to usher in."

"There should be no reluctance to abridge or regulate the fundamental rights to property if it was felt necessary to do so for changing the economic structure and attaining the objective contained in the Directive Principles." (at p. 1880).

Chandrachud J. has set the judicial sights straight in this passage (at p. 2050):

"What is fundamental in the governance of the country cannot surely be less significant than what is fundamental in the life of an individual. The freedoms of a few have to be abridged in order to ensure the freedom could be enjoyed by all, the freedom of all. If State fails to create conditions in which the Fundamental freedoms of the few will be at the mercy of the many and then all freedoms will vanish. In order, therefore, to preserve their freedom, the privileged few must part with a portion of it."

The upshot, after Bharati, is that Art. 46 has to be given emphatic expression while interpreting Art. 16(1) and (2). Indeed, Art. 335 is more specific and cannot be brushed aside or truncated in the operational ambit vis a vis Art. 16(1) and (2) without hubristic aberration.

To clear the clog of Art. 16 (2) as it stems from a confusion about caste in the terminology of Scheduled Castes and Scheduled Tribes. This latter expression has been defined in Arts. 341 and 342. A bare reading brings out the quintessential concept that they are no castes in the Hindu fold but an amalgam of castes, races, groups, tribes, communities or parts thereof found on investigation to be the lowliest and in need of massive State aid and notified as such by the President. To confuse this backward-most social composition with castes is to commit a constitutional error, misled by a compendious appellation. So that, to protect harijans is not to prejudice any caste but to promote citizen solidarity. Art. 16(2) is out of the way and to extend protective discrimination to this mixed bag of tribes, races, groups, communities and non-castes outside the four-fold Hindu division is not to compromise with the acceleration of castelessness enshrined in the sub-article. The discerning sense of the Indian Corpus Juris has generally regarded Scheduled Castes and Scheduled Tribes, not as caste but as a large backward group deserving of societal compassion.

'Reservation' based on classification of backward and forward classes, without detriment to administrative standards (as this Court has underscored) is but an application of the principle of equality within a class and grouping based on a rational differentia, the object being advancement of backward classes consistently with efficiency. Arts. 16(1) and (4) are concordant. The Supreme Court has viewed Art. 16(4) as an exception to Art. 16(1). Does classification based on desparate backwardness render Art. 16(4) redundant? No. Reservation confers pro tanto monopoly, but classification grants under Art. 16 (1) ordinarily a lesser order of advantage. The former is more rigid, the latter more flexible, although they may overlap sometimes. Art. 16 (4) covers all backward classes, but to earn the benefit of grouping under Art. 16(1) based on Arts. 46 and 335 as I have explained,, the twin considerations of terrible backwardness of the type harijans endure and maintenance of administrative efficiency must be satisfied.

The basic question thus is one of social dynamics implied in Art. 16 (1). In a spacious sense, 'equal opportunity' for members of a hierarchical society makes sense only if a strategy by which the underprivileged have environmental facilities for developing their full human potential. This consummation is accomplished only when the utterly depressed groups can claim a fair share in public life and economic activity, including employment under the State, or when a classless and casteless society blossoms as a result of positive State action. To help the lagging social segments, by special care, is a step towards and not against a larger and stabler equality. I had occasion to observe in J. & K. State v. T.N. Khosa, (1974) ISCR 771.

"In this unequal world the proposition that all men are equal has working limitations, since absolute equality leads to Procrustean cruelty or sanctions indolent inefficiency. Necessarily, therefore, an imaginative and constructive modus vivendi between commonness and excellence must be forged to make the equality clauses viable. This pragmatism produced the judicial gloss of 'classification' and 'differentia', with the by-products of equality among equals and dissimilar things having to be treated differently. The social meaning of Arts. 14 to 16 is neither dull uniformity nor specious 'talentism'. It is a process of producing quality out of larger areas of equality extending better facilities to the latent capabilities of the lowly. It is not a methodology of substitution of pervasive and slovenly mediocrity for activist and intelligent—but not snobbish and uncommitted—cadres. However, if the State uses classification casuistically for salvaging status and elitism, the point of no return is reached for Arts. 14 to 16 and the Court's jurisdiction awakens to deaden such manoeuvres. The soul of Art. 16 is the promotion of the common man's capabilities, overpowering environmental adversities and opening up full opportunities to develop in official life without succumbing to the sophistic argument of the elite that talent is the privilege of the few and they must rule, wriggling out of the democratic imperative of Arts. 14 and 16 by the theory of classified equality which at its worst degenerates into class domination."

This observation was approved later by this Court in Mohd. Shujat Ali v.Union of India, AIR 1974 SC 1631, 1653.

If Art. 14 admits of reasonable classification, so does Article 16(1) and this Court has held so. In the present case, the economic advancement and promotion of the claims of the grossly under-represented and pathetically neglected classes, otherwise described as Scheduled Castes and Scheduled Tribes, consistently with the maintenance of administrative efficiency, is the object, constitutionally sanctioned by Articles 46 and 335 and reasonably accommodated in Art. 16 (1). The differentia, so loudly obtrusive, is the dismal social milieu of harijans. Certainly this has a rational relation to the object set out above. Not all caste backwardness is recognised in this formula. To do so is subversive of both Arts. 16 (1) and (2). The social disparity must be so grim and substantial as to serve as a foundation for benign discrimination. If we search for such a class, we cannot find any targe segment other than the Scheduled Castes and Scheduled Tribes. Any other caste, securing exemption from Art. 16 (1) and (2), by exerting political pressure or other influence, will run the high risk of unconstitutional discrimination. If the real basis of classification is caste, masked as backward class, the Court must strike at such communal manipulation. Secondly, the Constitution recognizes the claims of only harijans (Art. 335) and not of every backward class. The profile of Art. 46 is more or less the same. Casteism cannot come back by the backdoor and, except in exceptionally rare cases, no class other than harijans can jump the gauntlet of 'equal opportunity' guarantee. Their only hope is in Article 16 (4).

Jurisprudence, to be living law, must respond to the bhangi colony and the black ghetto intelligently enough to equalise opportunities within the social, political and economic orders, by making up for long spells of deprivation. Hence, if a court is convinced that the purpose of a measure using a suspect classification is truly benign, that is, that the measure represents an effort to use the classification as part of a programme designed to achieve an equal position in society for all tribes and groups and communities, then it may be justified in permitting the State to choose the means for doing so, so long as the means chosen are reasonably related to achieving that end. The distinction would seem to be between handicaps imposed accidentally by nature and those resulting from societal arrangements such as caste structures and group suppression. Society being, in a broad sense, responsible for these latter conditions, it also has the duty to regard them as relevant differences among men and to compensate for them whenever they operate to prevent equal access to basic, minimal advantages enjoyed by other citizens. In a sense, the theory broadens the traditional concept of 'state action' to require government attention to those inequalities for which it is not directly responsible, but which nevertheless are concomitant features of the existence of the organized state. I quote from Harvard Law Review 1968-69, Vol. 82, excerpls from 'Developments in the Law—Equal Protection:

"A state might, for example, decide to give some racial groups an exemption from qualification examinations or establish a racial credit on such examinations to that often given to veterans" (pp. 1105-06).

"Where racial classifications are being used ostensibly to remedy deprivations arising from past and continuing racial discrimination, however a court might think it proper to judge the measures by a less stringent standard of review, possibly even the permissive or rationality standard normally used in constitutional appraisal of regulatory measures" (p. 1107).

"Moreover, even if racial classifications do have some negative educative effects, the classifications may be so effective that they should be instituted despite this drawback. If the measures succeed in aiding blacks to obtain opportunities within the social, political and economic orders that have formerly been denied to them, they may be worth the cost of emphasizing men's differences. It may be that the actual participation of blacks in positions alongside whites will ultimately prove to have the most important and long-lasting educative effect against discrimination." (p. 1113)

"Hence, if a court is convinced that the purpose of a measure using a racial classification is truly benign, that is, that the measure represents an effort to use the classification as part of a programme designed to achieve an equal position in society for all races, then it may be justified in permitting the state to choose the means for doing so, so long as the means chosen are reasonably related to achieving that end" (p. 1115).

Illustrative of an allied type of State action to eliminate gross group inequality for attaining general equality is a recent ruling of the U.S. Supreme Court The good omen for American women in Schlosinger v. Ballard. (1975) 42 Law Ed 2d 610, is indicative of high judicial hunch in understanding the classificatory clue to promotion of employment equality. The case related to a male challenge of a provision entitling women officers in the U.S. Navy to longer years of commissioned service. The Court remarked upholding the unequal step to promote eventual gender equality, that "in enacting and retaining of Section 640 Congress may thus quite rationally have believed that women line officers had less opportunity for promotion than did their male counterparts and that a longer period of tenure for women officers would therefore be consistent with the goal to provide women officers with fair" and equitable career advancement programmes."

The key thought is the broader test of constitutional classification.

It is a statistically proved social reality in India that the depressed employment position of harijans is the master problem in the battle against generations of retardation, and "reservation" and other solutions have made no significant impact on their employment in public services. In such an unjust situtation, to maintain mechanical equality is to perpetuate actual inequality. A battery of several programmes to fight down this fell backwardness must be tried out by the State. Relaxation of "tests' qualification at the floor level of clerical posts (lower or upper division) is part of this multiform strategy to establish broader, though seemingly 'differential' equality. If the Court has its listening posts on raw Indian earth, its assessment of 'equal opportunity' cannot remain legalistic or individualistic but should see the age-old inequality to mend which is also the means to real equality, a demanding command of our Constitution. The poignant and ominous words of Sterling Tucker, in his book 'For Blacks Only" will awaken the judicial vision to the harijan situation and so I quote:

"If white Americans had learned to see us as we are, human beings, like themselves without individual burdens of hope, or fear, they could have understood our rage and our defiance. They might have wished to accommodate to it, but they could have comprehended it. They could have understood our need for pride and grasped what black power meant to us. But as Relph Ellison potently expressed, they never really saw us:

I am an invisible man .... I am a man of substance, of flesh and bone, fiber and liquids, and I might even be said to possess a mind. I am invisible, understand, simply because people refuse to see me .... When they approach me they see only my surrounding, themselves or figments of their imagination—indeed, everything and anything except me.

That invisibility to which I refer occurs because of a peculiar disposition of the eyes of those with whom I come in contact. A matter of the construction of their inner eyes, those eyes with which they look through their physical eyes upon reality .... You wonder whether you aren't simply a phantom in other people's minds .... You ache with the need to convince yourself that you do exist in the real world, that you're a part of all the sound and anguish, and you strike out with your field, you curse and you swear to make them recognize you. And, alas, it is seldom successful."

No caste, however seemingly backward, or claiming to be derelict, can be allowed to breach the dukes of equality of opportunity guaranteed to all citizens. To them the answer is that, save in rare cases of 'chill penury repressing their noble rage', equality is equality—nothing less and nothing else. The heady upper berth occupants from 'backward' classes do double injury. They beguile the broad community into believing the backwardness is being banished. They rob the need-based bulk of the backward of the 'office' advantages, the nation by classification reserves or proffers. The constitutional dharma, however, is not an unending deification of 'backwardness'and showering "classified" homage, regardless of advancement registered, but progressive exorcising of the social evil and gradual withdrawal of artificial crutches. Here the Court has to be objective, resisting mawkish politics. But, by that standard, as statistically shown to us in this case, harijan have-nots have 'miles to go' and so long, the Administration has 'promises to keep'.

In the case of K.C Vasamh Kumar v. State of Kerala (AIR 1985 SC 1495), the Chief Justice Y.V. Chandrachud observed that the reservation in favour of Scheduled Castes and Scheduled Tribes must continue as at present, there is, without the application of a means test, for a further period not exceeding fifteen years. The means test, that is to say, the test of economic backwardness ought to be made applicable even to the Scheduled Castes and Scheduled Tribes after 2000 AD. In so far as the Other Backward Classes are concerned, two tests should be conjunctively applied for identifying them for the purpose of reservations in employment and education: One, that they should be comparable to the Scheduled Castes and Scheduled Tribes in the matter of their backwardness; and two, that they should satisfy the means test such as a State Government may lay down in the context of prevailing economic conditions. The policy of reservations in employment, education and legislative institutions should be reviewed every five years or so. That will at once afford an opportunity (i) to the State to rectify distortions arising out of particular facets of the reservation policy, and (ii) to the people, both backward and non-backward, to ventilate their views in a public debate on the practical impact of the policy of reservations.

Justice D.A. Desai, after reviewing various decisions of the Supreme Court, observed that this would put into focus, the dithering and the vacillation on the part of Judiciary in dealing with the question of reservation in favour of Scheduled Castes, Scheduled Tribes as well as other socially and educationally backward classes. Judiciary retained its traditional blindfold on its eyes and thereby ignored perceived realities. A perceptive viewer of judicial intervention observed that 'the courts turned out to be more limited as a vantage point than I naively assumed at the outset. They act as a balance wheel channelling compensatory policies and accommodating them to other commitments, but it is the political process that shapes the larger contour of these policies and gives them their motive force. Official doctrine—judicial pronouncements or administrative regulations—proved insufficient guide to the shape of the policies in action and the result they produced.' Marc Galanter, Competing Equalities, 1980, p, XVIII. The Indian social scene apart from being disturbing presented the picture of stratified society hierarchically fragmented. At the lowest rung of the ladder stand Scheduled Castes and Scheduled Tribes and any preferential treatment in their favour has more or less met with judicial approval. But when it came to preferential treatment or affirmative action or what is also called compensatory discrimination in favour of socially and educationally backward classes of citizens, the caste ridden society raised its ugly face. By its existence over thousands of years,more or less it was assumed that caste should be the criterion for determinin social and educational backwardness. In other words, it was said, look at the caste, its traditional functions, its position in relation to upper castes by the standard of purity and pollution, pure and not so pure occupation, once these questions are satisfactorily answered without anything more, those who belong to that caste must be labelled socially and educationally backward.This over-simplified approach ignored a very realistic situation existing in each caste that in every such caste whose members claim to be socially and educationally backward, has an economically well-placed segments. But that may wait. We are at present concerned with the judicial response to the attempt of the Executive to accord preferential treatment to socially and educationally backward classes of citizens. The litigation which came to the court was more often by those who relied on meritocracy and complained that the merit is crucified at the altar of the mirage of equality. The outcomeof judicial intervention against preferred treatment is summed up as under. Marc Gallanter, Competing Equalities, p. 511:

"Summing up, we may surmise that the gross effect of litigation on the compensatory discrimination policy has been to curtail and confine it. Those who have attacked compensatory discrimination schemes in court have compiled a remarkable record of success, while those seeking to extend compensatory discrimination have been less successful."

The controversy now has shifted to identifying socially and educationally backward classes of citizens. The expression 'backward classes' is not defined. Courts have more or less in the absence of well-defined criteria not based on caste label has veered round to the view that in order to be socially and educationally backward classes, the group must have the same indicia as Scheduled Castes and Scheduled Tribes. The narrow question that is being examined here is whether caste label should be sufficient to identify social and educational backwardness? Number of Commissions have attempted to tackle this complex problem.

However, both Mandal Commision and the Havanur Commission of Karnataka and Bakshi Commission of Gujarat have finally accepted caste as the identifying criterion for determining social and educational backwardness, though it will be presently pointed out that Mandal Commission had serious reservations about caste criterion. Most of these Commissions and the Government orders based on their recommendations used communal units to discriminate the backward class. Rane Commission of Gujarat has chalked out a different path, rejecting caste as the basis for ascertaining social and educational backwardness. The question we must pose and answer is whether caste should be the basis for determining social and educational backwardness. In other words, by what yardstick, groups which are to be treated as socially and educationally backward are to be identified? To simplify the question: should membership of caste signify a class of citizens as being socially and educationally backward? If 'caste' is adopted as the criterion for determining social and educational backwardness does it provide a valid test or it would violate Art. 15(1) which prohibits discrimination against any citizen on grounds of religion, race, caste, sex, place of birth or any of them.

What then is a caste? Though caste has been discussed by scholars and jurists, no precise definition of the expression has emerged. A caste is a horizontal segmental division of society spread over a district or a region or the whole State and also sometimes outside it I.P.Desai: Should 'caste' be the Basis for Recognising Backwardness (1985). Homo Hierarchies is expected to be the central and substantive element of the caste system which differentiate if from other social systems. The concept of purity and impurity conceptualises the caste system. Louis Dumont asserts that the principle of the opposition of the pure and the impure underlies hie:archy, which is the superiority of the pure to the impure, underlies separation because pure and the impure must be kept separate and underlies the division of labour because pure and impure occupation must likewise, be kept separate. Louise, Dumont Homo Hierarchicus (1970). There are four essential features of the caste system which maintained its homo hierarchicus character: (1) hierarchy; (2) commensaiity; (3) restrictions on marriage; and (4) hereditary occupation. Caste in Contemporary

India: G. Shah (1985). Most of the castes are endogamous groups. Inter-marriage between two groups is impermissible. But 'Pratilom' marriages are not wholly unknown. Similarly with the onward movement of urbanisation, members of various castes are slowly giving up, traditional occupations and the pure and impure avocations is being frowned upon by developing notion of dignity of labour. As the fruits of indepen-dence were unequally distributed amongst various segments of the society, in each caste there came into existence a triple division based on economic resurgence amongst the members of the caste. Those who have become economically well off have acquired an upper class status (class consciousness) and the one on the step below is the middle class and the third one belongs to poorer section of the caste. This led to the realisation that caste culture does not help economic interest. In fact the upper crust of the same caste is verily accused of exploiting the lower strata of the same caste. It is therefore, rightly argued thai the basis of the caste system namely, purity and pollution is slowly being displaced by the economic condition of the various segments of the same caste. It is recognised on almost all hands that the important feature of the caste structure are progressively suffering erosion. The new organisation, the so-called caste organisation, is substantially different from the traditional caste structure and caste councils. Economic differentiation amongst the members of the caste has become sharp, but not so sharp as to bury caste sentiments and ties.

If the transformation of the caste structure as herein indicated is realistically accepted, should the caste label be still accepted as the basis for determining social and educational backwardness. In a recent paper by the noted sociologist Shri IP, Desai (Alas, he is no more), it has been ably argued that not a caste but the class or the social group should be examined with a view to determining their social and educational backwardness. Rejecting the recommendations of the Mandal Commission for caste based reservation, he argues in favour of class based reservation. He says that if the Stale accepts caste as the basis for backwardness, it legitimises the caste system which contradicts secular principles and secondly the traditional caste system has broken down and contractual relationship between individuals have emerged. This approach has been questioned in a recent paper by Mr. Ghanshyam Shah on Caste, Class and Reservation.

In order to appreciate the viewpoint advanced by Mr. Desai which appeals to me both for its indepth study of the problem, and a fresh outlook on this vexed problem. At the outset let me take a look at the futuristic view of the Indian Society as envisaged in the Constitution. No one is left in any doubt that the future Indian Society was to be casteless classless. Pandit Jawaharlal Nehru the first Prime Minister of India said that Mahatma Gandhi has shaken the foundations of caste and the masses have been powerfully affected. But an even greater power than Gandhi is at work, the conditions of modem life—and it seems at last this hoary and tenacious relic of past times must die. Discovery of India by Pandit Nehru, Ch. VI, p. 234. Mahatma Gandhi, the Father of the Nation said, "The caste system as we. know is an anachronism. It must go if both Hinduism and India are to live and grow from day to day." In its onward march towards realising the constitutional goal, every attempt has to be made to destroy caste stratification. It enjoins the State to strive to minimise the inequality in income and endeavour to eliminate inequalities in status, facilities and opportunities, not only amongst individuals but also amongst groups of people residing in different areas or engaged in different vocations. Art. 46 enjoins duty to promote with special care the educational and economic interests of the weaker sections of the people, and in particular, of the Scheduled Castes and Scheduled Tribes, and shall protect them from social injustice and all forms of exploitation. Continued retention of the division of the society into various castes simultaneously introduces inequality of status. And this inequality in status is largely responsible for retaining inequality in facilities and opportunities, ultimately resulting in bringing into existence an economically depressed class far transcending caste structure and caste barrier. The society therefore, was to be a classless casteless society. In order to set up such a society, steps have to be taken to weaken and progressively eliminate caste structure. Unfortunately, the movement is in the reverse gear. Caste stratification has become more rigid to some extent, and where concessions and preferred treatment schemes are introduced for economically disadvantaged classes, identifiable by caste label, the caste structure unfortunately received a fresh lease of life. In fact there is a mad rush for being recognised as belonging to a caste which by its nomenclature would be included in the Ist of socially and educationally backward classes. To illustrate : Bakshi Commission in Gujarat recognised as many as 82 castes as being socially and educationally backward. On the publication of its report, Government of Gujarat received representations by members of those castes who had not made any representation to the Bakshi Commission for treating them as socially and educationally backward. This phenomenon was noticed by Mandal Commission when it observed : "whereas the Commission has tried to make the Statewise lists of OBCs as comprehensive as possible, it is quite likely that several synonymies of the castes listed as backward have been left out. Certain castes are known by a number of synonymy which vary from one region to the other and their complete coverage is almost impossible." Mandal Commission found a way out by recommending that if a particular caste has been treated as backward then all its synonyms whether mentioned in the State lists or not should also be treated as backward. (Mandal Commission Report, Ch. XII, p. 55) Gujarat Government was forced to appoint a second commission known as Rane Commission. Rane Commission took note of the fact that was an organised effort for being considered socially and educationally backward castes. Rane Commission recalled the observations in Balaji's case (AIR 1963 SC 649) that 'Social backwardness is on the ultimate analysis the result of poverty to a very large extent. The Commission noticed that some of the castes just for the sake of being considered as socially and educationally backward, have degraded themselves to such an extent that, they had no hesitation in attributing different types of vices to and associating other factors indicative of backwardness, with their castes. The Commission noted that the malaise requires to be remedied. The Commission, therefore, devised a method for determining socially and educationally backward classes without reference to caste, beneficial to all sections of people irrespective of the caste to which they belong. The Commission came to an irrefutable conclusion that amongst certain castes and communities or class of people, only lower income groups amongst them are socially and educationally backward. We may recall here a trite observation in case of N.M. Thomas (AIR 1976 SC 490) which reads as under:

"A word of sociological caution. In the light of experience, here and elsewhere, the danger of 'reservation', it seems to me, is three-fold. Its benefits, by and large, are snatched away by the top creamy layer of the 'backward' caste or class, thus keeping the weakest amongst the weak always weak and leaving the fortunate layers to consume the whole cake. Secondly, this claim is overplayed extravagantly in democracy by large and vocal groups whose burden of backwardness has been substantially, lightened by the march of time and measures of better education and more opportunities of employment, but wish to wear the 'weaker section' label as a means to score over their near-equals formally categorised as the upper brackets."

A few other aspects for rejecting caste as the basis for identifying social and educational backwardness may be briefly noted. If State patronage for preferred treatment accepts caste as the only insignia for determining social and educational backwardness, the danger looms large that this approach alone would legitimise and perpetuate caste system. It does not go well with our proclaimed secular character as enshrined in the Preamble to the Constitution, The assumption that all members of some caste are equally socially and educationally backward is not well-founded. Such an approach provides an oversimplification of a complex problem of identifying the social and educational backwardness. The Chairman of the Backward Classes Commission, set up in 1953, after having finalised the report, concluded that 'it would have been better if we could determine the criteria of backwardness on principles other than caste'. Backward Classes Commission Report, Vol. I, Ch. XIV. Lastly it is recognised without dissent that the caste based reservation has been usurped by the economically well-placed section in the same caste. To illustrate, it may be pointed that some years ago I came across a petition for special leave against the decision of the Punjab and Haryana High Court in which the reservation of 21 per cent for admission to Medical and Engineering College in favour of Majhabi Sikhs was challenged by none other than the upper crust of the members of the Scheduled Castes amongst

Sikhs in Punjab, proving that the labelled weak exploits the really weaker. Add to this, the findings of the Research Planning-Scheme of Sociologists assisting the Mandal Commission when it observed : 'while determining the criteria of socially and educationally backward classes, social backwardness should be considered to be the critical element and educational backwardness to be the linked element though not necessarily derived from the former'. Part 3 Appendix XIII, p. 99 of the Report of the Team, The team ultimately concluded that 'social backwardness refers to ascribed status and educational backwardness to achieved status, and it considered social backwardness as the critical element and educational backwardness to be the linked though not derived element.' The attempt is to identify socially and educationally backward—classes of citizens. The caste, as is understood in Hindu Society, is unknown to Muslims, Christians, Parsis, Jews etc. Caste criterion would not furnish a reliable yardstick to identify socially and educationally backward group in the aforementioned communities though economic backwardness would.

Therefore, a time has come to review the criterion for identifying socially and educationally backward classes ignoring the caste label. The only criterion which can be realistically devised is the one of economic backwardness. To this may be added some relevant criteria such as the secular character of the group, its opportunity for earning livelihood etc., but by and large economic backwardness must be the load star. Why I say this?

Chronic poverty is the bane of Indian Society. Market economy and money spinning culture has transformed the general behaviour of the society towards its members. Upper caste does not enjoy the status or respect, traditional, voluntary or forced any more even in rural areas what to speak of highly westernised urban society. The bank balance, the property holding and the money power determine the social status of the individual and guarantee the opportunities to rise to the top echelon. How the wealth is acquired has lost significance. Purity of means disappeared with Mahatma Gandhi and we have reached a stage where ends determine the means. This is the present disturbing situation whether one likes it or not. Rane Commission on the evidence before it and after applying the relevant tests and criteria observed as under:

"We have found on applying relevant tests and criteria and on the basis of the evidence on record, that there are certain caste/communities or classes of people which are backward, but, only lower income groups amongst them are socially and educationally backward. In order to ensure that, no ambiguity remains in regard to the above aspect, we may add that, the above observations hold good even in respect of those classes which are identified as socially and educationally backward without reference to any caste." Report of Rane Commission, Chapter, XII, para 12.1.

Reservation in one or other form has been there for decades. If a survey is made with reference to families in various castes considered to be socially and educationally backward, about the benefits of preferred treatment, it would unmistakably show that the benefits of reservations are snatched away by the top creamy layer of the backward castes. This has to be avoided at any costs.

If poverty is to be the criterion for determining social and educational backwardness, we must deal with a fear expressed by sociologists. It is better to recapitulate these aspects in the words of a sociologist:

"Now, if the government changes the criteria of reservation from caste to class, persons from the upper strata of the lower castes who are otherwise not able to compete with the upper strata of the upper castes despite the reservations will be excluded from the white collar jobs. And the persons from the lower strata of lower castes will not be able to compete with their counterpart of the upper castes. They too will be excluded. This will bridge the gap which is otherwise widening between the rich and the poor of the upper castes and it will strengthen their caste identity. It will wipe out the small poor strata of the upper castes at the cost of the poor strata of the lower castes, and in the name of secularism. In course of time, the upper caste will also become the upper class. Such a process would hamper the growth of secular forces."

This fear psychosis is effectively answered by an eminent academic. He says that 'if the poor can be operationally defined, categorised and sub-categorised and reservation benefits be stratified accordingly, would the scenario still haunt us? I think not'. He recognised that this point is valuable in terms of alerting everyone to the need for further refinement of the notions of poor strata. He recognised that the State is, with all its limitations and resources, to direct and plan social transformation. (The non-revolutionary) choice is between reinforcing 'caste' or reinforcing the extant constitutional values.' Upendra Baxi, the then Vice-Chancellor, South Gujarat University, in 'Caste, Class and Reservations; A Rejoinder to Ghanshyam Shah.'

If economic criterion for compensatory discrimination or affirmative action is accepted, it would strike at the root cause of social and educational backwardness, and simultaneously take a vital' step in the direction of de,struction of caste structure which in turn would' advance the secular character of the Nation. This approach seeks translate into reality the twin constitutional goals: one, to strike at the perpetuation of the caste stratification of the Indian Society so as to arrest progressive movement and to take a firm step towards establishing a casteless society; and two, to progressively eliminate poverty by giving an opportunity to the disadvantaged sections of the society to raise their position and be part of the mainstream of life which means eradication of poverty.

It should be made abundantly clear that this approach does not deal with reservation in favour of Scheduled Castes and Scheduled Tribes. Thousands of years of discrimination and exploitation cannot be wiped out in one generation. But even here economic criterion is worth applying by refusing preferred treatment to those amongst them who have already benefited by it and improved their position. And finally reservation must have a time span otherwise concessions tend to become vested interests. This is not a judgement in a lis in an adversary system. When the arguments concluded, a statement was made that the Government of State of Karnataka would appoint a Commission to determine constitutionally sound and nationally acceptable criteria for identifying socially and educationally backward classes of citizens for whose benefit the State action would be taken. This does not purport to be an exhaustive essay on guidelines but may point to some extent, the direction in which the proposed Commission should move.

Justice Chinnappa Reddy observed that one of the results of the superior, elitist approach is that the question of reservation is invariably viewed as the conflict between the meritarian principle and the compensatory principle. No, it is not so. The real conflict is between the class of people, who have never been in or who have already moved out of the desert of poverty,illiteracy and backwardness and are entrenched in the oasis of convenient living and those who are still in the desert and want to reach the oasis. Efficiency is very much on the lips of the privileged whenever reservation is mentioned. There is neither statistical basis nor expert evidence to support the assumptions that efficiency will necessarily be impaired if reservation exceeds 50 per cent, if reservation is carried forward or if reservation is extended to promotional posts.

In view of Arts. 15(4) and 16(4), the so called controversy between the meritarian and compensatory principles is not of any great significance, though, it is true that efficiency should not be sacrificed. The question really is, who are the scheduled castes, scheduled tribes and backward classes, who are entitled to special provision and reservation in regard to admission into educational institutions and representation in the services.

If poverty be the cause, caste is the primary index of social backwardness, so that social backwardness is often readily identifiable with reference to a person's caste. So sadly and oppressively deep-rooted is caste in our country that it has cut across even the barriers of religion. The caste system has penetrated other religious and dissentient Hindu sects to whom the practice of caste should be anathema and today we find that practitioner of other religious faiths and Hindu dissentients are sometimes as rigid adherents to the system of caste as the conservative Hindus.

Class poverty, not individual poverty, is the primary test. Other ancillary tests are the way of life, the standard of living, the place in the social hierarchy, the habits and customs, etc. Despite individual exceptions, it may be possible and easy to identify social backwardness with reference to caste, with reference to residence, with reference to occupation or some other dominant feature. Notwithstanding our antipathy to caste and sub-regionalism, these are facts of life which cannot be wished away. If they reflect poverty which is the primary source of social and educational backwardness, they must be recognised for what they are along with other less primary sources. There is and there can be nothing wrong in recognising poverty wherever it is reflected as an identifiable group phenomena whether it is seen as a caste group, a sub-regional group, an occupational group or some other class. Once the relevant factors are taken into consideration, how and where to draw the line is a question for each State to consider since the economic and social conditions differ from area to area. Once the relevant conditions are taken into consideration and the backwardness of a class of people is determined, it will not be for the court to interfere in the matter. But lest there be any misunderstanding, judicial review will not stand excluded.

Justice A.P. Sen observed that economic backwardness is only one of the tests to determine social and educational backwardness. If that test were to be the sole criterion of social and educational backwardness, the reservation for the advancement of such classes to special treatment under Art. 15(4) would fail. The predominant and the only factor for making special provisions under Art. 15(4) or for reservations of posts and appointments under Art. 16(4) should be poverty, and caste or a sub-caste or a group should be used only for purposes of identification of persons comparable to Scheduled Castes or Scheduled Tribes, till such members of backward classes attain a state of enlightenment and there is eradication of poverty amongst them and they become equal partners in a new social order in our national life.

Since the problems pertaining to reservation can never be resolved through litigation in the Courts, the Central Government should consider the feasibility of appointing a permanent National Commission for Backward Classes which must constantly carry out sociological and economic study from State to State and from region to region within a State. The framers of the Constitution by enacting Art. 340 clearly envisaged the setting up of such a high powered National Commission for Backward Classes at the Centre.

The doctrine of protective discrimination embodied in Art. 15(4) and 16(4) and the mandate of Art. 29(2) cannot be stretched beyond a particular limit. The State exists to serve its people. There are some services where expertise and skill are of the essence. In such services or posts under the Union or States there can be no room for reservation of posts; merit alone must be the sole and decisive consideration for appointments.

Justice E.S.Venkataramiah observed that the questions have to be tackled with sympathy for persons who are really in need of the benign assistance at the hands of the State and with due regard to the interests of the general public.

It is now necessary to redetermine the question of backwardness of the various castes, tribes and communities for purposes of Art. 15(4) and Art. 16(4) in the light of the latest figures to be collected on the various relevant factors and to refix the extent of reservation for backward classes. The reservation of 15 per cent now made under Art. 15(4) and Art. 16(4) but which may be traced to Art, 14 and Art. 16(1) to "special group" based on occupation-cum-income can in any event be availed of by members of all communities and castes. At this stage it should be made clear that if on a fresh determination some castes or communities have to go out of the list of backward classes prepared for Art. 15 (4) and Art. 16 (4), the Government may still pursue the policy of amelioration of weaker sections of the population amongst them in accordance with the directive principle contained in Art. 46 of the Constitution. There are in all castes and communities poor people who if they are given adequate opportunity and training may be able to compete successfully with persons belonging to richer classes. The Government may provide for them liberal grants of scholarships, free studentships, free boarding and lodging facilities, free uniforms, free mid-day meals etc., to make the life of poor students comfortable. The Government may also provide extra tutorial facilities, stationery and books free of cost and library facilities. These and other steps should be taken in the lower classes so that by the time a student appears for the qualifying examination he may be able to attain a high degree of proficiency in his studies.

The judgements cited in the preceding pages lay down broadly the following criteria to determine the test of backwardness:

	Criteria	*No. of Judges*
1.	Poverty as exclusive or predominant test.	3 Judges (Desai. Reddy and Sen, JJ.)
2.	Caste-cum-means or caste as subsidiary test.	2 Judges (Chinnappa Reddy and Venkataramiah, JJ.)
3.	Means test.	1 Judge (Chandrachud, CJ)
4.	Comparability with S.Cs. and S.Ts	1 Judge (Chandrachud, CJ)
5.	Caste as sole or dominant criterion.	No Judge.

The matter is now resting with a 9-Judge Constitution Bench of the Supreme Court of India.

In the meanwhile the Government is seriously considering the criteria recommended by the Chinnappa Reddy Commission's Report set up by the Government of Karnataka. The Chinnappa Reddy Committee submitted its report in 1990: It identified three categories of SEBCs: backward communit-ties, more backward communities and backward occupations (like landless agriculture labourers, construction workers, sweepers, carpenters, cobblers and butchers). Thus, the Reddy formula takes the constitutional concept of SEBCs beyond the caste parameter.

Mr. Justice Chinnappa Reddy further suggested that the candidates belonging to any of these three categories be subjected to an economic test to eliminate the less deserving ones. He made six economic classifications and recommended that no SEBC candidates coming under any of them be entitled to the benefit of reservations.

These economic classifications are:

- Either of whose parents is a Class I or Class II officer in the service of the government or holds an equivalent post in a public sector undertaking or is employed under a private employer and draws a salary which is not less than that of a Class II officer.

- Either of whose parents is a professional i.e. doctor, chartered accountant, income-tax consultant, financial or management consultant, dentist, engineer or architect.
- Both of whose parents are graduates.
- Either of whose parents is an income tax assessee.
- Either of whose parents is a sales tax assessee.
- Either of whose parents or both together own more than eight hectares of rain-fed dry land or its equivalent.

But the Centre's approach differs from the Reddy formula in one important respect. The government has made it clear in the office memorandum of September 1991 that the economic test would be only to give "preference" to the poorer sections among the SEBCs.

The office memorandum said "in case sufficient number of such candidates are not available, unfilled vacancies shall be filled by the other SEBC candidates." Thus, no SEBC candidate is altogether debarred from the reservations.

In a judgement of far-reaching consequences, the Constitution Bench of the Supreme Court by a majority 6:3 verdict noted that the notification issued by the National Front Government in 1990, for providing 27 per cent job quota for Other Backward Classes (OBCs) was enforceable provided the Government removed the economically better off from the list of beneficiaries. The Court struck down the provision of the amended notification issued on September 25, 1991, by which ten per cent posts were reserved for other economically backward sections of the people who were not covered by any of the existing reservation schemes.

The judgement was delivered on November 16, 1992. The Judgement which was delivered by Mr. Justice B.P Jeevan Reddy, directed that reservation in jobs for the socially and educationally backward classes was restricted to employment alone and not for promotions. The six judges expressed similar views. Mr. Justice Reddy maintained the 50 per cent bar on the total reservation of jobs for both Scheduled Castes. and Scheduled Tribes and OBCs.

While 50 per cent should be the rule, the Court said it was not necessary, to ignore certain extraordinary situations inherent in the great diversity of the country and its people.

The court allowed some relaxation in the rule for those living in far-flung areas. The rule of 50 per cent, the judges said, should be applied to each year, it cannot be related to the total strength of the class, category, service or cadre, the court said while cautioning against any abuse of the rule. Maintaining that it was necessary to express any opinion on the correctness and adequacy of the exercise done by the Mandal Commission, which submitted itsreport in 1981, the court said while reservation could not be called anti-Martian, there were certain services, including defence, where it may not be advisable to apply the rule of reservation.

A cross-section of society filed 10 Writ Petitions including some political parties challenging the National Front Government's order to implement, in a phased manner, the recommendations of the MandaI Commission's Report. On October 1, 1990, a five-Judge Bench of the Supreme Court stayed the operation of the Notification following reports of violence and self-immolation by youths who felt threatened on the outcome of the Government's policy.

The court at the outset framed eight questions arising for its consideration. First, whether Art. 16(4) of the Constitution is an exception to Art. 16(1) and would be exhaustive of the right to reservation to posts in services under the State. Article 16(4) stipulates: The State shall make any provision for the reservation of appointments or posts in favour of any backward class of citizens which, in the opinion of the state, is not adequately represented in the services under the State. Article (1) states: there shall be equality of opportunity for all citizens in matters relating to employment of appointment to any office under the State.

Second, what would be the content of the phrase 'backward class' under Art. 16(4) and whether caste by itself constitute a class and, whether economic criterion by itself could identify a class for Art. 16(4) would include the Art. 46 as well.

Third, if the economic criterion could not constitute a backward class whether reservation of posts in services based exclusively on economic criteria would be covered by Art. 16(1).

Fourth, whether the extent of reservation in the posts could exceed 50 per cent in any particular year and whether such an extent could be determined without determining the inadequacy of representation of each class in the different categories and grades of services.

Fifth, whether Art. 16(4) permits the classification of 'backward classes' into backward classes and most backward class or permit classification among them based on economic or other consideration.

Six, whether any provision by the state under Art. 16(4) would necessarily have to be made by the legislature or Parliament. Or could such provisions be made by an executive order.

Seventh, whether the extent of judicial review would be restricted to identification of backward classes.

Lastly, would reservation of appointments in favour of any backward class be restricted to the initial appointment to the post or would it extend to promotions as well. Dealing with each issue independently and after considering the arguments made by counsel for the parties, the majority judgement noted that it was not necessary that the provision under Art. 16(4) should necessarily be made by the legislature or Parliament. Such a provision could made by an executive mandate, the court ruled.

An executive order making a proving under Art. 16(4) would be enforceable the moment it was made, the judges ruled and added that Art. 16(4) is not an exception to Art. 16(1). Similarly, Art. 16(4) is exhaustive of the subject of reservation in favour of backward classes. Reservation could also be extended under Art. 16(1). Such an extension would not be confined to extending of preferences, concessions or exemptions alone, the court said.

Significantly, the judges noted, a caste could be and quite often is a social class in India, if it is socially backward it would be a backward class for the purposes of Art. 16(4), the court ruled. Among non-Hindus, there are several occupational groups, sects and denominations, which for historical reasons are socially backward. They too represent backward social collectives for the purpose of Art. 16(4), the court added. Neither the constitution nor the law prescribes the procedure for identification of backward classes, the court said adding that it would be advisable for it not to recommend method for determination.

The judges said that identification of the backward classes could be determined with reference to caste among and along with, other occupational groups, classes and sections of people. One can start the process either with the occupational groups or with castes or with the occupational groups and with caste or with some other groups, the judges said.

The salient features of the majority judgement are:

(i) Reservations not to exceed 50 per cent;

(ii) No reservations in promotion; and

(iii) No reservations based on economic criteria.

The Supreme Court further directed the Centre, the States and the Union Territories to constitute within four months a permanent body for entertaining, examining and recommending requests for inclusion and complaints of over-inclusion and under-inclusion in the lists of other backward classes of citizens. The Court said that within four months the government should specify the bases, applying the relevant and requisite socio-economic criteria to exclude socially advanced persons and sections from Other Backward Classes. The implementation of the order issued on September 13, 1990, will be subject to exclusion of such socially advanced persons (creamy layer), the judges said.

This direction shall not, however, apply to states where the reservations in favour of backward classes are already in operation. They can continue to operate them. Such states shall, however, evolve the criteria within six months from today and apply the same to exclude the socially advanced persons and sections from the designated other backward classes, the judgement said.

The judges said any objection to the criteria that might be evolved by the government and the states in pursuance of the directions as well as to the classifications among backward classes and equitable distribution of the benefits of reservations among them should be preferred only before the Supreme Court.

While this historic judgement directs the skimming off the creamy layer, to set right the distortions that have crept into the reservation system with the beneficiaries who have long outgrown the need for special treatment still clamouring for and enjoying the privileges, the court has entered an intriguing caveat by calling upon the governments at the Centre and the States, to set up commissions both to include more groups in the list of backward classes and to exclude those among them which are socially advanced. The judgement, instead of helping the caste system to wither off, may foster the same, as the proposed commissions will in effect continue the work of the Mandal Commission.

5

The Dalits

According to scholar statesman and the late President S. Radha Krishnan, Manu had based his chaturvarna concept of priest teacher, warrior, businessman and worker with a view to accord equal status, equal prestige and equal value to all sections of the society but winds of change and waves of history turned function based Chaturvarna into heredity based the jajmani system that ultimately turned out to be the greatest curse for the country. Of all the sections the shudras, once put on the lowest rung of the social hierarchy were destined to suffer all types of deprivations. These untouchables and depressed classes came to be designated as Scheduled Castes-the term appeared for the first time in the Government of India Act 1935. In April 1936, the British Government had issued the Government of India (Scheduled Castes) order, 1936 specifying certain castes, races and tribes as scheduled castes in the provinces of Assam, Bengal, Bihar, Mumbai, Central provinces and Berar, Chennai, Orissa, Punjab and United Provinces.

Under Article 341 of the Constitution, certain backward classes/communities suffering from untouchability and social disabilities were declared as scheduled castes. After the Constitution came into force, the list of scheduled castes was notified under the Constitution (Scheduled Castes) Order 1950 by the President of India. So far 15 President orders specifying

Scheduled Castes and Scheduled Tribes for various states and Union territories have been issued. Any amendment to the existing list of scheduled castes/scheduled tribes is made by a Parliamentary enactment on the part of the Government, no definition of a Scheduled Caste or a Tribe has even been given. Only at the pleasure of authorities a community becomes a Scheduled Caste or a Scheduled Tribe. No wonder, a community having some socio-cultural-economic characteristics is a Scheduled Caste or a Tribe in one state/UT but not in other. Not only that on purely political considerations, some communities on the advice of some, sociologists have been scheduled to draw benefits whereas the Ladakhis, totally similar to their neighbours in Himachal Pradesh have ultimately resorted to violence to get themselves scheduled. By 1971 there were 612 Scheduled Castes in India.

Position of the Community

According to 1981 census, the Scheduled Castes and Scheduled Tribes constitute 15.47 per cent and 7.85 per cent respectively of the total population of the country. In other words, Harijans and 'Girijans' that is, Tribes, constitute about one fourth of the country's population. The major concentration of Scheduled Castes is in Uttar Pradesh (22.3 per cent) followed by West Bengal (11.46%), Bihar (9.8%), Tamil Nadu (8.48%), Andhra Pradesh (7.6%); Madhya Pradesh (7.02%), Rajasthan (5.57%), Karnataka (5.34%), Punjab (4.31%), Maharashtra (4.28%), Kerala (2.43%), Haryana (2.35%), Gujarat (2.33%), Himachal Pradesh (1.01%), Jammu and Kashmir (0.47%), Tripura (0.30%), Sikkim (0.02%) and Manipur (0.2%);

In Nagaland, Andaman and Nicobar Islands and Lakshadweep there are no Scheduled Castes and in Meghalaya, Arunachal Pradesh, Dadra and Nagar Haveli and Mizoram their number is very insignificant.

An overwhelming number of the Harijans (88 per cent) resides in the countryside. Although until recent past, a Harijan dreaded to move out of his moorings, but owing to agricultural development (particularly the Green Revolution) in some parts of the country, industrial progress in certain regions, rapidly expanding urbanisation and the breaking of the jajmani system as also the steeply declining demand for rural good prepared by artisans, the

Harijans have become quite a mobile class. About 52 per cent of all scheduled caste workers are agricultural labourers and 28 per cent are small and marginal farmers, and share croppers. In the western part of the country, almost all weavers are from Scheduled Castes and in the eastern part of the country almost all fishermen are from the Scheduled Castes. Unclean occupations like scavenging, flaying, tanning etc are almost entirely left to the Scheduled Castes. In the urban areas a substantial proportion of rickshaw pullers, cart pullers, construction labourers, beedi workers and other unorganised non-agricultural wage labourers and civic sanitation workers belong to Scheduled Castes. They are amongst the poorest of those who live below the poverty line.

Although there are have-nots and downtrodden among other sections of the populace, the major chunk of the deprived section of India's population that is living in object poverty, abnormal ignorance and unparallelled superstition comes from the Scheduled Castes. Among deprived people top, it was the Harijans who for centuries lived practically the life of servitude, humiliation and utter helplessness.

Statutory Provisions

The Constitution prescribes protection and safeguards for the scheduled castes and scheduled tribes, and other weaker sections either specially or by way of insisting on their general rights as citizens with the object of promoting their educational and economic interests and of removing the social disabilities. The main safeguards are:

(i) the abolition of untouchability and the forbidding of its practice in any form (Art. 17);

(ii) the promotion of their educational and economic interests and their protection from social injustice and all forms of exploitation (Art. 46);

(iii) the throwing open by law of Hindu religious institutions of a public character to all classes and sections of Hindus (Art. 25b);

(iv) to removal of any disability, liability, restriction or condition with regard to access to shops, public restaurants, hotels and places of public entertainment or the use of wells, tanks, bathing ghats, roads and places of public resort maintained wholly or partially out of state funds or dedicated to the use of the general public [Art. 15(2)];

(v) the curtailment by law in the interest of any scheduled tribes of the general rights of all citizens to move freely, settle in and acquire property [Art. 19(5)];

(vi) the forbidding or any denial of admission to educational institutions maintained by the state or receiving grant out of State funds [Art. 29(2)];

(vii) permitting the State to make reservation for the backward classes in public services in case of inadequate representations and requiring the State to consider the claims of the scheduled castes and scheduled tribes in the making of appointments to public services (Arts. 16 and 335);

(viii) special representation in the Lok Sabha and the State Vidhan Sabhas to Scheduled Castes and Tribes till 25 January 2000 (Articles 330, 332 and 334); the setting up of Tribes Advisory Councils and separate departments in the State and the appointment of a special officer at the centre to promote their welfare and safeguard their interests (Arts. 164 and 338 and Fifth Schedule);

(ix) special provision for the administration and control of scheduled and tribes areas (Article 244 and Fifth and Sixth schedules); and prohibition of traffic in human beings and forced labour (Article 23).

Elected Leaders

Under Articles 330 and 332 of the Constitution, seats are reserved for scheduled castes and scheduled tribes in the Lok Sabha and State Legislative Assemblies, in proportion to their population. This concession, initially for a period of 10 years from the commencement of the Constitution, has been extended through amendments upto 25 January 2000. Parliamentary Acts provide for such reservation in the Union Territories having legislatures. There is no reservation of seats in Rajya Sabha and Vidhan

Parishads. The enclosed table gives detail of their representation in the Lok Sabha and the Vidhan Sabhas.

Following the introduction of Panchayati Raj, safeguards have been, provided for proper representation of members of scheduled castes and tribes by reserving seats for them in the gram panchayats and other local bodies.

Benefits of Reservation

Article 335 of the Constitution provides that the claims of the members of scheduled castes and scheduled tribes shall be taken into consideration, consistent with the maintenance of efficiency of administration, in making appointment to posts and services, in connection with the affairs of the Union or the state. Article 16 (4) permits reservations in favour of citizens of backward classes, who may not be adequately represented in services. In pursuance of these provisions, the Government has made reservation for scheduled castes and scheduled tribes in the services under their control.

For the scheduled castes, reservation is 15 per cent of the vacancies for which recruitment is made by open competition on all India basis and 16-2/3 per cent of the vacancies to which recruitment is made on All India basis otherwise than by open competition for the scheduled tribes, the reservation is 75 per cent in both cases. Reservation in direct recruitment to Group C and D posts, which normally attract candidates from Cine locality or region is fixed in proportion to the population of Scheduled Castes and tribes in the respective states and union territories:

Reservation is also made at 15 per cent of the vacancies for the Scheduled Castes and 7.5 per cent for the Scheduled Tribes in promotions on the result of the competitive examinations limited to departmental candidates in Group B, C and D and to the lowest rung of Group A in grades or services to which direct recruitment, if any, does not exceed 66-2/3 per cent. Reservation has been provided for Scheduled Castes and Scheduled Tribes in promotion on the basis of seniority subject to fitness in Group A, B, C and D posts in Grades or services to which direct recruitment if any, does not exceed 66-2/3 per cent.

To facilitate their adequate representation, concessions such as relaxation of age limit, standard of suitability, qualification regarding experience in the case of direct recruitment only, wherever necessary and inclusion of scientific and technical posts upto the lowest grade of Group. A required for research in the scheme of reservations, have been provided for. Simultaneously, with notification to employment exchanges or advertisements in newspapers, vacancies reservations. For scheduled castes and scheduled tribes in Group C and D (Class III and IV) posts are announced over the stations of all India Radio located in areas having a concentration of scheduled castes and scheduled tribes population, notified to the voluntary associations of scheduled castes and scheduled tribes enlisted for this purpose and to the Directors of SC/ST Welfare of the States and Union Territories. Vacancies filled through the Union Public Service Commission otherwise than through examination, are advertised on the first occasion as exclusively reserved for scheduled castes/scheduled tribes and are re-advertised if the first advertisement is infructuous. After the second advertisement, other community candidates can also be considered, if no, scheduled castes/tribes candidates still become available. Reservations for scheduled castes and scheduled tribes (including vacancies carried forward) is subject to the ceiling of 50 per cent of the total number of vacancies, This scheme of reservations is also being followed by the public sector undertakings. The voluntary agencies, which are in receipt of substantial grants-in-aid from the Government, are also required as a condition to adopt certain specific features of the reservation scheme in their establishments, The government was examining the feasibility of directing the private sector undertakings to reserve seats for SC/ST.

Annual statements are required to be submitted by the recruiting authorities for scrutiny by the Government. For ensuring implementation of the special representation orders, liaison officers have been appointed in different ministries of the Central Government.

State Governments have also framed rules under the power given to them by item 41 of the State list of the Seventh Schedule to the Constitution for the reservation of posts for these classes and have taken steps to increase their representation in the state services. Reservation in State Government services, however, is under the exclusive jurisdiction of the State Governments.

Welfare Officials

Article 338 of the Constitution provides for the appointment of a Special Officer for the Scheduled Castes and Scheduled Tribes who is charged with the duty to investigate all matters relating to the safeguards provided for the Scheduled Castes and Scheduled Tribes under the Constitution and to report to the President upon the working of these safeguards at prescribed intervals. In pursuance thereto, a Special Officer, commonly known as Commissioner for Scheduled Castes and Scheduled Tribes, is appointed by the President from time to time. Considering the magnitude of the problem, the Government was of the view that in addition to the functioning and authority of the Special Officer, these matters should appropriately be entrusted to a high level Commission consisting of persons of eminence and status in public life. The functioning of the Commission would not be lessening the authority of the Special Officer.

Government had accordingly decided to set up a Commission for this purpose which was to consist of a Chairman and not more than four other Members, including the Special Officer appointed under Article 338 of the Constitution. The term of office of the Chairman and the Members of the Commission would not ordinarily exceed three years. The headquarters of the Commission would be located at New Delhi.

The functions of the proposed Commission would broadly correspond with the functions fit present, entrusted to the Special Officer under Article 338 of the Constitution and would be as follows:

(i) To investigate all matters relating to safeguards provided for Scheduled Castes and Scheduled Tribes in the Constitution. This should inter alia, include a review of the manner in which reservations stipulated in public services for Scheduled Castes and Scheduled Tribes are in practice, implemented.

(ii) To study the implementation of protection of Civil Rights Act, 1955, with particular reference to the objective of removal of untouchability and individual discrimination arising there from within a period of five years.

(iii) To ascertain the socio-economic and other relevant circumstances accounting for the commission of offences against persons belonging to Scheduled Castes or Schedule Tribes with a view to ensuring the removal of impediments in the laws in force and to recommend appropriate remedial measures including measures to ensure prompt investigation of the offences.

(iv) To enquire into individual complaints regarding denial of any safeguards provided to any person claiming to belong to Scheduled Castes or Scheduled Tribes.

The Commission would devise its own procedure in the discharge of its functions. All the Ministries and Departments of the Government of India would furnish such information and documents and provide such assistance as may be required by the Commission.

From time to time the Government of India trusts that the State Governments and Union Territory Administrations and others concerned will extend their fullest cooperation and assistance to the Commission.

The Commission would submit an annual report to the President detailing its activities and recommendations. This would however, not preclude the Commission from submitting reports to the Government at any time they consider necessary on matters within their scope of work. The Annual Report together with a memorandum outlining the action taken on the recommendations and explaining. The reasons for non-acceptance of recommendations, if any, in so far as it relates to the Central Government will be laid before each House of Parliament.

The Commission was set up in 1978. It is assisted by a Secretariat with headquarters at Delhi and seventeen field offices located in the States. Twelve of the field offices are headed by Directors and five by Deputy Directors. The Secretariat is headed by an officer of the rank of Secretary to Government.

The Commission for Scheduled Castes and Scheduled Tribes has been renamed as National Commission for Scheduled Castes and Scheduled Tribes. It will function as an Advisory Body on broad issue to policies and levels of development of the SCs and STs. It shall consist of a Chairman and not more than eleven other members and may include experts in the field of social anthropology, social work and other related social sciences. The terms and conditions of the Chairman and the Members shall be as determined by the Government in each case, provided that their term of office shall not normally exceed three years. The functions of the National Commission for Scheduled Castes and Scheduled Tribes will be as follows :

(i) To study the extent and ramifications of untouchability and social discrimination arising therefrom and effectiveness of the present measures and recommend further measures to be taken;

(ii) To study socio-economic and other relevant circumstances leading to the Commission of offences against persons belonging Scheduled Castes and Scheduled Tribes; and to recommend appropriate remedial measures to ensure prompt investigation of such offences;

(iii) To make studies on different aspects of development to the Scheduled Castes and Scheduled Tribes with a view to ensuring integration of these groups with the main stream of the society in all aspects. These would include studies in the field of socio-economic development, education, commerce, trade, art, literature, language, housing, communication, agriculture, forestry, horticulture, fisheries, rehabilitation, pollution and environment; and

(iv) Such other functions as may be entrusted to the National Commission for Scheduled Castes and Scheduled Tribes in evolving general policies relating to any aspect of development of the Scheduled Castes and Scheduled Tribes as may be thought proper by the Central Government.

Union Government's Role

Post-matric Scholarships for Scheduled Castes and Scheduled Tribes Students : The Post matric Scholarships scheme is the most important Centrally sponsored scheme meant for providing financial assistance to Scheduled Caste and Scheduled Tribe students to enable them to pursue post-matriculate education. All eligible Scheduled Caste and Scheduled Tribe students whose parents/guardian's satisfy the means of test prescribed under the rules are entitled to scholarship on admission to any recognised educational institutions. The scheme is implemented by the State Governments/Uniỏn Territory Administrations according to the rules framed by the Government of India and ,the students get the scholarship through the Government of State to which the students belong irrespective of the place of study. The scholarships are sanctioned on a year to year basis.

Under the scheme, the level of expenditure reached in the last year of each plan stands committed on the part of States/Union Territories and is borne by them out of their own funds. The Central Government assist the States/Union Territories financially by reimbursing the expenditure over and above the committed liability. The committed liability for all the State Governments/ Union Territories Administrations during the Seventh Plan is Rs 88.53 crores. Starting with a meagre 114 awards to the Scheduled Caste students in 1944-45 and 89 to Scheduled Tribes in 1948-49, the number of awards in 1985-86 for these two categories together stood at 10 lakhs and had gone upto 12 lakhs by the end of 1987-88.

The question of enhancement of rates of maintenance allowance, upward revision in the means test etc, had been engaging the attention of the Government of India for quite some time. A high level Official Committee under the Chairmanship of the Additional Secretary in the Ministry with representatives from the Ministry of Human Resource Development, Finance and Planning Commission set up to review the scheme has submitted its report. The recommendations made by the Committee are under active consideration.

Pre-matric Scholarships for the Children of those Engaged in Unclean Occupations : The main object of this scheme is to provide good quality of education to the children of those engaged in unclean occupations viz. Scavenging, flaying, tanning and sweepers who have traditional link with the job of scavenging by keeping them in hostels away from unhygienic surroundings in which their parents live. Under this scheme a scholarship of Rs 200/-per month per child is given to the students studying in classes VI to VII and Rs 250/ per month per child to classes IX to X. Provision is also made of providing hostel buildings on rent where government accommodation is not available. Provisions are also made to appoint full time hostel warden where the number of students are more than 20, otherwise one of the school teachers is appointed as hostel warden for some extra remuneration. During the year 1986-87 a central assistance of Rs 13.12 lakh was sanctioned to various States/Union Territories over and above the committed expenditure under this scheme. For the year 1987-88 a provision of Rs 2 crores was made. The number of beneficiaries under this scheme during 1986-87 was 894.

Books Banks for Scheduled Caste/Tribes Students Studying in Medical and Engineering Colleges : This scheme is intended for Scheduled Caste and Scheduled Tribe students pursuing Medical and Engineering degree courses in the country. Under this scheme Central assistance is given to the State Governments/Union Territories on 50:50 basis for establishment of books banks for Scheduled Caste/Tribe students. Under this scheme a set of text books is given to a group of three students. The life period of a set is fixed for three years. During the year 1986-87 Central assistance of Rs 46.56 lakhs was sanctioned to various States/ Union Territories for 19,631 scheduled caste/tribe students as against an outlay of Rs 55 lakhs. For the year 1987-88 a provision of Rs 55 lakhs was made for this scheme.

Girls Hostels Scheme for Scheduled Castes : Under this scheme Central assistance is provided to the State Governments/Union Territories administration on 50:50 basis for the construction of hostel buildings to provide hostel facilities to the girls belonging to Scheduled Castes studying in middle, high, higher secondary school, colleges and universities Central assistance is also given to the Voluntary Organisations through the concerned State Governments for the needful extension of existing hostel buildings but not for the construction of new hostels. In this case of 10 per cent of the total cost is to be borne by the grantee organisations and remaining 90 percent is to be shared between Central and State Government on 50:50 basis. Upto 100 inmates can be accommodated in each hostel out of which 10 per cent seats are reserved for non-scheduled castes/tribes. During the year 1986-87 an amount of Rs 3.15 crores was sanctioned as Central Assistance to various States/Union Territories. A provision of Rs 3.50 crores was made for this scheme during the year 1987-88. The physical achievements during the year 1986-87 was 143 hostels for 7,204 inmates.

Coaching and Allied Scheme for Scheduled Castes and Scheduled Tribes : In order to improve the representation of Scheduled Castes and Scheduled Tribes in various posts and services under the Central Government and public undertakings, the Ministry of Welfare has taken up a Centrally sponsored programme of coaching and allied scheme. Under this scheme pre-examination coaching facilities are provided to the Scheduled Caste and. Scheduled Tribe candidates who intend to appear for the various competitive examinations held by the U.P.S.C., Staff Selection Commission, State Public Service Commission and other recruiting agencies. At present more that 80 coaching centres are being run. Central Assistance is also given to the State Governments, and Union Territories for coaching centres on 50:50 basis. According to Mrs. Dr. Rajendra Kumari Bajpai, former Minister of State for Welfare the government had also decided to provide coaching facilities for examinations for entrance to medical and engineering institutions with effect from 1999.

During the year 1986-87 a central assistance of Rs 35 lakhs was given to State Governments/Union Territories and for the year 1987-88 a provision of Rs. 52 lakhs was made for this scheme.

Scheduled Castes Development Corporation : The Scheduled Castes Development Corporations in the States envisage providing an interface between, Scheduled Castes families and financial institutions in respect of bankable scheme of economic development. Eighteen states and three Union Territories with a sizeable population of Scheduled Castes, have set up Scheduled Castes Development Corporations. The Government of India provides assistance to States for share capital investment in their Corporations at the rate of 49 per cent against States share at the rate of 51 per cent and this has helped the Corporations in expanding their activities.

The Third National Conference of Scheduled Castes Development Corporations was convened at Delhi in April 1987 jointly by the Ministry of Welfare and the Agricultural Finance Corporation. The participants in the conference included Secretaries of State Social Welfare/Scheduled Castes Welfare Departments, Managing Directors and other Senior Officers of Scheduled Castes Development Corporations, representatives of Reserve Bank of India, State Bank of India, NABARD, Deposit Insurance and Credit Guarantee Corporation (DICGC) and Banking Institutions, Ministry of Welfare and the Department of Rural Development, the Commission for Scheduled Castes and Scheduled Tribes, Office of the Commissioner for scheduled castes and scheduled tribes. The theme of the conference was the New Pattern of Assistance (NPA) for the Economic Development of Scheduled Castes families through Scheduled Castes Development Corporations which was evolved as an alternative to the Margin Money Loan Pro-gramme.

Aid to Voluntary Organisations for Scheduled Castes : Under this scheme Central Assistance is provided on 100 per cent basis to the voluntary organisations of All India character who are engaged in the welfare of Scheduled Castes and Scheduled Tribes. A central grant-in-aid of Rs 80.40 lacs was released to 13 voluntary organisations during the year 1986-87, and an outlay of Rs 1 crore was made for this scheme for the year 1987-88.

National Overseas Scholarships : The scheme of National Overseas Scholarships is a non-plan scheme for enabling the candidates belonging to the Scheduled Castes/Scheduled Tribes, Denotified, Nomadic and Semi-Nomadic Tribes to go abroad for higher education for Post-graduate studies leading to Ph.D. and Post-doctoral Research etc. in Engineering Technology and other subjects for which adequate facilities are not available in the country.

Crimes against Scheduled Castes : The problem of crimes against scheduled castes and their protection has been continuously engaging the attention of the Government of India. This comes out of the fact that the members of Scheduled Castes are particularly in a weak and vulnerable position and hence deserve special consideration. In pursuance of this policy, comprehensive guidelines covering precautionary and preventive measures are formulated and communicated to the States for necessary action. A number of States have reported inter-alia, that the following measures and steps have been taken or are proposed to be taken to eliminate the phenomenon of crimes against Scheduled Castes and also to ensure a sense of confidence and security amongst them:

(i) Machinery has been geared up in order that the States may apprise themselves of disputes of land, wages, etc, concerning Scheduled Castes;

(ii) All efforts will be made to see that they are put in effective possession of lands belonging to them or allotted to them and enabled to carry cultivation without any hindrance and that the land reforms machinery in the states/Union territories will be made aware of their responsibilities particularly in respect of protection of tenants and distribution of ceiling surplus lands.

(iii) Police authorities in States have been specifically instructed to intervene in instances of criminal trespass into lands belonging to Scheduled Castes by others. Besides, they are under orders to treat serious cases of crimes against them as Special Report cases, register the complaints promptly and start investigation forthwith and to arrange for quick trial with efficient prosecution with a view to ensuring deterrent punishment to be awarded to the offenders.

(iv) Machinery has been set up to ensure that the agricultural labourers get wages not less than the statutory minimum wages for them.

(v) High level revenue and police officers have been instructed to go to the spot for resolving the disputes in a manner fair to the Scheduled Castes. They have been entrusted with the responsibilities to supervise the steps for the apprehension of the culprits and keep a watch on the progress of investigation etc.

(vi) In order to ensure quick disposal of the cases registered, special Courts have been set up. These courts are functioning in the States of Andhra Pradesh, Bihar, Madhya Pradesh, Rajasthan and Tamil Nadu. The State Government of Uttar Pradesh has issued instructions to nominate one Magistrate in each district to hear PCR Act cases.

(vii) The States of Gujarat, Haryana, Himachal Pradesh, Karnataka, Maharashtra, Orissa, Uttar Pradesh and West Bengal have accepted the standing scheme for relief/ compensation to SC/ST victims of crimes and have adopted the enhanced scale recommended by the Commission for SCs/STs. While the States of Andhra Pradesh, Bihar, Madhya Pradesh, Rajasthan have accepted the scheme with some modification, the States of Kerala and Tamil Nadu have drawn up schemes of laying down different rates of compensation. The State of Punjab is considering the proposed scheme.

(viii) Eleven police stations in Bihar and seven sub-police stations in Madhya Pradesh have been set up exclusively to register cases of crimes against Scheduled Castes.

(ix) High ranking officers have been made personally responsible for prompt and effective action.

(x) While an official tours, the officers have been specifically instructed to spend a good part of their time in residential areas of SCs in the villages.

(xi) In most of the States, Special Scheduled Castes, cells have been set up under DIG with a complement of staff to ensure that crimes against SCs are properly registered, promptly and correctly investigated and expeditiously prosecuted.

(xii) In most of the States, State level Committees, under the Chairmanship of the Chief Ministers have been set up to look after the aspects concerning welfare of Scheduled Castes.

The State Governments of Bihar, Gujarat, Haryana, Karnataka, Punjab, Madhya Pradesh and Maharashtra have identified a total of 48 districts as sensitive from the point of view of crimes against Scheduled Castes. The information regarding postings of SC/ST officers as District Magistrates, Sup. of Police, Sub Divisional Magistrates and Sub-Divisional Police Officers is also collected from the State Governments from time to time with a view to assess the action taken on the advice of the Union-Home Ministry earlier given to States in this regard.

Legal Protection

In pursuance of Section 14 A of the PCR Act, Government of India provide matching assistance to the States for the strengthening of machinery for the effective enforcement of PCR Act and Liberation of Scavengers by converting dry latrines into water-borne latrines in the whole town approach basis and rehabilitation of liberated scavengers in alternative occupations. During 1986-87, the Central Government had released an amount of Rs 8.57 crores to 16 states for improving and strengthening the provisions of the PCR Act, 1955 including the scheme of liberating of scavengers. Assistance has been provided to 121 towns in 16 States of liberation of scavengers since 1980-81. So far 25 towns in 11 states have been made scavenging free towns by conversion of dry latrines into water borne ones. For speedy trial of untouchability offences, special courts or special mobile courts have been set up in different states. Eight such courts in Rajasthan, 17 in Andhra Pradesh, 11 in Madhya Pradesh, 8 in Tamil Nadu and 4 each in Orissa and Bihar States have been set up. Officers have also been appointed in 19 states to man special Cell/squads for initiating or exercising supervision over prosecution of PCR Act cases. Committee with official and non-official members in 18 States have been set up to review/supervise the working and implementation of PCR Act, 1955. A provision of Rs 11 crores was made for this scheme during 1987-88.

In Great Leader's Memory

The 99th birth anniversary of Dr. B.R. Ambedkar, the great son of India, the Chairman of the Drafting Committee of the Constitution of India, the greatest champion of the cause of the downtrodden, the mesiah of the Scheduled Castes and Scheduled Tribes on April 13, 1990. The Government concerned the highest civil award of the country "Bharat Ratna" on Baba Saheb posthumously and put his portrait in the central hall of Parliament in recognition of his services in nation building and upliftment of the downtrodden and declared that the centenary year of Baba Saheb would be observed as the Year of Social Justice. Mr V.P. Singh, the Prime Minister of India had also announced the intention of the National Front government to include all the laws geared towards social justice in the Ninth Schedule of the Constitution so that their implementation was ensured. There were more than 59 laws enacted by the various states which were yet to be implemented. In order to rid these laws of any interference in implementation, a Bill will be introduced in Parliament to make them free from the hurdle of judicial review. The Prime Minister also announced that constitutional status was being conferred on the SC/ST Commission, referred to the introduction of a Bill aimed at providing an all the SC/ST benefits to the neo-Buddhists and resolve of the government to fill the SC-ST quota in civil services within a years.

Various State Governments had also launched welfare programmes for the Scheduled Castes/Scheduled Tribes and other Voucherable sections of society as a part of the continently celebrations. For example, the Kerala Government had announced a package of time bound programmes -more educational and housing facilities and rehabilitation of the freed SC/ST labourers, financial assistance for continued education of Scheduled Castes. Tribes students who had failed in the pre-degree examinations, incentives to students with special talent in sports and arts, encourage to Law graduates to take up practice of law, construction of 30 hostels all over the State to facilitate the education of SC/ ST students. Andhra Pradesh government announced a Rs 100 crore action plan for the welfare of Scheduled Castes and Scheduled Tribe and the appointment of three officers to monitor the scheme in the Telengana, Andhra and Rayalseema region. The speakers at a public meeting held at Jalandhar (Punjab), called for tagging the stipends and scholarships given-to SC/ST students with the price index. The Ambedkar Joint Council at Agra (UP) in one of the several resolutions, demanded declaration of Ambedkar Jayanti as public holiday and nationalisation of land, to end exploitation and atrocities and the implementation of prohibition policy. All these decisions/demands would give a momentum to the welfare programmes of the Scheduled Castes/Scheduled Tribes.

State Governments' Role

Various State Governments/Union Territory Administrations administer a number of programmes for the welfare of scheduled castes and backward classes through their Departments of Welfare of Scheduled Castes and Backward Classes. The Punjab Government Department (Directorate of Welfare of Scheduled Castes and Backward Classes) functions under the supervision of the Director assisted by two Joint Directors, one Deputy Director, one Accounts Officer and three Assistant Directors at the headquarter. District Welfare Officers at district level and 45 Tehsil Welfare Officers at tehsil level and, one lady Welfare Officer incharge of all the Community Centres Training-cum-production Centres in the state.

The Welfare Programmes comprise:

Educational and Training Programme : Pre-matric Coaching to Scheduled Castes Student's grant for the purchase of books and stationery to students studying in 6th to 8th classes; subsidy for the purchase of Law, Medical and Engineering books; Stereography Training; J.B.T./B.Ed. Training; grant to Scheduled Caste girl students studying in post-matric and post-graduate classes; Coaching centres for competitive examinations (centrally sponsored scheme); girls hostels (Centrally Sponsored Scheme); technical training in Industrial trades;

Economic Uplift : Subsidy for the purchase of agricultural lands, stamp duty, houses, wells; Socio-economic survey to identify the families below poverty line under the special Component Plan.

Health, Housing and other Programmes : Legal aid to defend the cases registered under the Untouchability Act and those pertaining to ejectment from land and other immovable property etc. subsidy for construction of Dharmashalas and Chaupals; environmental improvement in Harijans Basties; drinking water wells scheme; subsidy for construction of new houses for sweepers/ scavengers, tanners, etc.; assistance for development of manorial pits; construction of houses for vimukat jaties; community centres and training-cum-production centres for village women; opening of creches/centres for children of working mothers/sweepers and scavengers; employment Cell; Post-matric Scholarship (Centrally Sponsored Scheme).

The Punjab Scheduled Castes Land Development and Finance Corporation was set up in 1970 to undertake the task of economic upliftment of the Scheduled Castes in the State, and was assigned the following functions:

(i) to plan, promote and undertake, on its own or in collaboration with or through such Scheduled Castes organisations or other agencies as may be approved by the Board, Programmes of agricultural development, marketing processing, supply and storage of agricultural produce, small scale industries, building construction, transport and such other business, trade or aciivity as may be approved in this behalf by the State Government.

(ii) provide financial assistance to members of Scheduled Castes or Scheduled Castes organisations by advancing to them in cash or in kind loans including loans under hire purchase system for any of the purpose specified in Clause (i) either directly or through such agency, organisation or institution as may be approved by the Board.

(iii) to give on hire agricultural or industrial machinery or equipment to the members of Scheduled Castes or Scheduled Castes organisations.

(iv) to give grants and subsidies to, and to guarantee loans taken by the member Scheduled Castes or Scheduled Castes organisations.

The State Government has provided the corporation with a capital of Rs. 5.00 crores, enhanced to Rs 10.00 crores in 1979, to Rs 20.00 crores in 1983 and Rs 30.00 crores w.e.f. April, 1985.

The Punjab Backward Classes Land Development and Finance Corpn., popularly known as BACKFINCO was established in 1976 for âmeliorating the lot of those belonging to Backward classes duly notified by the State Government and those belonging to economically weaker sections of the society whose annual family in come from all sources is less than Rs 3,600/-by liberal advancement of financial assistance, either free of interest or nominal rate of interest for various viable, productive and income generating schemes, relating to agricultural development, small scale cottage and village industries etc.

6

The OBC's

The term, "'Backward classes" is used to include Scheduled Castes, Scheduled tribes Denotified Tribes and Other Backward Classes (OBC's)'. These sections of the community have laboured under distinct disadvantages in consequence of the rigid caste-ridden hierarchy prevailed in the past in India's social structure. They have suffered from social and economic disabilities and have come to be known as Backward classes. Whereas the scheduled castes and scheduled tribes are identified as a result of the issue of revised lists under time: scheduled castes and scheduled tribes lists Modification Order, 1956, and the Denotified communities are defined under the Criminal Tribes Act, 1924, the precise definition of Other Backward Classes has eluded so far. It has been fully realised that special arrangements would have to be made for them in order to bring them to a position of equality with other citizens. The Constitution of India therefore provides protection and safeguard for Scheduled Castes, Scheduled Tribes and other Backward Classes either specifically or by way of general rights of citizens with the object of promoting their educational and economic interests and of removing certain special disabilities they were subject to.

Statutory Provisions

The relevant legal provisions are embodied in Part XVI of the constitution of India, which is entitled: "Special provisions relating to certain classes." From these provisions it is evident that in 1950 the Constitution-makers visualised the need to make special provisions only for the following classes: Scheduled Castes and Scheduled Tribes; Anglo-Indian Community; and Socially and Educationally Backward Classes.

For the above three special categories of persons, the Constitution makers provided for different level and types of concessions. For the Scheduled Castes and Scheduled Tribes, under Arts. 330 and 332 seats in the Lok Sabha and Vidhan Sabhas were required to be reserved on the basis of their population. It was envisaged that these reservations of seats would be available for a period of 10 years only. With subsequent amendments to the Constitution, this period has been extended from time to time and these provisions are still in force.

For the Anglo-Indian community, the facility of reservation of seats in the Lok Sabha was also provided to the extent of two seats by nomination by the President, in case he found that this community did not have enough representation. A similar provision was also made for the representation of Anglo-Indians to the Vidhan Sabhas. There is no provision in Part XVI for reservation of seats in legislatures for socially and educationally backward classes.

The other category of special provision under Part XVI relates to appointment to services and posts in connection with the affairs of the Union or of a state of the Scheduled Castes and Scheduled Tribes and the Anglo-Indian community. For the Anglo-Indians, Article 336 provides reservation in the Railways, Customs, Postal and Telegraph services of the Union Government on the same basis as they were available to them immediately before August 15, 1947. These reservations, however, were to be available for a period of two years and were to be reduced every two years by 10 per cent and it was also envisaged that there should be no reservation for them from year 1990 onward. For the Scheduled Castes and Scheduled Tribes, however, Article 335 of the Constitution provides that consistent with the maintenance efficiency of the administration, the claims of the members of the Scheduled Castes and the Scheduled Tribes shall be taken into consideration in the making of appointment to services and posts in connection with the affairs of the Union or of the States. In other words, unlike in the case of Anglo-Indians, there was no fixed quota for the Scheduled Castes and Scheduled Tribes. Secondly, there was no cut-off period of two years or 10 years in the matter of recruitment of Scheduled Castes and Scheduled Tribes to the services and posts. Thirdly, the reservation for Anglo-Indians was to be enforced, irrespective of the effect of it on the efficiency of the administration, but in the case of the Scheduled Castes and Scheduled Tribes their claims for recruitment to public services had to be consistent with the requirement of maintenance of efficiency of administration. Lastly, while the Anglo-Indians could compete on merit and yet enjoy their quota, there was no such facility envisaged for the Scheduled Castes and Scheduled Tribes. Yet another special provision made available for Anglo-Indians by way of added facility, was for educational grants. It may be noted that the Constitution does not make provision for any such facility under. Part XIV for the Scheduled Castes and Scheduled Tribes or for socially and educationally backward classes.

As regards the socially and educationally backward classes now popularly called OBCs, the only special provision for them is under Article 340 of Part XIV of the Constitution which is extracted below:

340-Appointment of a Commission to investigate the conditions of backward classes.

(1) The President may by order appoint a Commission consisting of such persons as he thinks fit to investigate the conditions of socially educationally backward classes within the territory of India and the difficulties under which they labour and to make recommendations as to the steps that should be taken by the Union or any state to remove such difficulties and to improve their condition and as to the grants that should be made for the purpose by the Union or any state and the conditions subject to which such grants should be made and the order appointing such Commission shall define the procedure to be followed by the Commission.

(2) The Commission so appointed shall investigate the matters referred to them and present to the President a report

setting out the facts as found by them and making such recommendations as they think proper.

(3) The President shall cause a copy of the report so presented together with a memorandum explaining the action taken thereon to be laid before each House of Parliament.

The President of India had accordingly appointed a Backward Classes Commission headed by Shri Kaka Saheb Kalelkar in January 1953 under Art. 340 of the Constitution to determine the criteria for treating any sections of the people, other than the Scheduled Castes and Scheduled Tribes, as socially and educationally backward; and in accordance with the criteria thus determined, to prepare a list of such classes. The report of the Commission submitted in March, 1955 disclosed considerable divergence of opinion among its members, but the majority recommended that the basic criterion for identification of the "Other Backward Classes" should be their low social position in the traditional caste hierarchy of Hindu society and accordingly prepared a list of almost 2700 communities, and estimated that 930 of them would alone account for nearly a third of the country's population. The Commission also considered women as a Class to be backward. While placing the report of the Commission before Parliament in September 1956, the Government of India observed that if the bulk of the country's millions were to be regarded as coming within the category of backward classes, no useful purpose would be served by separate enumeration of such classes. Pt. Jawaharlal Nehru was of the view that it is basically wrong to label any section of the people as backward, even if they were so when 90 per cent of the people in the country were backward and poor. It is, therefore, clear that the classes to be specified should be distinctly and palpably more backward socially and educationally than the general rule of the population. Government also endorsed the view expressed by the Chairman of the Commission that acceptance of caste as a criterion of backwardness was not a correct approach and that the remedies suggested on the basis of caste would be worse than the evil of backwardness itself. The Report was rightly shelved by Pt. Nehru as such an approach was bound to lead to compartmentalisation of society.

The Government after finding the controversial recommendations of the Kalelkar Commission unacceptable, decided to undertake further studies to arrive at objective and workable criteria for identifying other backward classes. The Deputy Registrar General of Census was asked to conduct a pilot study of occupations which could be considered backward. But his effort did not yield any useful result because he found it impossible to draw up any precise and complete list of occupations, the members of which could be treated as socially and educationally backward. The Government of India elicited the views of the State Governments on the issue. One State advocated identification of backward areas rather than backward classes. The Planning Commission accepted this concept later on. Some States favoured adoption of economic backwardness as a criterion, while others stuck to their existing caste based lists of other Backward Classes. The Central Government was, however, under no legal compulsion to draw up an all India list of socially and educationally backward classes, and that even if such a list were to be drawn up, the State Governments were free to have their own lists. It was also felt that any further exercise in stratification of the population into special groups and classes would only foster existing divisive tendencies, and run counter to the national objective of establishing a casteless and classless society. The Government of India, therefore, informed the State Governments in 1961 that they had "after careful consideration, decided not to draw up any all-India list of backward classes (other than the existing lists of scheduled castes and scheduled tribes) and while the State Governments had the discretion to choose their own criteria for defining backwardness, it would be better to apply economic tests than to go by caste."

Historically, this concept of backward classes owes its origin to the thesis of Ram Manohar Lohia for upliftment of the castes next downtrodden to Harijans and Adivasis, who are economically worse than the higher strata of society, through land reforms and asset building to improve income of peasants and occupational status of artisans through loans and subsidies to modernise the jobs. He did not have the remotest idea this would degenerate into a short cut and populist vote-catching device of reservations in government jobs.

State Level Position

The position concerning other Backward Classes varies from State to State. At one end, Manipur, Nagaland, Sikkim, Tripura, West Bengal, Arunachal Pradesh, Andaman and Nicobar Islands, Chandigarh, Dadra and Nagar Haveli, Goa, Daman and Diu, Lakshadweep and Mizoram, have not recognised or maintained any official list of other backward classes. Orissa and Delhi had at one time prepared their lists of Other Backward Classes on the basis of caste, but had later on withdrawn them and adopted economic criteria for determining backwardness. The Southern States of Tamil Nadu, Karnataka, Kerala and Andhra Pradesh which contain sizeable numbers of scheduled Castes and other converts to Christianity, as well as groups on the periphery of Hindu society, have always followed a liberal policy towards these groups. They have a caste-wise lists of other backward classes but qualified with a family income limit. Besides scholarships or exemption from fees in schools and colleges, seats are also reserved for these classes in technical institutions. A substantial percentage of vacancies in all state services are also reserved for them to the extent of 25 per cent in Andhra Pradesh, 50 per cent in Tamil Nadu, 48 per cent in Karnataka, 40 per cent in Kerala, 20 per cent in Bihar, 10 per cent (in class III and IV jobs and services) and 5 per cent in Class I and Class-II jobs and services in Gujarat, 42 per cent in Jammu and Kashmir, 5 per cent in Punjab, 15 per cent in Uttar Pradesh. 10 per cent in Haryana and 5 per cent in Himachal Pradesh.

Social Welfare

Various State Governments are also providing some of the facilities like the promotion of education among the other Backward Classes by free education upto higher secondary level; exemption of examination and tuition fee; reservation of seats in educational institutions and holding of adult literacy classes; free supply of text books and clothes; relaxation in minimum qualifying marks at the time of admission; arranging study tours; award of scholarships and stipends; hostel facilities; running of coaching centres and special schools; establishment of mobile schools; and free training in workshops.

During the first three Five Year Plans, the Central Government had made a provision for Rs 1.62 crores (first plan), Rs 5.02 crores (Second Plan), and Rs 6.00 crores (Third Plan) for the welfare of Other Backward Classes and almost all the schemes implemented were in the field of education. And till the end of the Third Five Year Plan, an annual financial provision of Rs 40 lakhs used to be made in the Central Sector for post matric (university level) scholarships awarded on a merit cum means basis. From the Fourth Plan, the scheme had been transferred to the state sector. For the Fifth Year Plan, the total financial outlay for all States was Rs 17.25 crores of which more than two-thirds had been on educational programme, mostly for pre-matric scholarships and provisions of hostel facilities. Economic development schemes on which the expenditure was a little over. Rs 3 crores, included financial assistance in the from of loans and grants to artisans and industrial cooperatives to agriculturists for irrigation wells and purchase of bullocks and implements.

Besides such special assistance earmarked in the backward classes sector of the Central and State Plans, the Other Backward Classes had derived benefits during the fifth Plan from the special rural area programmes such as Programmes of Rural Development mostly in the agricultural sector, Minimum Needs Programme; Drought prone Areas Programme; Small Farmers Development Agencies; Marginal Farmers and Agricultural Labourers Projects; Food for Work Programme; Rural Employment Projects; Milk Production Programme; Rural Electrification Programme; Provision of House-sites for Landless Persons; and Liquidation of Bonded Labour and rural debt which were directed towards raising substantially the per capita monthly consumption of the lowest 30 per cent of the rural populations. In the Sixth Five Year Plan also much greater emphasis had been laid on the improvement of conditions of the families which were below poverty line.

There is no voluntary organisation operating at the national level, which caters exclusively to the Other Backward Classes. Voluntary organisations existing at the State, local and caste level are financially assisted by State Governments. The Government of India were however, affording an annual grant to the servants of India Society, Pune, which assists some other backward classes besides scheduled castes and scheduled tribes in Maharashtra to the Bharatiya Ghumantu Jan (Khana Badosh) Sevak Sangh, New Delhi for the Welfare of nomadic and semi-nomadic tribes, to the Indian Red Cross Society for operating maternity and child welfare services in some of backward areas of Uttar Pradesh (Tehri Garhwal and Jaunsar Bawar and to the Ramakrishna Ashrama, Puri (Orissa) for the maintenance of a hostel where Other Backward Classes students were admitted besides those belonging to Scheduled Castes and Scheduled Tribes.

No plan allocations are now being made by the Central Government for the welfare of Other Backward Classes. The Programmes for their welfare are launched by the respective State Governments/Union Territory administrations but the quantum of funds provided by them for the purpose is very meagre. For instance, Karnataka, Tamil Nadu, Jammu and Kashmir spent only 2.4 per cent, 0.27 per cent and 0.46 per cent respectively of their annual budget of recent years on schemes specifically prepared for the Other Backward classes.

Commission's Significance

It was left to the Janta Government to disturb the hornet's nest in 1978 by again taking up the issue by the appointment of Second Backward Classes Commission headed by Shri B.P. Mandal. The Mandal Commission was to determine the criteria for defining the socially and educationally backward classes. It was to recommend necessary measures for the advancement of the backward classes, so identified. In particular, it was required to examine the desirability or otherwise of making provision for reservation of appointments/posts in favour of these classes who otherwise do not find adequate representation in the public services.

The Commission applied 11 indicators grouped as social educational and economic for identification of the socially and educationally backward classes. It was guided by the thesis that social and educational backwardness would be directly linked with the low status of certain castes in respect of the Hindus, in the case of non-Hindus, all untouchable converts from the Hindu religion and those belonging to occupational groups such as dhobi, teli, jheemar, nai, gujar, kumhar, lohar, darji, and badhai, could be deemed as socially and educationally backward. Of the total population of India 52 per cent belong to these classes. These are other than the Scheduled Castes and Scheduled Tribes who make 22.5 per cent of the total.

The recommendations of the Mandal Commission can be summarised as follows:

1. Twenty seven per cent of the posts in public services should be reserved for OBCs. They do make 52 per cent of the total population yet the reservation quota for them cannot exceed this limit. This is because according to the law as interpreted by the Supreme Court of India, the total quantum of reservations under Articles 15(4) and (16) of the Constitution should be below 50 per cent and as at present, 22.5 per cent of the government jobs are already reserved for the Scheduled Castes (SCs) and Scheduled Tribes (STs) on priority basis of their share in the population.
2. Welfare programmes specially meant for OBCs should be financed by the Government of India in the same manner and to the same event already done in the case of SCs and STs.
3. Radical land reforms should be brought about in States to free small land holders from their heavy dependence on rich peasants for their subsistence.
4. OBCs should be encouraged and helped to set up small scale industries.
5. Special educational schemes, with emphasis on vocational training should be started for OBCs; they should also be given special coaching in technical and professional institutions to enable them to compete with the students from the open quota.

The Commission had submitted its Report to the Government on December 31,1980. It was presented to both the houses of the Parliament on April 30,1982. Even since then there has been a continuous and persistent demand for an outright acceptance, of its recommendations without any further scrutiny. But no government however favourably inclined could accept an additional 27 per cent representation in services to over 3000 castes thus making a total of 52 per cent taking into account the already existing reservation for Harijans and Adivasis. That is why the then Congress government even though keen to exploit this populist measure had to refer the report to a committee of Secretaries who found it full of infirmities and inconsistencies fraught with adverse consequences for the social fabric of the country. Most of the Chief Ministers also expressed their views against this caste and out caste based approach to backwardness and felt that in varying and different conditions from state to state (and in fact most of them having evolved a policy already providing reservations to backward classes -Andhra, Tamil Nadu, Karnataka, Gujarat, Maharashtra, U.P., Bihar allow 20 to 25 per cent reservation), there was no need of a Central scheme and the matter be left to the states. Mr V.P. Singh's action to refer the report to a Cabinet Committee, headed by Mr Devi Lal and the latter's resignation should be viewed in the context of controversies surrounding the report militating against its outright acceptance in totality.

Announcement for Implementation of the Report : National Front had promised in its poll manifesto to implement the Mandal Commission Report. But the, ruling party leaders had aired conflicting views about it. While both Mr Devi Lal and Mr Chandra Shekhar favoured the idea of imparting an economic basis to reservation in educational institutions and government jobs, Uttar Pradesh Chief Minister Mulayam Singh Yadav swore by the caste label alone. Prime Minister Mr V.P. Singh announced, all of sudden the acceptance of the Mandal Report on August 7,1990 in the Parliament without taking into confidence even his own Cabinet colleagues for reasons of political expediency to offset the political mileage that Mr Devi Lal could gain by convening the Kisan Sammelan at New Delhi on August 9,1990 immediately after his dismissal from the office of the Deputy Prime Minister. This miscalculated move of Mr V.P. Singh had alienated his senior most colleagues, provoked the Bharatiya Janta Party and C.P.M. to denounce publicly this decision, antagonised the bureaucracy and upset his sympathetic constituents academics, journalists, students and lawyers who were openly demanding his resignation Mr. Vasant Sathe and Dr. Karan casteist carnage.

The student community that had been seriously hit by the implementation of the Report had launched a massive movement throughout the country and initially brought the government to a collapsing point. The anger and anguish of the student was manifesting itself in protest rallies, violence, clashes with the police, hijacking and burning of buses and private property and even self-immolation in an unprecedented manner. The student had succeeded in mobilising the support of various professional bodies and unions who were openly denouncing Mr. V.P. Singh retro-gessive move that would upset the social balance and cohesiveness of our society.

The anti-reservationists had reached a new peak of frenzied violence especially in New Delhi, Chandigarh, Jammu, Jaipur and many other cities of north India. It had been reported that a larger number of students had self-immolated themselves several died and hundred of students injured on account of police repression and indiscriminate firings. The harrowing incidents had naturally sent shock waves all round and the deep and anguished voices were openly articulated in the print media by political leaders and sensitive people.

A Critique of the Report : There seems to be no rationable behind the commitment of the National Front government at the Centre to implement the much maligned and highly controversial recommendations of the Mandal Commission; it is only the political compulsion to win over the vote bank of erstwhile Lok Dal, consisting of middle peasantry in rural areas, Ahirs, Yadavs, Kurmis and traditional artisans both in urban and rural areas. They constitute 40 to 50 per cent of the population in U.P. and Bihar. The appointment of the Mandal Commission itself was a politically motivated action and its outcome a hastily drawn up half back-baked report with a clear bias and lacking in any study in depth of serious problem. The main points of criticism of the Report are:

1. The Commission seems to have been carried away by its enthusiasm in inviting castes to come forward with such a claim. Otherwise, how is it that between the Kalelkar commission and 1978 over 1000 have gone "backward" increasing the number from 2700 to over 3700. This has further released forces for population based representation

from among Muslims Jains and Buddhists. In fact, when the report came out, it was demanded that the entire Muslim community, should be declared as "backward" and granted special representation in proportion to its population.

2. The Mandal Commission violates the constitutional provision prohibiting any discrimination based on caste or religion in recruitment to services and goes against the special provisions for Harijans and Adivasis treated as impure and hence ritually excluded by hierarchy-ridden traditional Hindu society.
3. The Mandal Commission, by recommending 27 per cent representation for backward classes has exceeded the 50 per cent limit laid down by Supreme Court including representation for SC and ST. And what a farce of special representation if 70 per cent of population is clubbed as "backward" and keeping floodgates open for more and more castes competing for "backwardness". Why not define the "forward classes" which would be much easier provide special representation to them and leave the rest to the backward castes?
4. The Mandal Commission recommendations open the floodgates of special representation to Muslims, Jains, Buddhists, Christians and so on, leading to disintegration rather than harmony in the society.
5. The Commission has disregarded the observations of the Supreme Court that "social backwardness is a result of poverty to a large extent. Caste and poverty both are relevant to backwardness but neither caste nor poverty alone could be a determining, factor." To illustrate, how could a barber by caste setting up a modern haircutting saloon or a tailor with an up-to-date cutting unit or a dhobi starting a modern laundry be considered "backward"?
6. In fact, changes have taken place by abolition of zamindari, jagirdari and other land reforms as well as liberal loans for self-employed resulting in upper mobility so as to remove all vestiges of "backwardness". Even though

this process is not yet complete, we shall allow this to take a quick forward direction rather than reverse the order by creating vested interest in backwardness just to obtain a few thousand government jobs.

7. A pernicious result of the Mandal Commission recommendations is to create multiple leadership in 4,000 castes to serve the political ends of the parties-serving as vote gatherers, and agents a backward class elite appropriating all concessions to themselves and in the process exploiting their own community.

In October, 1981, the Ministry of Home Affairs had asked for the views of the Commission on certain aspects of the Mandal Commission Report. The Ministry wanted the opinion of the Minorities Commission on the question whether adoption of different criteria for identifying backwardness of classes of people amongst Hindus and non-Hindus is vitiated in law due to discrimination. The Commission held the view that caste could not be made the test of backwardness amongst non-Hindus whose religion does not permit caste classifications. The recommendation of the Mandal Commission appeared to the Commission to be constitutionally unacceptable as they did not disclose justifiable discrimination bearing a rational relationship to the object of such discrimination which should always be removal of backwardness. The Mandal Commission had not appreciated the force of the decisions of the Supreme Court of India in cases such as Balaji's case where poverty was treated as the primary cause of social and educational backwardness. An economic test of backwardness rather than caste-wise classifications even amongst Hindus seemed more just to the Commission.

In the words of an eminent academician, " The Mandal Commission Report is casually and hastily prepared document which is replete with errors of all kinds. In order to give itself a veneer of rationally and objectivity, the Mandal Commission sought to impart to its report a research base, but even a superficial reading would disprove the claim. The caste-data used by the Mandal Commission are based on the census report of 1931. Since then nothing short of a qualitative change has occurred in the Indian scenario but Mandal takes no account of it".

Haryana government had appointed Justice Gurnam Singh Panel to identify the castes which should get the facility of reservation in government jobs. Most of the deputations of various communities and castes pleaded for reservation for members of their respective castes. Jat deputation pleaded that they were still being discriminated against in the rural society. They were not allowed to share a "hokah" with the members of the forward castes. The average land holding among this community was only 2.5 acres. The Jats were under heavy debt and their representation in the IAS and other top services was minimal. The Sainis leaders pleaded that the Sainis were socially educationally and economically most backward. The delegation of Christians requested to entertain their claim for inclusion of Christians among the backward castes.

The deputation of Brahmins however opposed reservation on caste basis. It said the benefit should be extended to all castes and communities on the basis of their economic, educational and social backwardness. It pointed out that the benefit of reservation to certain castes since independence had not proved successful. The system had instead divided society on caste lines.

The Commission had received representations from 63 communities which wanted themselves to be included in the list of other backward classes. Persons, who migrated from Punjab to Haryana recently also wanted to be declared as backward.

The Haryana Cabinet on Jan. 24,1991 accepted with certain modifications the recommendations of the Gurnam Singh Commission, raising the reservation limit in government services and professional institutions in Haryana to 69 per cent, and adding 10 castes to the "other backward classes" (OBC) category. This decision was to be made applicable for recruitment to all jobs from January 26, 1991.

It was decided to recommend to the Central Government that the representation of these backward classes in all-India services etc. Being lower than that in state services, the centre should include them in Mandal Commission list relating to Haryana so that they could get the benefits of reservation in Central Government jobs also.

The Cabinet decided to include Rajputs also in the OBC category in addition to the nine castes recommended by the commission. These are Jats, Jat Sikhs, Gujjars, Sainis, Meos, Ahirs, Rors, Bishnois and Tyagis. With the acceptance of the commission recommendations the purpose for which the commission was set up under the direction of Mr Devi Lal, Deputy Prime Minister was fulfilled. The commission was constituted when Mr Devi Lal was sacked as Deputy Prime Minister by Mr V.P. Singh. In the day of the anti-Mandal agitation no one gave attention to the clever move of the Haryana patriarch.

This decision will have far reaching consequences on government services as the Deputy Prime Minister had been hammering the point that the bureaucracy is dominated by the upper classes and hence they could not feel the pulse of the rural folk. In fact, he had announced even before the submission of the report that these castes would be declared backward by it.

The reservation of 69 per cent will include 5 per cent reservation for the economically backward among the forward classes also. The criteria to determine this was also approved. The commission had suggested that only those owning two hectares or less of dry rainfed land or having an income of Rs 15,000 per year should be included in this. However, the Cabinet while agreeing to the proposal in regard to land modified the criteria of income by raising the limit to Rs 20,000 per year. The Cabinet also did not agree with the recommendation of the commission that Meos should be treated as a separate backward group and that a reservation of 2 per cent should be made for them. It was pointed out that this would amount to violation of the Constitution as reservation could not be given group-wise. Hence Meos were also included in the OBC category along with nine other castes.

At present, there is reservation of 50 per cent (20 per cent for the Scheduled Castes, 10 per cent for the backward classes, 17 per cent for ex-servicemen and 3 per cent for the handicapped) for class III and IV posts and 38 per cent (20 per cent for the Scheduled Castes, 10 per cent for the backward classes, 5 per cent for ex-servicemen and three per cent for the handicapped) for Class I and II posts in the State. With the new decision, 26 per cent posts would be reserved for "other backward classes" in class I and II posts and 14 per cent in Class III and IV posts in government services.

The Cabinet also did not agree with the recommendation that the students belonging to the OBC category should be given scholar ships as given to the students belonging to the Scheduled Castes. However the benefit of reservation would not pass on to the children of the following categories. Either of his parents is a Class-I or Class-II officer in the government service or holds an equivalent post in a public sector undertaking or is employed under a private employer and draws a salary which is not less than that of a Class-II officer either of his parents, is a professional a doctor, lawyer, chartered accountant, income tax consultant, financial or management consultant, dental surgeon and engineer or architect; either of his parents is an income tax assessee either of his parents is assessed for sales tax and either of his parents or both together own more than 8 hectares of rainfed land or its equivalent.

Difficulties Ahead

The Constitutional validity of the Mandal Commission Report and the Central Government decision to implement it reserving 27 per cent jobs for backward classes in the Central Government and public sector units was challenged before the Supreme Court of India. The arguments put before the court are: The Mandal Commission report has no constitutional sanctity to recommend 27 per cent job reservation for the backward castes. The Commission had generously thought that it was its duty under Article 340 of the Constitution to recommend job reservation for the backward classes. The Mandal report virtually "rewrites the Constitution" by providing preference to the 3, 743 backward castes by reducing the status of forward castes as of second class citizens. Casteism which the Constitution emphatically intended to end was reviewed by the report and ideals were buried by it. The Commission had ignored certain principles laid by the apex court that efficiency of administration should be borne in mind when reservations were made and unreasonable excessive or extravagant reservation was a "fraud" on the Constitution. There had never been a more flagrant disregard of these principles, except by the Mandal Commission. There was no express provision in the Constitution for the appointment of a commission to consider advisability or otherwise of reservation of government jobs. Any backward class might be given the benefit of reservation and other preferences but the class must consist of a homogenous group the element to homogeneity would be backwardness characterising the class. In other words the link or the thread holding the class together would be the backwardness of the members. Any determination of a backward class, which was wholly and exclusively based on caste, was prohibited by the Constitution. The Commission had violated all norms of law governing the reservation in government jobs. It had avowedly adopted the sole and exclusive test and ground of caste for determining their entitlement to the benefit of reservation. The implementation of the Mandal Commission report will give a fresh lease to the canker of casteism and undo independent India's efforts over the past 55 years to create a unified and cohesive society. The report was against the basic structure of the Constitution as it revitalised casteism, cleaved the nation into two—forward and backward and opened up new vistas for internecine conflict and fissiparous forces, and made backwardness a vested interest. The Commission did not investigate whether reservations in different states had resulted in "substandard replacing standard" and the reins of power passing from "meritocracy to mediocrity".

The Mandal Commission's recommendations are not justified also because they are based on outmoded and obsolete data from the 1891 and 1931 census reports, which were irrelevant in identifying the population of castes and current distribution of castes in India. The entire burden of establishing that conditions existed for departing from the principle of equality enshrined in Article 16(1) of the Constitution, that correct tests had been applied to identify backward classes under Article 16(4) and that such tests had been correctly implemented by collection of necessary statistics so that it was proved to the satisfaction of the court that each of the castes was backward lay squarely on the government. The Mandal Commission treated economic criterion as a separate head and devalued its importance by not including it as a criterion for social backwardness and by giving it only one point for each one of the four economic criteria as against three for each one of the social backwardness criteria. Even the four tests of economic backwardness laid down by the Mandal Commission had no relevance to economic backwardness, while the single most important factor of either household income or household consumption expenditure was ignored by striking off the particulars of household income in the tables of the socio educational survey; and caste could be identified as a backward class only if practically the whole or the entirety of the caste was backward which meant a percentage of three to five alone need not be backward for the entirety to claim the status of a backward class.

"Fact of non-existence" of several of the castes identified by the report had been examined and stated by the Anthropological Survey of India in its compendium of 120 volumes called "People of India" that 1,100 castes had been erroneously included by the commission in the list in so far as these were "mere synonyms for certain castes"; 224 castes mentioned as other backward classes in Orissa were also "non-existent" as the State had shown as "nil" the list of other backward classes. The Mandal report ought to be discarded as it was "totally opposed to the facts as they exist" and the decision of the Government of India in accepting the same had to be struck down as being without any basis or authority; the deliberate exercise in the Constitution was to abjure the term "caste" and to provide for socially and educationally backward classes. If at all the word caste had been used it was to negate it and to state that it shall be not be the basis of discrimination. The Constitution-makers had not defined "backward classes" as people of backwardness and it was hoped that reservation would be temporary and short-lived. The Constitution-makers had left it to the judges of the Supreme Court to interpret the constitutional provisions when the occasion arose.

Political Strategies

The verdict of the Supreme Court to be announced some time after the conclusion of the arguments by the parties concerned notwithstanding all the major political parties swear by reservation. The Mandal Commission report, which threatened to divide society on caste lines, has become an important instrument to woo the voters as is evident from the election manifestos of all major political parties. While the National Front and the Left parties, in their manifestos have clearly spelt out their policy on the implementation of the report, other parties appear to have taken an ambiguous stand on the issue. All the major political parties had bitterly criticised the manner in which the government had sought to implement the Mandal Commission recommendations but they now appear to have realised the report's vote-catching potential.

The Congress (I) in its manifesto, says it is committed to reservations as an important instrument of social justice. The party says that if it comes to power, it will launch a concerted drive to ensure that reservation quotas for thee Scheduled Castes and Tribes are duly filled. It will bring forward necessary legislation to establish a backward classes development corporation, it is committed to ensuring that the benefits of reservation are provided to other economically Backward sections of people who are not covered by the existing schemes. Interestingly the manifesto does not make any mention of the Mandal Commission report directly.

The BJP pledging to the socio-economic uplift of the backward classes says reservation should be continued for the Scheduled Castes and Tribes as before reservation should also be made for other backward classes broadly on the basis of the Mandal Commission report with preference to the poor among these very classes reservation should also be provided for members of the other castes on the basis of their economic conditions. The party says the reservation policy should be used as an instrument of social justice and for promoting social harmony as well. The question of reservation has to be viewed with an open mind free from all prejudices of any kind.

The National Front says reservation of 27 per cent jobs in Central Government and central undertakings for the socially and educationally backward classes shall be fully implemented. In addition 5 to 10 per cent jobs will be similarly reserved for the economically backward sections not covered by the Mandal Commission recommendations or any other reservation schemes. The Front says it will set up an experts committee to recommend steps for removing anomalies in the Mandal Commission recommendations and for considering representation that may be received in this connection.

The Samajwadi Janta Party (SJP) says that the implementation of the Mandal Commission report is imperative. However it has to be done in a scientific manner for contributing to the process of nation building and not for promoting castes war, it pledges to give preference to the most backward sections of society in an endeavour for social justice.

The Left parties allies of the National Front have also taken a clear stand on the Mandal Issue. The CPM says it supports the implementation of the Mandal Commission report for reservation of jobs in central services for the backward classes. It is a step towards social justice which will provide some opportunities for those socially backward due to the oppressive caste structure for entering employment in the state sector. The party is opposed to any move to scuttle reservation and wants this benefit to reach the really deserving sections amongst the backward classes.

The CPI says it is for the speedy implementation of comprehensive measures of social justice including job reservation for other backward classes (OBCs), on the lines of the Mandal Commission report, with 10 per cent reservation for the economically weaker sections of the forward castes and 30 per cent job for women in all categories.

As explained above opinion is sharply decided about the implementation of the recommendations of Mandal Commission, the pendulum swinging from one extreme position to another. But there is a general consensus that the criteria for reservation should be a socio-economic and not caste identity. Instead of correcting the age old imbalances, it perpetuates new imbalances and new wrongs. It will not end the old inequality but create a new one by rigging the competition in favour of those who do poorly at the entrance examination. The remedy lies in providing special and generous provision to the disadvantaged groups in terms of education, hygiene, nutrition and other areas to raise their overall living standards and so their competitiveness. The government can institute limitless scholarships to help children of backward castes with good schooling.

One moot question is whether, the backwardness should be measured purely on the basis of social and educational criteria or in terms of economic considerations also. True, that social and economic backwardness of various castes are interrelated yet, it can not be denied that this relationship is not that perfect. It is, also to be conceded that at the heart of the matter is the economic upliftment of all concerned. Hence poverty emerges as an additional criterion for the purpose. It will certainly take care of all the members of the OBCs except those who have already gone higher on the ladder. If a blanket reservation policy in favour of the other backward castes (not classes) is adopted, the gains of it will be cornered by only few who are better off among them. On the other hand, a poverty based reservation policy will benefit not only the vast majority of the OBCs but also the poor amongst the remaining castes. In any case, the division of society along caste lines must be avoided as far as possible.

The benefits of the reservations in public services may therefore be extended to those also who are living below the poverty line but are not listed among the backward classes. These could be defined as the families whose annual income from all sources is less than Rs 7500/-. Scheduled Castes and Scheduled Tribes constitute 22.5 per cent of the country's population. A pro-rata reservation has been made for them in all the central public services. In States also, the reservation for them is directly proportional to their population in each state. The fact is that even amongst the Scheduled Castes and Scheduled Tribes, who have been enjoying the fruits of reservation in public services for the last 40 years, the top echelons have skimmed off most of the benefits. Now they from an impervious layer disallowing any percolation of benefits to more disadvantaged members of their own groups. Consequently, a few Scheduled Caste and Scheduled Tribes families are reaping the institutional benefits repeatedly at the cost of the others. Therefore, the policy of reservation for backward classes should be followed with discretion. Benefits must flow to as many members of the backward classes possible. This is possible only when we do not allow them to be cornered by a few. Hence, once a particular family has benefitted from a policy provision, it should be subsequently asked to be self-reliant and compete for the jobs with the candidates in the open category.

The recommendations of the Mandal Commission may be accepted for the social, educational and economic advancement of the OBCs with a provision that other economically backward households with an annual income of less than Rs 7500 from all sources, are also included. In fact, the initial thrust of the policy could be directed to all household below the poverty line.

Article 46 of the Constitution may be put to a greater use by the government and some special programmes may be drawn up for the economic and educational advancement of OBCs and other below poverty line households. The benefits of the reservation of seats in public services should be given as a one-time measure, otherwise a few families keep on monopolising the benefits of the provisions and do not allow these to percolate downward. This will have another indirect advantage also. The sooner a family is freed from its dependence on reservations the better, because a prolonged dependence of any kind is self-degenerating.

The efficiency in performance of the government jobs has to be maintained at all costs. To ensure this, the pre-service and in-service training programme may be organised for the candidates belonging to the reserved categories.

The Mandal Commission and the action of Former Prime Minister V.P. Singh to implement its recommendations in a precipitate manner had agitated the mind of the Indian public particularly in the Hindi heartland. There had been unprecedented loss of young lives and of valuable property which had caused extreme distress. It is regrettable that the government had shown insensitivity towards the young people and had been a silent spectator of the agonising confrontation taking place between the pro-reservationists and anti-reservationists in different parts of the country. The matter is now before the highest judicial forum of the country—the Supreme Court of India. It is expected that the highest judicial forum will clear the mist and settle the issues involved in the report and its implementation in the best interests of the country.

7

Tribal People

The term Scheduled Tribes has been used for the first time in the Constitution only and the earlier expressions used in pre-independence days were aboriginal tribes, backward tribes, etc. There is no universal definition of a tribe acceptable to all social scientists. But the definition of a tribe given by the late Dr. D.N. Majumdar, has maximum acceptance. He defined a tribe "a social group with territorial affiliation, endogamous, with no specialization of functions, ruled by tribal officers, hereditary or otherwise, united in language, or dialect, recognising social distance from other tribes or castes but without any stigma attached in the case of a caste structure, following tribal traditions, beliefs and customs, above all conscious of a homogeneity of ethnic and territorial integration." Tribal, origin, primitive way of life and habitation and less easily accessible areas; and general backwardness in all respects, are the features common to the tribes in various states.

Statutory Provisions

The Constitution provides various safe guards far promotion and protection of the interests of the Scheduled Tribes. Provisions contained in Articles 19, 46, 164, 244, 275, 330, 332, 334, 338, 339, 34 and the 5th and 6th Schedules of the Constitution are relevant in this regard. The Government of India's responsibility in relation to the development of Scheduled Tribes and the Schedule Areas extend not only to the provision of funds (Article 275) for their development but also to evolving polices and programmes for their rapid and harmonious development in consultation with and cooperation of the State Governments.

Special Programme

The importance attached to tribal development is also reflected in the new 20 Point Economic Promamme 1986 which lays special emphasis on the development of Scheduled Tribes. Being the nodal Ministry for overall policy, planning and coordination of programmes for the development of Scheduled Tribes, the Welfare Ministry is concerned with the following points relating to tribals:

(a) Point 11 : Justice to scheduled castes and scheduled tribes.

(b) Point 7 : Pay special attention to water supply for scheduled castes and scheduled tribes.

(c) Point 14 (3): Lay special emphasis on construction of houses for scheduled castes and scheduled tribes.

(d) Point 16(2): Protect the traditional right of tribal, population and local communities of access to fire, wood and forest produce.

The British Government in India was mainly concerned with the maintenance or law and order rather than with economic and social development in tribal areas. In Assam the policy of 'exclusion' was followed and no outsiders except missionaries with known antecedents were allowed to go there. Since independence of the country, the chief programmes for the scheduled tribes have been directed to raising their standard of living, developing agriculture and industry in tribal areas, and providing for their educational, social and economic development.

Welfare Measures

Schemes for tribal welfare must fulfil two essential conditions, namely, conformity to the social values and patterns of the life of the people for whom they are intended and the psychological receptivity and the ability of the tribal population to absorb them. Theoretical perfection of a scheme or its suitability to the people, in general, must not be regarded as the criterion for tribal people. Ignorance of these basic facts and inability to appreciate them are responsible for the failure of many development schemes which by themselves are unexceptionable. The Third Five Year Plan also said: "It would be an error to over-administer them in the name of development. In facilitating the development, the tribal people should be enabled to develop along the lines of their own genius, with genuine respect and support for their own traditional arts and culture and without pressure or imposition from outside. In Tribal areas every effort should be made to train and build up a team of their own people to do the work of administration and development, the constant aim being to develop local personnel both as official functionaries and as social workers.

The Population of the Scheduled Tribes as per 1981 census was about 5.38 crores (including the projected figures in respect of Assam) constituting about 7.8 per cent of the total population. Tribal development has from the beginning been based on a two-pronged policy, viz., (i) protection and promotion of their interests, thorough legal-administrative support and (ii) implementation of developmental schemes to raise their level of living. The Tribal Sub-Plan (TSP)-concept evolved and implemented during the Fifth Five Year Plan period continues to be the main instrument for development of tribal people and tribal areas. The TSP is in operation in 17 States and 2 Union Territories, viz., Andhra Pradesh, Assam, Bihar, Gujarat, Himachal Pradesh, Karnataka, Kerala, Madhya Pradesh, Maharashtra, Manipur, Orissa, Rajasthan, Sikkim, Tamil Nadu; Tripura, Uttar Pradesh, West Bengal, Andaman and Nicobar Islands and Goa, Daman and Diu. It covers 26 districts fully and 97 districts partly in the country. The TSP does not cover tribal majority States and Union Territories of Meghalaya, Mizoram, Nagaland, Arunachal Pradesh, Dadra and Nagar Haveli and Lakshadweep as their respective plans are primarily meant for the majority tribal population.

The TSP approach consists of three main components, viz., (a) Integrated Tribal Development Projects (ITDPs) comprising generally administrative units like Sub-Divisions of Tehsils/ Talukas with 5% or more Scheduled Tribe population, (b) 248 pockets of tribal Concentration (MADA pockets) having a total population of 10.000 or more and Scheduled Tribe population of 50% or more and (c) 73 Primitive Tribal Group Projects. In addition, during the Seventh Five Year Plan period clusters having a total population of 5,000 and 50% or more Scheduled Tribe concentration therein are being identified.

Aims and Goals

During the Sixth Plan the major objectives in tribal development were: (i) taking up family oriented beneficiary programmes through raising productivity levels of the beneficiary families in the fields of agriculture, horticulture, animal husbandry, small industries, etc. (ii) elimination of exploitation of tribals in the spheres of alienation of land, money lending, debt-bondage, forest, etc.; (iii) human resources development through education and training programmes; and (iv) infrastructure development.

Fiscal Support

The TSP is funded through resources drawn from: (i) State Plans, (ii) Special Central Assistance of the Ministry of Welfare, (iii) Central and Centrally Sponsored Programmes, and (iv) Institutional Finance.

The State Plan investment includes amounts proposed under various sectors of activity of the State Government and also includes amounts earmarked towards the State's share of the Centrally Sponsored Schemes. According to the guidelines for quantification of funds for the TSP the total financial outlay in a State Plan is to be divided into divisible and non-divisible components. The non-divisible components would represent investments where the benefits cannot be identified to have flown to and specific area or region or any target group. During the Sixth Plan the State Governments were advised that they should earmark an amount of outlay for the TSP keeping in view: (i) proportion of the TSP area in the total geographical area of the State, (ii) relative level of development of tribal areas vis-a-vis other areas in the State and (iii) percentage which the tribal population in the State bears to the total population. The flow to the TSP for the country as a whole was 8.25% of the total State Plans (Rs. 3495.24 crores out of Rs. 42390.60 crores).

The Special Central Assistance (SCA) was instituted in the beginning of the Fifth Plan period. The purpose of the SCA was that it should be an additive and catalyst for spurring financial investment by the State Governments and financial institutions. The SCA from Rs. 190 crores in the Fifth Plan period was increased to Rs. 486.11 crores in the Sixth Plan period. The expenditure under the SCA is reported to have been Rs. 441.51 crores.

The Central Government wholly finance certain schemes of national importance and these are known as Central Sector Schemes. Besides there are certain Centrally Sponsored Schemes in most of the Plan sectors which are usually common to all the States end which are financed by the Central Government and the State Governments usually in the ratio of 50:50. Most of these schemes are concerned with anti-poverty goal and are based on part-subsidy to be drawn from the State and the Central Plans and part-loan drawn from financial institutions. The proportion between subsidy and loan is generally 50:50. The idea that earmarking of funds also under the Centrally Sponsored Schemes should be done under the TSP was mooted in the Fifth Plan period, but the progress in this regard was not satisfactory. According to available data only six States viz., Andhra Pradesh, Gujarat, Madhya Pradesh, Orissa, Rajasthan and Tamil Nadu, could quantify Rs 197.49 crores from their Centrally Sponsored Schemes during the Sixth Plan period.

The Report of the Working Group of Tribal Development during the Sixth Plan have observed that in formulation of programmes specific problems of each area and the target group in terms of family should be clearly defined and schemes directly benefiting the individual tribal family given the highest priority. A tribal family is given 50% subsidy and 50% loan in the field of agriculture. However, the relative percentage of subsidy and loan component may vary from State to State and further in a State from scheme to scheme. In the field of credit-cum-marketing the part to be played in institutional finance is vital. Both production and consumption credit have come to occupy a pivotal position in the promotion of tribal economy. Institutional finance is thus an important ingredient in the entire beneficiary oriented programme. While subsidy element is available from the Central and State funds, the loan component has to flow from financial institutions.

The Finance Commission allocated funds amounting to Rs 88.70 crores to 13 Tribal Sub-Plan States for raising the level of administration in tribal areas. The award was for grant of compensatory allowance to personnel working in tribal areas and construction of residential quarter for transferable-government employees posted in tribal areas. The Eighth Finance Commission in addition to providing enhanced grants compared to the recommendations of the Seventh Finance Commission has provided funds for creation of infrastructure facilities in selected tribal villages as Rs 5 lakhs per village. The Commission also provided Rs 19.27 crores as compensatory allowance, Rs 30.97 crores for residential quarters and Rs 38.45 crores for infrastructural facilities in villages for a period of four years (1985-89) in respect of 13 states, namely, Andhra Pradesh, Assam, Bihar, Himachal Pradesh, Kerala, Madhya Pradesh, Manipur, Orissa, Rajasthan, Sikkim, Tripura, Uttar Pradesh, and West Bengal. The four Tribal Sub-Plan States, namely, Gujarat, Karnataka, Maharashtra and Tamil Nadu which are revenue surplus states have not been covered under this Award.

Union Government's Role

There are three Centrally Sponsored Schemes for Scheduled Tribes viz. (i) Girls Hostels for Scheduled Tribes; (ii) Research and Training; and (iii) Aid to Voluntary Organisations.

Girls Hostels : The scheme of girls hostels for scheduled tribes is in operation since Third Five Year Plan and has considerably helped promotion of girls education amongst tribal communities. The expenditure on this item is shared between the State and the Centre on a matching basis i.e. 50:50.

Under the Centrally Sponsored Schemes : Tribal Research Institutes have been set up at Hyderabad, Gauhati, Ranchi, Ahmedabad, Calicut, Bhopal, Pune, Bhubaneswar, Udaipur, Lucknow and Kolkatta. Another full-fledged Tribal Research Institute is to be set up at Imphal. These institutions are substantially contributing to the developmental efforts through research, evaluation, collection of statistical data, training and providing professional input in the preparation of Tribal Sub-plan documents. The scheme is operated on sharing basis, the expenditure on plan items are met by the Central and State Governments in the ratio of 50:50. A Central Tribal Research Advisory Council was set up in 1986-87 to guide and coordinate the activities of these institutions. Two other components of the scheme are: grant of research fellowships to students working on tribal problems and supporting research project by expert bodies. The scholarship holders are selected by a Selection Committee duly constituted in the Ministry of Welfare for the purpose.

Grants-in-aid to Voluntary Organisations : Grant-in-aid to Voluntary Organisations of All India character which are operating in more than one state for the development of Scheduled Tribes is given on year to year basis. The activities of the voluntary organisations include education, training, medical and public health. During 1987-88 a provision of Rs 80 lakhs existed for the purpose and about 25 organisations were assisted.

Steps for Betterment

To explore new markets to improve the marketing of tribal produce, eliminate intermediaries and obtain better value for tribal produce to augment the income of tribal families, a Tribal Cooperative Marketing Development Federation (TRIFED) at the national level was set up during 1987-88 and a sum of Rs 2 crores was provided as share capital assistance to TRIFED.

Schemes Implemented

Despite these efforts of the governments and voluntary organisations for development and welfare of the Scheduled Tribes it is alleged that the tribal people have experienced nothing but the backlash of development leading to disorganisation as a community and destitution as Individuals.

The Commissioner for Scheduled Castes and Tribes in his latest (Twenty-eighth) Report has lamented that the denial of right to life which is basic and self-created and is enshrined in our Constitution is the biggest anomaly of our national life and the worst sufferers are members of the scheduled castes and the scheduled tribes whose protection and welfare is the special responsibility of the state under the constitutions. In various states, the governments have not been finding it too easy to cut through bureaucratic maze, land reforms are often mythical, in specific pockets all over the country, quite a few tribals routinely end up as bonded labourers. And as the Commissioner puts it, "In implementing the law of bonded labour no action is usually taken against a person who violates the same, the emphasis is on liberation, it does not make any difference to the employer". Another important aspect of the scheme: the rehabilitation of bonded labourers is neglected. In many cases a person may be presented as bonded labourer for the sole objective of getting a rehabilitation grant. But the money meant for the labourer is misappropriated by the employer and the official. In this situation it is difficult even to identify the real bonded labour.

The condition of tribal masses in the country as a whole has been deteriorating from year to year. They have been alienated from the rest of society by moneylenders, landlords or their touts. Their customary rights in the forests have long been forgotten, and in many areas even the traditional "jhum" cultivation has been banned without arranging employment through other avenues. They are victims of eviction and displacement due to the construction of irrigation dams and other projects which take years to take off without any proper alternative land, compensation or even employment to the tribals. There are numerous cases of attacks on them. Furthermore, they are being driven out of forests by the same officials who along with contractors, are denuding the forests. All this, despite the fact that agro-forestry research clearly shows that inside these very forests crops of specific types can be grown without damage to the trees. No wonder that some of the tribals, aided by vested interest, are taking to the separatist path.

What is needed is some measure to end the transfer of tribal land to non-tribal people, protection of their customary right to forest produce and land, the protection of their right to the "jhumias" till rehabilitation is arranged satisfactorily, preventing the degradation of environment in tribal areas by mining companies and other enterprises, and ensuring pure drinking water to these people. Their exploitation by forest and police officials, contractors and timber merchants, who pay starvation wages, must be ended and they must be given full rights to participate in panchayat activities. A government with a vision has to look for forest-based industries and economic activities to make them self-reliant. The government will also have to recognise their cultural and linguistic distinctiveness. Moreover, where they are in majority they should be granted regional or local autonomy within the state concerned.

There is need for a political will to create a climate of goodwill, particularly in the tribal areas. A unilateral process of development should not be imposed on voiceless people. Their lives should not be staked in the name of national development and high ideals.

NGO's in Action

Voluntary organisations play a significant role in advancing socio-economic progress of the community in general and that of the Scheduled Castes and Scheduled Tribes in particular. Some of the agencies of all India character receive direct grants-in-aid from the Ministry of Welfare.

Some of the prominent organisation working for Scheduled Castes are: Harijan Sevak Sang, Delhi; Divyayan Krishi Vigyan Kendra, Ranchi; Ramakrishan Mission Ashrama, Puri (Orissa); Sri Rama-Krishna Advait Ashram, Kalady (Kerala); Ramakrishna Mission Ashrama, P.O. Narendrapur, 24 parganas District (West Bengal); and Ramakrishna Mission Vidyapith, P.O. Vivekananda Nagar, District purulia (West Bengal) and those working for the Scheduled Tribes are: Bharatiya Adimjati Sevak Sangh, New Delhi; The Nilgiris Adivasi Welfare Association, Kotagiri; The Nilgiris District (Tamil Nadu); Banasthali Vidyapith (Rajasthan); Rama-krishna Mission, Shillong; Gharmora Model Satra Mills & Plains Cultural Institution, North Lakhimpur (Assam); and Ramakrishna Mission Boys Home, P.O. Rahara, District 24 parganas (West Bengal).

In view of the fact that the important role which voluntary organisations play in the development of weaker sections, the Working Groups on the Development of Scheduled Castes and Scheduled Tribes during the Seventh Five Year Plan made a number of important observations and recommendations. The Planning Commission themselves gave a set of criteria for recognising voluntary agencies working in the field of development. This, inter alia, envisaged that these agencies should not be linked directly or indirectly with any political party. They will adopt legal and non-violent means in the furtherance of their goals and objectives. These guidelines are unexceptionable and should be adopted by the State Government as well. Voluntary agencies in tribal development work can play a crucial role in the remote areas where the functioning of the governmental agencies is not satisfactory for a variety of reasons. These areas can be effectively covered by selfless voluntary workers. Even elsewhere the voluntary organisation; can play an important role in mobilisation of the tribal people and organising them into voluntary groups for social and economic development programmes. The basic problem in the tribal areas is lack of confidence between the people and the administration and the voluntary workers can serve as a valuable bridge between them.

A number of voluntary organisations in the tribal areas are receiving foreign assistance. Though the clearance from the Government of India is obtained by them before receiving foreign assistance a special check by the Ministry of Welfare is not made. This needs a careful consideration in view of the rise in the flow of foreign money into the tribal areas.

Progress of Tribes

Protective laws and multi-pronged programmes have helped tribals of Himachal Pradesh emerge from the cesspool of illiteracy and backwardness. The tribals-the Swanglas, the Pangwalas, the Lahbals, the Gujjars and the Bhots-have benefited both from laws protecting them against exploitation and programmes which set aside funds for their uplift. The tribal sub-plan for instance set aside 9 per cent of the annual plans funds for tribal development though they account for only 4 per cent of the State's population.

Similarly, the Himachal Pradesh Transfer of Land Act prevents their alienation from land the prime asset of the 1.33 lakh tribal population. Under the Act tribals cannot sell, mortgage or lease their land to non-tribals without prior permission of the Deputy Commissioner. Also no land right or title held by a tribal in any land can be attached or sold under a court decree. The Act has been further amended so that its protection can be sought to set aside a Court decree at any stage of proceedings. The Act imposes restriction on the power of the decendants to contest that alienation of immovable property is contrary to custom.

Money lending has been regulated by another legislation which prescribes registration of all money lenders. Ceilings have been provided of the amount returnable in case of both secure and unsecure loans taken before and after the enforcement of the Act. The provisions of Himachal Pradesh Relief of Agricultural indebtedness have also provided relief to certain farmers, agricultural labourers and rural artisans. Every outstanding debt, including the amount of interest payable by a marginal farmer, landless agricultural labourer or rural artisan, has been deemed to be wholly discharged. There is no bonded labour in the tribal areas of the State—Kinnaur, Lahul-Spiti, Pangi and Bharmour. The Himachal Pradesh Tenancy and Land Reforms Act has put an end to all forms of tenancy except under certain legal disabilities. The law provides suo moto conferment of proprietary rights on tenants.

A study conducted by a team of university experts headed by Dr. D.S. Thakur, Deputy Director (Planning) to evaluate the impact of the tribal development project on the Pangi and Spiti valleys has revealed that the efforts being put in by the State Government to develop these remote and backward pockets have significantly increased the agricultural and livestock production. The average yield of crops in the tribal areas is in fact comparatively higher than the overall average yield in Himachal. This fact makes the impact of the tribal project quite evident. However, the study has pointed out that the actual physical achievements under various schemes in these areas are not commensurate with the expenditure incurred. The Pangi valley has remained more backward than the cold desert area of Spiti because the former is not connected by a motorable road is and thus lacks the mobility of men and material required for rapid development.

To ensure better results the Government should introduce the system of single line administration, post additional officers on special duty during the summer and send an inter-discipline valuation team of experts to these areas every year to supervise and report the progress of work. Besides, the construction of roads and bridges and implementation of afforestation schemes should be given priority.

The Scheduled Castes and Scheduled Tribes committee of the Himachal Vidhan Sabha in its report laid on the table of the House by its Chairman, Mr Roop Dass Kashyap on Feb. 27,1990 had pointed out that many members of these castes had been deprived of facilities due to them because several schemes launched by the government needed more publicity and the funds remained unutilised because many people in several areas were ignorant of such schemes.

Chosen Groups

Denotified Communities consist of several groups which may broadly be divided into two sections: (1) nomadic and (2) settled. The nomadic group includes gypsy like people while the settled and the semi-settled groups trace their descent from 'irregular fighting men' who were uprooted from their original homes on account of invasions or political upheavals in the distant past. Before settlement in colonies they used to make a living by hunting, selling jungle products, exhibiting bear and monkey dances, snake-charming, selling medicinal herbs and other goods and supplemented their earnings by begging. The innate spirit of adventure inherited from their forefathers together with extreme poverty, lack of openings for better economic conditions and also other psychological factors led them to take to criminal practices which later became a tradition and a part of their heritage.

Under the Criminal Tribes Act, 1924, these groups which numbered about 127 and whose population was 24.64 lakhs in 1951 were dubbed as criminals. Thus when a child was born of these tribes, he was considered to be criminal from the very beginning and on his attaining the age of majority, he was automatically registered criminal even though he might have been totally innocent. These people were kept in colonies, sometimes fenced with barbed wire and under strict vigilance of the police. Quite often they were made scapegoats for undetected crimes. In these settlements, the registered persons were interned for a prescribed period, during which they were taught agriculture or certain handicrafts. The movement of these settlers was restricted within that area. Thus these notified groups had to wear a dark cloak of notoriety around them. This deprived them of all channel of employment.

After independence, the national Government realised the injustice of dubbing the whole community as criminal without exception. Apart from being repugnant to the fundamental principles of jurisprudence, it was socially unjustifiable and nationally wasteful to maintain a whole community, generation after generation, in bondage. The government, therefore appointed a Criminal Tribes Enquiry Committee in 1949 and on its recommendation repealed the Criminal Tribes Act with effect from August 31,1952 and the restrictions imposed on those people were withdrawn. The Backward Classes Commission 1955 had inter alia recommended that: (i) The nomenclature of these classes may be changed from 'Criminal' or 'Excriminal' Tribes to 'Denotified Communities'; (ii) These communities may be divided into Scheduled Tribes, Scheduled Castes and other Backward Classes for getting the benefits available to the categories concerned; (iii) These communities may be distributed in small groups in towns and villages where they will ultimately come into the contact with other people and will eventually be assimilated in society; (iv) Normal instruction together with basic education followed by vocational and technical education at secondary level should be given to them. The children of criminal groups should be removed from their parents on attaining the age of seven and should be put in suitable hostels. After the legal withdrawal of the limitations and restrictions in 1952, the first problem was to wean them away from the criminal tendencies, particularly the younger generation and remove the stigma attached to them and secondly to put before them openings to useful occupations which would make-responsible for them to live honourably. The total allotment under the First Five Year Plan both at the centre and the states for these communities and other backward classes was As 3.5 crores. By the end of the First Five Year Plan about 17 settlements and 30 colonies had been setup; more then 36000 families had received assistance for agricultural development; 113 co-operatives had been organised and 337 industrial centres were set up for their benefit. The Second Plan made an allocation of Rs 3.12 crores for the welfare of these communities. The major schemes were housing and educational development. Apart from agriculture and cottage industry, another possibility of leading a life of honest means can be by getting employed in Government services, private firms, factories etc. But even though the Act has been repealed and theoretically there is no bar to getting employment, yet the stigma attached to those belonging to these communities does not make it easy to secure them employments. With a view to removing the stigma, the Government should give a lead in offering them government employment.

In view of the small results achieved so far, their needs should be studied in each area and programmes could be drawn up on the basis of the following suggestions of the Study Team set up by the Committee on Plan Projects:

1. the need for a combined correctional and welfare approach for the rehabilitation of denotified communities which should be supported by a programme of social education;
2. formulation of special economic programmes which keep in view the character of the population, in particular, their adventurous spirit of traditional skills;
3. organisation of industrial and other cooperatives;
4. provision of opportunities for employment in the public services supported by way of additional training and orientation facilities; and
5. where the denotified tribes constitute a sizeable population, cadres of trained workers, who are familiar with their social and cultural background and can work closely with them, should be built up.

The objective of assimilation, emphasized the Third Plan should guide the programme of rehabilitation and development from the very start and progressive and forward-looking elements among the denotified tribes themselves should be assisted and encouraged to play an increasing part in this effort.

In pursuance of these observations and recommendations and in view of the urgency of early rehabilitation of the Denotified tribes all the schemes were implemented under the centrally sponsored programmes. Economic development and social progress of these communities were given due emphasis for which Rs 419 lakhs was made available. In the Fourth Plan all schemes were continued with an allocation of Rs. 439 lakhs.

The pattern of implementation of schemes was again changed in the Fifth Plan period when all the welfare schemes for the denotified tribes were transferred to the State plans sector. These schemes have continued to be implemented in the Sixth and Seventh

Five Year Plans by the respective State Governments. These schemes include (i) educational programmes in the form of granting of scholarships and stipends to eligible students, tuition and examination fees, provision of mid-day meals and establishment of Ashram school, residential schools and hostels; (ii) programmes of economic development, rehabilitation, colonisation, assistance for agriculture development, animal husbandry, poultry farming, cottage industries and organisation of cooperative societies; (iii) miscellaneous schemes-setting up of community welfare centres, balwadis, digging of drinking wells, etc.

Much more could have been done for the welfare of the Denotified Tribes, had there been a statutory provision for their welfare as there has been for the protection and promotion of interests of scheduled castes and scheduled tribes in the various articles of our constitution. The Denotified tribes are entitled to certain benefits and concessions under the general provision of Article 41 of the constitution which stipulates promotion of educational and economic interests of the scheduled castes, scheduled tribes and other weaker sections. It is desirable that the various safeguards, concessions and benefits available to scheduled castes/tribes should be extended to them also under statutory provisions to be made by the Parliament through an amendment of the constitution.

There is also the need to identify their complex problems which vary from state to state due to their habitational ecology, traditions and cultural ethos and to find their remedies especially of their rehabilitation in vocations suited to their genius and to wean them away from their criminal tendencies, particularly the children. This can be achieved to a great extent by formulating comprehensive and integrated plans to provide them land and the financial facilities in the form of loans/subsidies for agriculture, agro-based cottage industries, housing, education etc. Voluntary organisations, have been playing appreciable role in their rehabilitation and welfare. They need to be involved in larger measure to complement the government efforts in ameliorating the lot of the denotified tribes with a view to integrating them in the mainstream of the Indian society and enabling them to live as respectable citizens of the country.

The Government was satisfied with the soundness of the strategies adopted for the welfare and development of Scheduled

Castes and Scheduled Tribes since the Fifth Plan as former prime Minister V.P. Singh had told that the results of the strategy adopted so far have been encouraging and the targets had been achieved in many cases while in some cases the targets had in fact been exceeded. He had asked all Central Ministers and Chief Ministers to formulate innovative schemes in the Eighth Plan and make adequate allocations for the benefit of scheduled castes and scheduled tribes and sent to them copies of a letter sent by the late Prime Minister Indira Gandhi on March 12, 1980. He had suggested that out of the total plan outlay of each State/U.T., a proportion equal to the percentage of scheduled caste and scheduled tribe population in the State/U.T. should be set apart for the special Component Plan and the Tribes Sub-plan. There should be no division of the total plan outlay into so called divisible and non-divisible components with the SCP and TSP being combined to the divisible outlays alone. The Scheduled Castes and Scheduled Tribes are entitled to a share in the total plan size of the state equivalent to that of their population in the State/U.T. and no less. In fact they need justifiably more, considering the extent of their past and present deprivations and the magnitude of problems before them. Their development needs should be identified according to the order of priorities.

The fact of the matter however is that the condition of the Scheduled Castes and the Scheduled Tribes continues to be pathetic in spite of the numerous constitutional safeguards and exclusive programmes for their welfare. For millions of those belonging to the weaker sections with small land holdings, as also the landless, escape from the atrocities suffered for centuries is still a distant dream. On the one hand, caste-based inequity is being accentuated despite claims to the contrary and on the other hand, tribal regions all over the country are simmering with discontents. Technological advances, instead of helping them march towards a better tomorrow, are ravaging them with increased severity. The situation in tribal areas is particularly disturbing, as is evident from the demand for a separate Jharkand or Bodo land. The claims of the State, in utter disregard of their traditional rights and virtual forced displacement for making room for the so-called developmental projects, have made the tribals restive. Atrocities against the weaker sections have acquired a new economic dimension. With the consolidation of the vested interests, the task of ensuring an equitous deal to the under-privileged has now become more difficult.

Neither the ban on untouchability nor reservation of jobs had made the Harijans lot any better. The indifference of caste Hindus is more or less the same as was many decades earlier. Untouchability continues to be practised in one form or the other particularly in the rural areas of the country where the scheduled castes have not yet overcome the aversion for the Scheduled Castes and continue to exploit them. In a few urban pockets also especially in the States of Bihar, Orissa, Uttar Pradesh, Madhya Pradesh, Rajasthan, Karnataka, Andhra Pradesh and Tamil Nadu there have been instances of discrimination against the schedule castes. The Scheduled Castes are not allowed to draw water from the taps/wells used by the caste Hindus and are prevented from entering the temples. They are refused service at places commonly used by the caste Hindus and are served in separate containers or utensils. In some places they are denied the services of washermen, barbers etc. and are still compelled to pursue their age old unclean occupations due to socio-economic reasons. The late harijan leader, Jagjivan Ram had remarked, "The untouchability offences Act which provides for imprisonment and fine to those who practise discrimination is mostly on paper, particularly in rural areas." In the words of Sh. B.N. Singh former Assam Governor, "Dr B.R. Ambedkar fixed the limit of reservation for 10 years in the hope that within this period untouchability would end and a new social order would emerge. But it did not end 41 years after independence, we are still trying to solve the problem and fixing another limit, the end of the century to finally abolish scavenging which is the worst form of untouchability in the country.

The conversion of Harijans to Islam, Christianity or Buddhism are mainly attributed to the long-standing social discrimination based on untouchability and the indifference of Hindu society at large towards them. This is confirmed by the report of Tamil Nadu Scheduled Castes Director to the Union Home Ministry when some 560 Harijans in Meenakshipuram in Tirunelveli district of Tamil Nadu embraced Islam more than eight years ago. The report also said that the conversion was voluntary and not on account of any compulsion, allurement or inducement.

Even now all types of indignities are heaped upon Harijans. In U.P. people still recall how the statue of the Late U.P. Chief

Minister Sampurnanand was washed after it was unveiled by Jagjivan Ram then a Minister in the Central Government. There are reports that 400 to 500 Harijan girls between 12 to 20 years of age are taken every year from Karnataka to Mumbai's brothels. At many places in Rajasthan, Harijan bridegrooms are still not allowed to go on horse back.

Incidents of clashes between Harijans and Caste Hindus are on the increase. Traditional causes like land disputes, socio-economic exploitation of weaker sections, eviction of landless cultivators and entry of Harijans into temples are mainly responsible for these conflicts. Even 40 years of reservations and special concessions have not been able to break the shackles of social discrimination against Harijans. In concrete terms the situation has not improved. Exasperated Commissioners for the Scheduled Castes and the Scheduled Tribes submit reports on discrimination in Parliament every year.

Difficulties Ahead

It is thus clear that the objective of integrating the Scheduled Castes into the mainstream of society still remains a far cry. The penal provision of the Protection of Civil Rights Act 1955 play but a limited role in dealing with the problem of untouchability. A more concerted effort is therefore required to be made in this direction by all Government agencies at various levels. Administration/official machinery needs to shed its unusual prejudice in favour of the higher caste Hindus and to feel more responsible to and involved in the tasks of eradication practice of untouchability. Above all, the building up of a strong public opinion against the evil of untouchability is essential. The following steps also need to be taken to combat this menace:

1. In order to ensure that maximum number of offenders under the provisions of the PCR Act are punished, it would be advisable for the States to consider introduction of incentive schemes for police officials and other Government functionaries whose performance is considered laudable in matters of proper registration of cases, flawless investigation and resolute prosecution ending in conviction. Recording of good remarks in the Annual Confidential Reports of the dedicated and conscientious workers could be one such incentive.

2. Special drives/campaigns such as observances of 'fortnight' and 'week' for eradication of untouchability could also prove to be useful in this respect.
3. The practice of untouchability in covert or overt from in Government departments or educational institutions needs to be dealt with firmness. In addition to departmental action, prompt and strict legal action would also need to be taken up against the of fenders.
4. Since the urge to practice untouchability is too deep-rooted, it is necessary to find out ways and means of bringing about a change in the mental outlook ,and social attitudes of the people in general. To achieve this objective, Government would do involve, besides the voluntary organisations, selected educational and research institutions for carrying out broad based surveys to locate the areas where untouchability is being practised.
5. Necessary changes also need to be introduced in the educational system by way of in-corporating suitable reading material at the primary and middle school levels.
6. Adequate propaganda and publicity should also be organised through mass media viz., radio. T.V., press and cinema and also through debates, seminars, symposia, 'Prabhat-Pheris' and Padyatras.
7. Community feasts along with members of the Scheduled Castes and inter-caste marriages need to be further encouraged. Government may, also consider taking suitable remedial action with regard to objectionable portions, if any, in scriptures books or other publications explicitly or implicitly, advocating any kind of discrimination on grounds of caste.
8. An ironical situation arises out of some of the developmental schemes aimed at ameliorating the lot of the Scheduled Castes in so far as some such schemes tend to further segregate them from the rest of the population. For example, houses/house-sites being provided to the Scheduled Castes under various schemes are generally located away from the main village which impedes their coming closer to people belonging to other castes. Similarly,

educational institutions and, hostels that are being opened exclusively for Scheduled Castes tend to keep them away from students belonging to other castes. It is desirable that the programmes meant for economic advancement of the Scheduled Castes be implemented in such a manner that they in the process, also ensure the absorption of the Scheduled Castes into the main stream of society.

While discussing the various issues and programmes or welfare of Scheduled castes/tribes, suggestions have been made at appropriate places to remove their deficiencies and bring about changes and modifications in the administrative machinery, the following further suggestions are offered to achieve the desired objectives.

The Remedies

1. Flaws meant to Control the alienation of land from Scheduled Castes and Scheduled Tribes should be enforced.
2. Ways should be found to allot land to the landless Castes and Scheduled Tribes, and also to provide necessary agricultural inputs to them.
3. Centrally sponsored schemes meant for the protection of vulnerable groups should not be transferred to states.
4. The economic rehabilitation could be successful only when these vulnerable groups come up educationally also.
5. The Eighth Plan allocation for the vulnerable groups should be more than the percentage justified by their number to make up for the backlog. In formulating the detailed schemes, the Planning Commission should work in with the National Commission on Scheduled Castes and Scheduled Tribes.
6. So far had been considerable leakage in delivering the benefits and ways would to be found to plug them.
7. The regulations under the Fifth Schedule should be framed immediately to streamline administration in tribal areas vigorously. The automous district council might not be as effective as autonomous village Councils.

8. The provision relating to self-management available under the Sixth Schedule should also be suitably made applicable in the Fifth Scheduled Areas.
9. The country liquor shops should be closed down in the areas, whether declared scheduled areas or not.
10. The National Commission for Scheduled Castes and Tribes should undertake a comprehensive evaluation of programmes for Scheduled Castes and Scheduled Tribes to effect midterm corrections.
11. There should be a price commission for fixing procurement price for minor forest produce in line with the Agricultural Price Commission.
12. The functioning of the financial and development corporations in the states for the benefit of the Scheduled Castes and Scheduled Tribes should be supervised by the National commission of Scheduled Castes and Scheduled Tribes.

The implementation of all welfare programmes for the socioeconomic development of scheduled castes/tribes as also atrocities against them is dealt with in the ministry of Welfare. It shall be desirable that the subject of atrocities against scheduled castes/tribes be re-entrusted to the Ministry of Home affairs who have all the machinery for law and order and channel of communication of orders and instructions at their command.

At the state level, welfare of Scheduled Castes is taken care of by the Department of General Welfare of Scheduled Castes having multi dimensional facets of great magnitude, it is advisable that there should be separate exclusive department of their welfare to implement the programmes of their welfare.

The Commission for Scheduled Castes/Tribes has been recommending to the Government in its successive annual reports for the conferment of constitutional status and vesting it with the power of a Commission of Enquiry under the Commission of Enquiry Act, 1952. The Commission is handicapped to do its best without the required status/power. The National Front Government is committed to accept this recommendation. The State Government fail to supply information relating to implementation of constitutional safeguards for Scheduled Castes/ Tribes that impedes the functioning of the Commission. The State Governments should therefore supply the required information regularly and speedily.

The two institutions of Commissioner for Scheduled Castes/ Tribe and the Commission. For Scheduled Castes/Tribes have been assigned similar and overlapping functions. The Commissioner was an ex-officio member of the Commission until 1st September 1987 when it was reconstituted as the National Commission for Scheduled Castes and Scheduled Tribes with separate functions. The Commissioner's post had remained vacant for about seven years (24th November 1981 to 10th Feb. 1986)) and his report for that period was covered by the Report of the Commission of Scheduled Castes/Tribes. The Commissioner does not have enough powers while the Commission had no statutory powers. To avoid the duplication of functions and the lacuna the two institutions suffer from the Ministry of Welfare has a proposal to merge the office of Commissioner with the Commission and give it statutory powers. This proposal when implemented will go a long way in improving and streamlining the functioning of the institution charged under the Constitution with the duty to investigate all matters relating to the safeguards for the Scheduled Castes and Scheduled Tribes.

It is alleged that the Government at the Centre and those in the States are concerned only with the funds they make available for to use their cliche, the amelioration of the downtrodden. And they do not bother whether they reach the beneficiary or not. Again the political parties are interested in the extension of reservations and the grant of specific concessions to scheduled castes tribe as vote catching instruments. These charges though quite valid need to be met with by political parties in showing genuine concern for the upliftment of the weaker sections of society by initiating programmes at the grass roots to eradicate untouchability and ensure that the underprivileged sections of today acquire a position of honour and dignity due to all citizens of our great country.

8

Minority Groups

The term "minority" has not been defined in the Constitution or in any other enactment or in the Government Resolution under which the Minorities Commission was established. However, the Commission has been treating Muslims, Christians, Sikhs, Buddhists and Zoroastrians as religious minorities at the national level because their numerical strengths as compared with rests of Indian citizens is smaller and as such they ate entitled to any protections that may be designed for religious minorities. According to the 1981 census; the religious (minority) communities constitute about 16.46% of the population of India (excluding Assam) comprising 11.35% Muslims, 2.43% Christians, 1.96% Sikhs, 0.71 Buddhists and 0.01 % Zoroastrians (parsees).

The picture of the population by religions at the national level is different from that at the State levels. At the national level Hindus are the dominant majority but at the State level they are not in a few states and Union Territories. The Muslims are in majority in Jammu and Kashmir State and Lakshadweep, whereas Christians are in majority in the States of Meghalaya, Nagaland and Mizoram. Sikhs in the State of Punjab and the followers of other than Hinduism, Islam, Christianity, Sikhism, Buddhists, Jainism and Zorostrianism are in majority in the state of Arunachal Pradesh.

The linguistic minorities are those who have separate spoken language without necessarily having a distinct script and which constitute numerically smaller sections of the people in a State. In other words, linguistic minorities are determined on a State wise basis. Majority of the population speak 15 major languages mentioned in the Eighth Schedule of the constitution viz. Assamees (speaks 0.7%), Bengali (3%), Gujarati (4.7%), Hindi (38.4%), Kannada (3.9%), Kashmiri (0.4%), Malayalam (4%), Marathi (7.6%), Oriya (3.6%), Punjabi (2.5%), Sanskrit (.00004%) , Sindhi (0.3%), Tamil (6.9%), Telugu (8.1%), Urdu (5.2%), and other languages (4.60%).

Ours is a multi-religious, multi-lingual and multi-cultural society. Secularism is the bedrock of our nationhood. Uniquely among world civilisations, ours has combined antiquity and continuity with a heterogeneity. Our diversity is not a weakness but the basic source of our strength as a nation. We have built our nationhood on the values of tolerance and self-confident synthesis, of openness to the best in all cultures without losing our distinctive identity, of co-existence among different ways of life and the cross-fertilisation of ideas. Ours is a tradition of "sarva dharma sambhava," equal respect for all religions and full freedom for all religions to be practised and propagated. Safeguards for the protection of the minorities and provision for their welfare were provided in the constitution, and necessary measures initiated in pursuance thereof. National Integration Council was constituted by Pt Jawaharlal Nehru in 1961; Prime Minister's 15-Point Programme for the upliftment of the minorities was devised by Mrs Indira Gandhi and the Minorities Commission was constituted by her in 1978. All these institutions and various programmes and schemes being implemented for the welfare of minorities are discussed in detail as follows:

Statutory Provisions

The Constitution is replete with provisions for the welfare of the minorities. Specific articles in this respect are the following:

Article 15—Prohibition of Discrimination on Grounds of Religion Race, Caste, Sex or Place of Birth : (i) state shall not discriminate against any citizen on grounds only of religion, race, caste, sex, place of birth, or any of them; (ii) No citizen shall, on grounds only of religion, race, caste, sex, place of birth or any of them, be subject to any disability, liability, restriction or condition with regard to (a) access to shops, public restaurants, hotels and place of public entertainment; or (b) the use of wells, tanks, bathing ghats, roads and places of public resort maintained wholly or partly out of State funds or dedicated to the use of the general public; (iii) Nothing in this article shall prevent the State from making any special provision for women and children; (iv) Nothing in this article or in clause (2) of Article 29 shall prevent the State from making any-special provision for the advancement of any socially and educationally backward classes of citizens or for the scheduled castes and scheduled tribes.

Article 16—Equality of Opportunity in Matters of Public Employment : (i) There shall be equality of opportunity for all citizens in matters relating to employment or appointment to any office under the state; (ii) No citizen shall, on grounds only of religion, race, caste sex, descent, place of birth, residence or any of them, be ineligible for, or discriminated against in respect of any employment or office under the State; (iii) Nothing in this Article shall prevent Parliament from making any law prescribing in regard to a class or classes of employment or appointment to an, office under the Government of or any local or other authority within a State or Union territory, any requirement as to residence within the State or Union territory prior to such employment or appointment; (iv) Nothing in this Article shall prevent the State from making any provision for the reservation of appointments or posts in favour of any backward class of citizens which in the opinion of the State is not adequately represented in the services under the State; (v) Nothing in this Article shall affect the operation of any law which provides that the incumbent of an office in connection with the affairs of any religious or denominational institution or any member of the governing body thereof shall be a person professing a particular religion or belonging to a particular denomination.

Article 25—Freedom of Conscience and Free Profession, Practice and Propagation of Religon : (i) subject to public order, morality and health, air persons are equally entitled to freedom of conscience and the right freely to profess, practise and propagate religion: (ii) Nothing in this article shall affect the operation of any existing law or prevent the State from making any law;- (a) regulating or restricting any economic, financial, political or other secular activity which may be associated with religious practice; (b) providing for social, welfare and reform or the throwing open of Hindu religious institutions of a public character to all classes and sections of Hindus.

Explanation : The wearing and carrying of kirpans shall be deemed to be included in the profession of the Sikh religion; In sub-clause (b) of Clause (2) the reference to Hindus shall be construed as including a reference to persons professing the Sikh, Jain, or Buddhist religion, and the reference to Hindu religious institutions shall be construed accordingly.

Article 26—Freedom to Manage Religious Affairs : Subject to public order, morality and health, every religious denomination or any section thereof shall have the right: (a) to establish and maintain institutions for religious and charitable purposes; (b) to manage its own affairs in matters of religion; (c) to own and acquire movable and immovable property; and (d) to administer such property in accordance with law.

Article 27—Freedom as to Payment of Taxes for Promotion of any Particular Religion : No person shall be compelled to pay any taxes, the proceeds of which are specifically appropriated in payment of expenses for the promotion or maintenance of any particular religion or religious denomination.

Article 28—Freedom as to Attendance at Religious Instruction or Religious Worship in Certain Educational Institutions : (i) No religious instructions shall be provided in any educational institutionally maintained out of State funds; (ii) Nothing in clause (1) shall apply to an educational institution which is administered by the state but has been established under any endowment or trust which requires that religious instruction shall be, imparted in such institutions; (iii) No person attending any educational institution recognised by the State or receiving aid out of State funds shall be required to taken part in any religious instruction that may be imparted in such institution or to attend any religious worship that may be conducted in such institution or any premises attached thereto unless such person or, if such person is a minor, his guardian has given his consent thereto;

Article 29—Protection of Interests of Minorities : (i) Any section of the citizens residing in the territory of India or any part thereof having a distinct language, script or culture of its own shall have the right to conserve the same; (ii) No citizen shall be denied admission into any educational institution maintained by the state or receiving aid out of states funds on grounds only of religion, race, caste, language or any of them.

Article 30—Right of Minorities to Establish and Administer Educational Institutions : (i) All minorities, whether based on religion or language shall have the right to establish and administer educational institutions of their choice; (i) In making any law providing for the compulsory acquisition of any property of an educational institution established and administered by a minority, referred to in clause (i), the State shall ensure that the amount fixed by or determined under such law for the acquisition of such as would not restrict or abrogate the right guaranteed under that clause; (ii) The state shall not, in granting aid to educational institutions, discriminate against any educational institution on the ground that it is under the management of a minority, whether based on religion or language.

Article 347—Special Provision Relating to Language spoken by a Section of the Population of a Section of the Population of a State : On a demand being made in that behalf the President may, if he is satisfied that a substantial proportion of the population of State desire the use of any language spoken by them to be recognised by that State direct that such language shall also be officially recognised throughout that State or any part there of for such purpose as he may specify.

Article 350—Language to be Used in Representations for Readers of Grievances : Every person shall be entitled to submit a representation for the redress of any grievance to any officer or authority of the Union or a State in any of the language used in the Union or in the State, as the case may be.

Article 350A—Facilities for Instruction in Mother-tongue at Primary Stage : It shall be the endeavour of every State and of every local authority within the State to provide adequate facilities for instruction in the mother tongue at the primary stage of education to children belonging to linguistic minority groups; and the President may issue such directions to any State as he considers necessary or proper for securing the provision of such facilities.

Article 350B—Special Officer for Linguistic Minorities : (i) There shall be a Special Officer for linguistic minorities to be appointed by the President; (ii) It shall be the duty of the special officer to investigate all matters relating to the safeguards provided for linguistic minorities under this Constitution and report to the President upon those matters at such intervals as the President may direct, and the President shall cause all such reports to be laid before each House of Parliament, and sent to the Governments of the States concerned.

These constitutional provisions constitute "magna carta" or "Charter of Rights" for the religious and linguistic minorities. They are intended for the well-being and all round development of the minority communities. The government at the Centre, State and Local levels are to comply with them in letter and spirit. Any law made by them in contravention of these provisions can be challenged in the course of law and declared ultravires of the constitution. The aggrieved minority individuals and organisations have approached the Supreme Court and High Courts whenever any Act against their interest has been passed by the legislature and injustice done to them has been undone by the judiciary. The government has constituted the Minorities Commission who inter-alia ensures that the Constitutional provisions and the laws made by the governments for the welfare of the minority are properly implemented. The government takes necessary action on the findings of the Minorities Commission.

Various Commissions

The Minorities Commission was set up by the Government of India, Resolution in 1978. Resolution provides that the Commission shall consist of a Chairman and two other Members. However, subsequently its strength was increased from three to five. The Commission now consists of the Chairman and four Members. The Resolution also provides that the Officer appointed as Special Officer in terms of Article 350-6 of the Constitution will function as the Secretary of the Commission but has not been given effect to as the proposed Constitutional amendment to confer statutory status on the Commission and to merge the duties of the Special Officer for Linguistic Minorities in India with those of the Commission, under a Constitutional provision, have not yet materialised. Consequently, the Commission has been looking into specific grievances of the linguistic minorities quite apart provisions of Article 350-6 of the Constitution.

Functions of the Commission : The Commission was established out of concern for secular traditions and to promote national integration. Effective enforcement and implementation of safeguards provided for religious and linguistic minorities in the Constitution, in Central and State laws and in Governmental policies and administrative schemes, enunciated from time to time were intended so that feelings of inequality and discrimination prevalent amongst minorities, whether based on religion or language, are removed. To carry out these objects, the Commission was entrusted with the following functions:

(i) to evaluate the working of the various safeguards provided in the constitution for the protection of minorities and in laws passed by the Union and State Governments;

(ii) to make recommendations with a view to ensuring effective implementation and enforcement of all the safeguards and the laws;

(iii) to undertake a review of the implementation of the policies pursued by the Union and State Government with respect to minorities;

(iv) to look into specific complaints regarding deprivation of rights and safeguards of minorities;

(v) to conduct studies, research and analyses on the question of avoidance of discrimination against minorities;

(vi) to suggest appropriate legal and welfare measures in respect of any minorities to be undertaken by the Central or the State Governments;

(vii) to serve as a national clearing house for information in respect of the conditions of minorities; and

(viii) to make periodical reports at prescribed intervals to the Government.

The Commission considers various complaints received by it from aggrieved individuals and associations of minority communities or which come to its notice through any other source. It also gives hearings to individually or collectively visit various States to investigate important general and specific issues relating to minorities. The Commission also entrusts studies on identified subjects to persons having expertise in the matter. It also gives detailed opinions on matters referred to it.

The Commission has been considering various grievances of minorities and making recommendations for appropriate action to redress them. For example, the Commission looked into the grievances of Muslims regarding demolition of Muslim graveyards in Mirzauddin area, Delhi for the construction of a fly-over, creation of the post of Urdu Officer in Delhi Administration for development of Urdu, problems of Urdu medium schools in Delhi, conversion of Harijan to Islam in Meenakshipuram, Tiruniveli, Tamil Nadu etc; investigating into the grievances of Sikhs regarding the status of Punjabi language in the Union Territory of Delhi, threatened eviction of Punjabi settlers in Terai region of Uttar Pradesh, permanent settlement rights of ex-serviceman of Indian Army in districts Kurukshetra, Karnal, Haryana.

The Commission had also considered the issue of "Khalistan" raised by some members of the Sikh Community in August, 1981. It had felt that the grievances of Sikhs if any, should be examined with a view to finding constructive solutions for them. Gyani Sujan Singh accompanied by the Secretary of the Council had visited Punjab to assess the feelings of the Sikhs in general about their grievances and the Khalistan issue in particular. In the meantime, the Government had decided to study the demands and grievances of the sikh community and opened a dialogue with leaders of the Sikh community and others. The Commission decided that before taking any further action in the matter. It may be ascertained from the Home Ministry whether it would like the Minorities commission to go ahead with the study of the grievances with a view to suggesting constructive solutions for them. The Ministry of Home Affairs informed the Commission that since the grievances of the Sikhs already being considered by the government, it was not necessary for the Commission to take up the matter. The Commission had therefore not taken any further action in the matter.

Similarly, the Commission had gone into the complaints of alleged atrocities against Buddhists in Hupari district Kolahpur, and the request of the Trustees of Parsis Panchayat Fund and properties for exemption of their properties from the operation of Bombay Rent Act.

The Commission has been receiving representations from various religious minorities that they have been under represented in the State and Central Services and that they have also been excluded from the benefits of higher technical education in Engineering, Medical and other disciplines, causing strong resentment and frustration among the minorities. In fact, this is one of the main grievances of minorities in general and of Muslims in particular. The Commission noted that an inter-Ministerial Committee had already made certain recommendations with regard to sponsoring of candidates belonging to the minorities for Government employment by the Employment Exchanges. The Commission is ascertaining the action taken by the Ministry of Labour on the various recommendations made in this regard. However, it was felt that, for a more purposeful consideration of the manner, it would be necessary to make a detailed study of the problem with a view to evolve measures to ensure adequate representation of the minorities in Government employment in, general and for the provision of educational and professional training facilities to the deserving candidates of minority communities. A change in the recruitment policy is urgently called for so that, other things being equal, preference may be given to candidates from minority communities to make up for the backlog whatever may be the reasons for an increasing drop in the proportion of members of minority communities in Government services so that this situation could be remedied. In the selection bodies, too, there should be adequate representation of minorities.

In addition to the Annual Report, the Commission has been submitting separate reports on various subjects such as dispute over Jama Masjid at Sidhpur, District Mehsana, Gujarat; its opinion on Mandal Commission Report; Religious Freedom as adopted to conditions in India; Demands from a section of the Parsis for exclusion of the Parsi community from the purview of the Adoption of Children Bill, 1970, grievances of St. John's Medical college, Bangalore, proposed amendments to the Central Wakf Act of 1954, matters connected with National Integration etc.

The Commission had submitted ten Annual Reports during the Congress (I) rule. The Tenth Report for the period April 1, 1987 to March 31,1988 was submitted to Dr. (Smt.) Rajendra Kumari Bajpai, Minister of State for Welfare on March 30,1989 containing various activities of the Commission, studies undertaken by it and action taken on representations received by it as well as review of the implementation of 15 Point programmes and other schemes for the welfare of minorities and suitable recommendations to the Government. It is regrettable that out of the ten reports presented to the government only four reports were laid in Parliament. That reflects the casual concern of the Congress governments at the centre towards the problems facing the minorities. The 11th report of the Commission was presented to the Government on January 31,1990 and it was proposed to place four reports in Parliament during the Budget session 1990.

As an evidence of its concern for the welfare of minorities, the National Front Government has set up a Cabinet committee, under the Chairmanship of former Prime Minister V.P. Singh to give a new thrust to the 15-Point programme for the welfare of the minorities and to ensure its effective implementation. The Committee at its first meeting on January 12, 1990 had decided to have a concrete programme of action comprising specific projects covering various aspects of the 15-Point Programme. (i) The projects were to be taken up by different Ministries in 41 minority concentration districts. It had also taken a number of other decisions, including better representation of the minorities in services especially in the police and creation of composite police battalions consisting of members of minority and majority communities in the States for law and order duty; (ii) Special courts would be set up exclusively to try communal offences in places where large scale riots break out. While special courts in Delhi and Meerut had already been constituted, a court at Bhagalpur in Bihar has been set up shortly and the progress in the disposal of cases would be closely monitored; (iii) The amount of ex-gratia relief granted for cases of death or permanent incapacitation fixed at Rs 20,000 per case is being revised upwards to Rs 50,000 for every case; (iv) A pension of Rs 500 per month would also be given to widows and riot victims with low income. These would become effective for case occurring from April; 990 onwards; and (v) A special programme for the rehabilitation of weavers, most of whom belonged to minorities and who have been affected by Communal riots in Bhagalpur and Meerut was being taken up.

Article 350 B of the Constitution provided for the office of the Special Officer for Linguistic Minorities (CLM) designated as Commissioner for Linguistic Minorities in pursuance of the recommendations of States Reorganisation commission. Accordingly it was created in July 1957. At present the ClM Organisation consists of the Headquarters. Office at Allahabad and the three Regional Offices at Kolkatta, Chennai and Belgaum. The post of the Commissioner for Linguistic Minorities has not been filled since the last incumbent left it in May 1977. The Deputy Commissioner for Linguistic Minorities is overall administrative incharge of the Headquarters office and the Regional Offices.

The office of the Commissioner for Linguistic Minorities investigates all matters relating to safeguards provided for linguistic minorities under the constitution as also those agreed to at the national level. It also looks into the representations and complaints received from various institutions, bodies and individuals belonging to linguistic Minorities for redressal of their grievances. It submits its reports annually to the Government. So far it has submitted 27 reports out of which 26 have been laid before the Parliament.

Anomalous Position : The Deputy Commissioner for Linguistic Minorities also acts as the Deputy Secretary of the Minorities Commission. He is not responsible for his work in the former capacity to the Minorities Commission and reports directly to the President. This position is very anomalous, and needs to be rectified either by filling up the post of Commissioner for linguistic minorities or by transferring his functions to the Minorities Commission itself and merging his duties with those of the Minorities Commission as already suggested to the Government by the Commission. This will bring the position in consonance with the Government Resolution creating the Commission making the whole. Commission responsible to look after the interests of both religious and linguistic minorities. The amalgamation of the two institutions as envisaged above will also result in economy and efficiency as it would enable investigations into the conditions of religious and linguistic minorities simultaneously.

Streamlining the Organisation and Administrative Setup of the Commission : The Commission suffers from certain weaknesses and shortcomings in its organisation and administrative set up and therefore is unable to discharge its functions to achieve its laudable objectives in an efficient and effective manner:

(i) It has not been granted constitutional status so far. The constitutional (Forty sixth) Amendment Bill, 1978 was introduced in the Parliament to this effect but had failed to be carried through due to lack of prescribed quorum during the budget session of 1979. Since then, no fresh constitution amendment bill has been introduced on this subject. Lack of constitutional status to the Commission has hampered its working. The Government should therefore take necessary steps in the matter without any further delay.

(ii) The Commission does not enjoy any statutory investigative powers. The government is under the impression that not only would all government agencies reasonably and effectively but all other management bodies or private citizens whose help is often indispensable, will voluntarily come forward to give information whenever required by the Commission. But it has not happened. The Commission therefore needs to be equipped with adequate powers of enquiry under the Commission of Enquiry Act, 1952.

(iii) The post of the Commissioner of Linguistic Minorities should be filled up or his powers transferred constitutionally to the Minorities Commission for removing the existing anomaly and fulfilling the obligations of the two institutions.

(iv) Some of the State Governments have appointed State Minorities Commission/Committee/Cell to look into the problems of religious and linguistic minorities in their respective jurisdiction. It is desirable that every state should have an institution to look into specific grievances of the members of minority communities. Arrangements for coordination of activities of state commissions or Panels with those of the Central Minorities Commission are also imperative.

(v) The restructuring of the Secretariat of the Commission is desired by the establishment of Research and Studies Division, Legal Division, Information and Publications Division, and Establishment of Regional Offices.

(vi) The administrative infrastructure available to the Commission for the discharge of its functions is quite unequal to its ask both quantitatively and qualitatively. Staffed as it is at present, it has been able to do precious little to carry out its numerous functions assigned to it in its terms of reference. The staffing pattern therefore needs to be reviewed and the Commission requirement for adequately qualified staff of its choice to be met with.

(vii) References made to state/Central Government by the Commission are not attended to promptly and the reports received from them are found to be routine, sometimes, perfunctory and sketchy: Some cases remain pending for years together. The instructions issued by the Ministry of Home Affairs, to the Chief Secretaries/U.T. Administrations seem to be of little avail. This not only delays redressal of grievances but also lowers the image of the Commission.

State Minorities Commissions/Boards exist in some states also. These are Andhra Pradesh Minorities Commission, Assam Minorities Development Board, Bihar Religious and Linguistic Minorities Commission, Gujarat minorities Board, Madhya Pradesh Minorities Commission and Uttar Pradesh Minorities Commission. Other State Government has also been requested to set up minority Commission/Boards.

In addition, separate Development/Financial Corporations have also been set up for the economic upliftment of minorities. These are Andhra Pradesh State Minorities Financial Corporation, Assam Minorities Development Corporation, Bihar State Minorities Financial Corporation, Karnataka Minorities Development Corporation, U.P. Minorities Financial Development Corporation. In Tamil Nadu, the Backward Classes Economic Development Corporation provides assistance to the minorities as a special case, while in Haryana, the Mewat Development Board has been set up for the welfare of the Muslim community inhabiting this area.

An annual conference of the Chairman and members of the Central and State Minorities Commission/Boards which is also attended by the representatives of the State Minorities Development/Finance Corporations, the representatives of the concerned Ministries of the Government of India and Reserve Bank of India is held to discuss the problems of the minorities. At the conference held in 1988, the Chairman of the Central Minorities Commission had highlighted the fact that even amongst the religious and linguistic minorities there were some sections which could be regarded as the poorest of the poor. To them, economic development seemed distant, social equality a dream, education advancement an illusion and alienation a constant fear. It was decided at the conference inter alia that the Central and a State Minorities Commission should be vested with statutory powers of investigation as contained in Section 5 of the Commission of Enquiry Act, socio-economic survey of minorities be conducted by the State Minorities Commission with the assistance of the State Governments as was done by Andhra Pradesh State Minorities

Commission, the Planning Commission be requested to set up a working group on the welfare of minorities, and to prepare a separate component plan for the welfare of minorities as is being done for the scheduled castes/tribes, and State Minorities Commission should be involved in the review of the implementation of 15 Point Programme at the State level and also at the District level etc.

Special Programme

The 15-Point Programme for the welfare of the minorities was formulated by Late Prime Minister Smt. Indira Gandhi as a result of the deliberations of the National Integration Council. It is intended to ensure fuller participation of the minorities in all aspects of national life. These points are:

Communal Harmony

1. The State Governments are advised that in the areas which have been identified as communally sensitive and riot prone, District and Police officials of the highest known efficiency, impartiality and secular record must be posted. In such areas and even else where, the prevention of communal tension should be one of the primary duties of DM and SP. Their performances in this regard should be an important factor in determining their promotion prospects.
2. Good work done in this regard by District, and Police officials should be rewarded.
3. Severe action should be taken against all those, who incite communal tensions or take part in violence.
4. Special Court or Courts specifically earmarked to try communal offences should be set up so that offenders are brought to book speedily.
5. Victims of communal riots should be given immediate relief and provided prompt and adequate financial assistance for their rehabilitation.
6. Radio and TV must also help in restoring confidence, communal harmony and peace in such affected areas.

7. It is unfortunate that certain sections of the press some times indulge in tendentious reporting and publication of objectionable and inflammatory material which may incite communal tension. It is hoped that editors, printers, publishers and other concerned will cooperate in finding a way to avoid publication of such material.

Recruitment to State and Central Services

8. In the recruitment of police personnel, State Government should be advised to give special consideration to minorities. For this purpose, the composition of Selection Committees should be representative.
9. The Central Government should take similar action in the recruitment of personnel to the Central Police Forces.
10. Large scale employment opportunities are provided by the Railways, nationalised banks and Public sector enterprises. In these cases also the concerned departments should ensure that special consideration is given to recruitment from minority communities.
11. In many areas recruitment is done through competitive examinations. Often minority groups have been handicapped in taking advantage of the educational system to compete on equal terms in such examinations. To help them to overcome these handicaps steps should be taken to encourage the starting of coaching classes in minority educational institutions to train persons to compete successfully in these examinations.
12. The acquisition of technical skills by those minorities who are today lagging behind would also help in national development. Arrangements should be made to set up ITIs and Polytechnics by Government or private agencies in predominantly minority areas to encourage admission in such institutions of adequate number of persons belonging to these communities.

Other Measures

13. In various development programmes, including the 20 Point Programme, care should be taken to see that

minorities secure a fair and adequate measure the benefits flowing therefrom. In the various committees which are set up to oversee the implementation of such programmes, members of those communities should be actively involved.

14. Apart from the general issues to which reference has been made, there are various local problems which develop into needless irritants to minorities. For instance encroachment of wakf properties and on grave yards have led to protests and grievances in some places. Suitable steps should be taken to deal with such problems on an expeditious and satisfactory basis.

15. Problems relating to minorities need to be attended to on a continuing basis so that apprehensions are allayed and genuine grievances redressed. To facilitate this, a special cell will be created in the Ministry of Home Affairs to deal with matters relating to minorities.

Implementing Machinery : The Progress of the implementation of the programme is monitored by the Minorities Cell in the Ministry of Welfare headed by an Additional Secretary. The Minorities Cell obtains quarterly reports on progress of the implementation of the programme from State Governments, Union Territory Administrations and Central Ministries/Departments, The quarterly reports are analysed and reviewed and the deficiency noticed in the implementation of the programme are brought to the notice of the authorities concerned through meetings, discussions and field visits etc.

The concerned Central Ministries/Departments and the State Governments, have nominated Nodal Officers to coordinate the implementation of the activities connected with the programme. All State and Union Territories with very few exceptions, have also set up Minorities Cells to oversee implementation of the programme. A few State Governments have also set up Research Units to take up random sample surveys to assess the benefits of development programme reaching the minorities. The States of Uttar Pradesh, Bihar, Madhya Pradesh and Andhra Pradesh have State Minorities Commissions whereas the States of Gujarat and

Assam have Minority Welfare Boards to deal with minority grievances and minority welfare measures. States of Uttar Pradesh, Bihar, Andhra Pradesh and Karnataka have also established State Minorities Financial Corporations to help for economic development of minorities.

Review of Implementation of the Programme : The implementation of the 15-Point Programme was earlier reviewed in a Conference of the State Nodal Officers in June 1986. It was, felt that the programme required a further review at a higher level. The Ministry of Welfare accordingly organised a conference of Chief Ministers/State Ministers in charge of 15-Point Programme on 19 June 1987 at New Delhi to review implementation of the Programme. The Conference was attended by the Chief Ministers of Uttar Pradesh, Sikkim and Pondicherry and Ministers incharge of Minorities Welfare in the States of Andhra Pradesh, Assam, Bihar, Gujarat, Himachal Pradesh, Jammu and Kashmir, Karnataka, Kerala, Maharashtra, Mizoram, Tamil Nadu and West Bengal. The remaining States and Union Territories were represented by the Secretaries to respective Government/Nodal Officers. The representative, of the concerned Central Ministries/Departments as well as chairman and members and Secretary of the Minorities Commission also attended the conference.

In his message to the conference then Prime Minister Shri Rajiv Gandhi had emphasized the need for ensuring a fair deal to minorities in term of opportunities for employment and economic betterment and protection from any kind of discrimination. Following were the important action points which had emanated as a result of the discussions in the aforesaid conference.

(i) Quarterly review meetings shall be held at the level of Chief Minister and also at the level of Chief Secretary in each state on regular basis;

(ii) Monthly review meetings to be held at Divisional Commissioner/District Collector's level;

(iii) State Minorities Commissions/Boards in the respective States would be associated with the review at the state level;

(iv) Quarterly review meetings would be held at the State

level with Nationalised Banks and Financial Corporations to review the processing of applications for financial assistance;

(v) Orientation courses for improving awareness of development schemes amongst minorities would be organised at the field level involving District Collector to create awareness of various developmental schemes in which minorities are largely employed;

(vi) Measures would be taken to improve registration of minority candidates in employment exchanges to minority educational institutions and minority concentration areas;

(vii) Reviews at State level regarding credit flow and credit plan evolved by the State Lead Banks;

(viii) In the context of Programme of Action under the National Policy on Education, 1986 relating to the educationally backward minority groups, State Government will draw up a time bound action plan for implementation;

(ix) Selection Committees for recruitment to various posts to include a representative of minority community;

(x) Minorities' Cell would be set up in those States which have not yet set up;

(xi) Random sample surveys to be carried out by the States in selected areas for assessing the extent to which benefits of developmental programme reach the minority communities; and

(xii) Special stress on orientation training of officers at various levels to deal with problems of minorities and minorities welfare.

In order to make the quarterly reports more result oriented with emphasis on physical progress achieved and to monitor the progress of implementation of Programme in qualitative terms, wherever possible, the conference adopted a format suggested by the Ministry of Welfare for the submission of the Information every quarter by the State Governments and Union Territory Administrations. Likewise the concerned Central Ministries/ Departments were asked to finalise formats for reporting on action taken in implementing the points in the Programme. Though it is not possible to indicate the progress achieved in qualitative terms, the analysis of the information received does indicate that programme is being taken very seriously and the same has generated fair amount of awareness about the problems of minorities amongst officers not only at the State or District levels but also at the Block and Village levels.

Inter-community Peace

State Government which have riot prone areas have shown positive response to the measures for prevention and control of communal violence and promotion of communal harmony. Most states have accepted the Central guidelines on relief to communal riot victims.

State Police Recruitment : Some states have taken action or making selection committees for recruitment to State police representative but some of the States are yet to do so. None of the states have provided for nominating non-official members on the Committee in case of non-availability of suitable minority officials.

Central Police Recruitment : Selection Committees for recruitment to Group C and D Categories have been made representative in five Central Police organisations namely Central Reserve Police Force, Border Security Force, Central Industrial Security Force, Assam Rifles and Indo Tibetan Border Police.

Making Selection Committee Representative : The Ministry of Personnel, Public Grievances and Pension have issued instructions to all Central Ministries Departments to ensure that the selection committee for Group C and D posts comprise representatives from minority community. Some of the State Governments and Union Territory Administrations have also issued orders making the selection committees for recruitment to various posts and particularly police service broad based by inclusion of representatives of minority communities.

Instructions to Employment Exchange : Director General Employment and Training (DGE & T), New Delhi has issued detailed instructions to State Governments to ensure that there is no discrimination against minorities in registering names and in sponsoring names to recruitment agencies by the employment exchanges. Instructions have also been issued by the DGE & T for conducting special registration drives in minority concentration areas and in minority educational institutions. The State Governments have been requested to review the arrangements for monitoring effective implementation of these instructions. The States of Assam, Gujarat, Kerala, Madhya Pradesh, Orissa, Rajasthan, Sikkim and Delhi Administration have set up Monitoring Cells for the purpose. The State of Uttar Pradesh has set up a Coaching Centre together with an Inspection Cell to help larger number of minority candidates to obtain jobs.

Educating Masses

University Grants Commission operates the scheme for coaching of weaker sections amongst minority communities through 20 universities and 14 coaching centers. The monitoring of the results of this scheme is done by the Department of Education of the Ministry of Human Resource Development. Analysis conducted by the UGC of the reports received, however, showed that the scheme had been rather ineffective and there were very few successful minority community candidates. The entire scheme is therefore being reviewed by the Standing Committee of the UGC.

Ministry of Welfare also grants 100% financial assistance to committee, minorities institutions to set up coaching centres exclusively for minorities to prepare them for All India and State Competitions for entry into IAS and other allied services as also the State services.

Official Schemes

Programme of Action under the National Policy for Education, 1986 contains an exclusive chapter on the education of the educationally backward minorities. The programme of action contains concrete measures to raise the literacy standard of the minorities. It provides for the drawing up a time bound action plan for implementation of the progress on items contained in the

Programme of Action and also for setting up a Monitoring Cell in the State Education Departments to monitor the programme of educationally backward minority groups. It lays emphasis on in-service training for teachers from educationally backward minority managed institutions in Science, Maths, English and provision of career guidance through National Council of Educational Research and Training, State Educational Research and Training and other resource centres. It also provides for adequate representation of minority educational institutions in computer literacy scheme, vocational education at higher secondary levels in minority managed institutions, adequate thrust to adult education and early childhood education programme in minority concentration areas, survey of available facilities for girls' education and for setting up girls' institutions/hostels in minority concentration areas wherever necessary. The Programme also provides for ensuring minority representation in all educational advisory committees/bodies at the Central/State level. The Programme also provides for drawing up clear guidelines for recognition of minority educational institutions and for timely disposal of pending applications. The programme of Action also requires introducing Maths, Science and English in Madrasas on voluntary basis and also setting up of early childhood centres and introducing socially useful productive work in these institutions besides provision for drawing up clear for scholarships for weaker sections on merit-cum-means basis, inbuilt system of placement in good institutions, fee exemption/fee concession/ compensation for opportunities lost for artisans and other weaker sections and formulation of a scheme for remedial coaching in minority, managed educational institutions. The Programme of Action also provides for setting up craft training institute in identified minority artisans concentration blocks, with 80 per cent seats for artisans children. The Programme of Action also being monitored by the Department of Education in the Ministry of Human Resource Development which has devised a format collecting information from State Governments and Union Territory Administrations.

Progress and Prosperity

The State Government and Union Territory Administrations are urged to organise quarterly review meetings by Secretary incharge of institutional Finance with Commercial Banks at the State level to review flow of credit in minority concentration areas and to discuss the progress on flow of credit in minority concentration areas in the District Consultative Committee meetings. The States/Union Territories are also advised to take action on the following issues:

(i) Implementation of time bound action by the Lead Banks for setting up officers pre-recruitment centres for minority candidates at the State capitals;

(ii) Holding quarterly review meetings at state level with commercial banks and the state financial institutions to monitor progress in processing of application sponsored by Minorities, Financial Corporation for financial assistance;

(iii) Drawing up phased programme on research studies to identify sectors in industries, crafts and trades where minority communities are largely employed and on flow of credit to Minority artisan areas by State Government and Nationalised Banks; and

(iv) Drawing up a phased programme for organising orientation courses on creating awareness of schemes of financial assistance by banks and other financial institutions in minority, artisan concentration blocks and in minority educational institutions.

Cultural Protection

The Ministry celebrates "Welfare of the Minorities Day" every year as it did on 20th November 1987 as part of celebration of "Quomi Ekta Week". The Day is celebrated highlighting the implementation of Prime Minister's 15 Point Programme for Minorities Welfare. The State Government and Union Territory Administrations are also advised to celebrate this day in the following manner:

(i) Organisation of orientation courses at field levels involving District Collectors for creating awareness amongst minority groups of various development programmes undertaken by Central and State Governments and by

Financial institutions, with special focus on schemes involving community participation and voluntary organisations in the field of education, health, women and children's welfare;

(ii) To give adequate publicity the progress made in implementation of Prime Minister's 15 Point Programme; and

(iii) Publication of articles through newspaper etc. highlighting progress made in implementation of various aspects of Prime Minister's 15 Point Programme in local languages.

Safety for All

In 1988, Union Minister of State for Home, Mr Subodh Kant Sahay had said that the Centre has decided to raise a special task force to deal with communal riots and terrorism. The force shall be raised on the pattern of National Security Guards (NSG) and trained to strike at short notice at trouble spots. It will be equipped with sophisticated weapons. The Chief Ministers of all the states would raise similar task forces in their states to deal with emergencies. The rationale for creating the task force was: (1) The Centre was deeply concerned about the flare up of communal riots and growth of terrorism in various parts of the country. The governments did not consider it advisable to summon army to handle disturbances. The deployment of army had been so frequent in recent years that there were apprehensions that 'the armed forces might also become controversial; (2) The need of the hour was therefore to have a task force, which should inspire confidence among the people and cause terror among the troublemakers; (3) The state police forces have been found to be inadequately trained and equipped to handle such situations; (4) The army, in any case, was not trained to handle civil disturbances.

A cell had been created in the Home Ministry to monitor communal flare-ups in the country. It has also been assigned the task of keeping in touch with the social and voluntary organisations at the grassroots level which could be used to create communal harmony. The Home Ministry has identified sensitive areas and prepared guidelines for the states on how to handle communal flare-ups. The Government also proposes to set up a core group of media persons to evolve a mutually acceptable code for reporting communal riots and terrorists activities. The role of the electronic media in this context is also being assessed and film and TV. personalities will be asked to chalk out a strategy for using the electronic media to effectively spread the message of communal harmony and amity.

Deficiencies in the Proposal for Riot Task Force : The proposal for Riot Task Force has been criticised among others by Bharatiya Janata Party. It suffers from certain deficiencies some of which are as follows:

Lack of Political Will : It was when Indira Gandhi was Prime Minister that the suggestion for the creation of a task force to deal with communal riots was first made. Though communal riots ravaged the country during Mr Rajiv Gandhi's regime the idea was not pursued seriously. The V.P. Singh, government did not last long enough to be able to consider various aspects of the suggestion. Now the Union Minister of State for Home of JD(S) government has announced that his government has decided to set up a "special task force" to deal with communal riots and terrorism and he has written to the state Chief Ministers also to set up similar task forces. Accordingly Mr Chimanbhai Patel, Chief Minister of Gujarat decided to establish a special riot police force and asked, top officials of his government to work out the details and submit a report in ten days. The report was not in evidence by the stipulated deadline. The reason obviously is weakness of political will.

Action against Politicians Engineering Riots : It is common knowledge that most communal cases are engineered by Politicians or their supporters. To give a specific instance when Mr Patel was heading a coalition government; there were communal riots in Baroda and according to an intelligence report he had received one his cabinet colleagues was camping in the city and instigating the riots. Yet the Chief Minister did not take any action against him for fear of Bhartiya Janata Party withdrawing from the government leading to his fall. It has not been spell out clearly if the proposed task force will have power to round up politicians instigating communal riots or its jobs will be fire-fighting.

The Conception and Tasks of the Force Unclear : It appears that the centre does not have a comprehensive conception of what the force should be like and what tasks it should perform. It is expected to deal with both communal riots and acts of terrorism. The, two are totally different from each other and any force saddled with the twin responsibility of a dealing with both must necessarily find itself less than equal to the tasks. For instance, the recent communal trouble in Hyderabad was immediately preceded by acts of terrorism by Naxalites. A task force cannot cope with both the time gap between which was so small as to be almost negligible.

Difficulty of Coordination between Central and State Task Forces : As stated earlier the Centre is to have a task force and every state has to set up one of its own. That will create the problem of coordination of activities between the two. It has been an accepted convention that the Centre can send reinforcements only on the specific request of the State Government whose police force is unable to face a situation. Since the proposed task force will be a para-military organisation, it is not clear if the centre will decide suo moto to despatch it to a riot-torn state.

Nature of Composition of the Task Force : The Parliament had been told on August 21,1987 that the states had been advised to have "mixed riot squads". Considering the proven communalisation of Uttar Pradesh's PAC and to a lesser extent, that of Bihar Police, the advice was sound but no state has acted on it so far.

Unless the above mentioned lacunae are removed, it would be desirable to stream line the existing police and paramilitary forces and continue the practice of deploying CRPF and Army in an area rocked by communal riots as these provide a sigh of relief to the peace roving and law abiding members of both the communities.

Unity Factor

One of the main objectives of the Minorities Commission has been the promotion of national integration and secular outlook which is also one of the goals provided in the Preamble and the

Chapters on Fundamental Rights the Directive Principles of State Policy and Duties of citizens in our constitution. We had built a powerful psychological bond in the course of a common struggle for freedom against exploiting imperialism which had tried to defend themselves by the use of traditional, divisions, economic or religious, cultural or regional to prolong their rule. They had adopted a policy of 'divide and rule', hence we could, throw off the foreign yoke without experiencing the trauma of a rather distressing and disastrous partition which resulted primarily from the manipulations of the foreign ruler who exploited all our weaknesses. Now our country is politically free. But both internal and external forces of exploitation still try to use the same weaknesses and fissiparous tendencies whether they be based on religion, culture or region, to serve their own supposed interests. Even the struggle of political parties for power is not free from exploitation of caste, language and region for obtaining votes in an unscrupulous fashion. In this context, national integration has a relevance and importance in our national life which is perhaps unprecedented.

National Integration can only take place satisfactorily if there is a cooperation both from minorities as well as majorities in every part of the country to secure this objective. The Minorities Commission has been trying to explore means of promoting national recommendations such as: Establishment of an institute of National Integration with departments for study as well as of teaching of every aspect of national integration under a highly qualified director helped by experts formulating schemes of education for national, and coordination of all the agencies of national integration both voluntary and official; a national integration week should be observed every year commencing with the observance of communal harmony day; citizens belonging to the religious minorities should be encouraged to participate in each other's religious festivals and social and cultural festivities like Holi, Id, Dushehra, Milad, Guru Nanak Day, Christmas, etc; Teachers' and students' camps from national to regional at university, college and school levels; may also the desirable, where feasible, to introduce nap-denominational students hostels and, to encourage willing young people to marry according to their free choice irrespective of creed, caste or community; Persons who exploit communal and caste sentiments should be dealt with firmly; special programmes for the education of women to bring about a genuine understanding and synthesis of the Indian culture should be undertaken. The women, as mothers, wives, teachers and influential citizens set best examples of human understanding tolerance and respect for different religious beliefs, cultures and customs and can built the strongest bridges in their homes conducive to children intermingling without differences of religion, castes or creed; No particular caste or community should be allowed to have a dominant position, in the para-military and police organisations; Special forces, should be created to combat riots; and administrators have an important role to play, maintaining communal harmony and peace. In sensitive areas, specially trained senior officers with broad cultural outlook should be posted.

The most revolutionary recommendation was however, the formulation of a very comprehensive scheme for the promotion of national integration and secular traditions and protection of human lights of all sections including minorities such a scheme involved the setting up of appropriate institutional machinery such as National Integration cum Human Rights Institute to help a National Integration-cum-Human Rights Commission to be provided for by the Constitution itself in place of multiplicity of Commission and panels looking after the interests of the minorities, scheduled castes/tribes and backward classes as naming Commissions as those meant for minority communities or scheduled castes etc was by itself misleading and encouraged decisiveness. The proposed Commission could have sub-commissions or sections separately with the problems of Minorities and those of scheduled castes and scheduled tribes and a Human Rights sub-commission as apart of it could cover cases of all citizens alleging discrimination against them on any illegal grounds. While all the suggestions except the last one are being implemented, the Government would do well in giving serious consideration to the establishment of National Integration-cum-Human Rights Commission to obliterate the concept of exclusiveness among different segments of our society and welding them into one nation.

Minorities in our country have been disadvantaged by educational backwardness or other social and economic disabilities. The constitution has therefore provided certain protection and safeguards for them to secure social justice to them and to achieve national integration. Multi-social, multi-culture, multi-lingual and multi-religious societies all over the world have enacted legislations to safeguard the interests of minorities and protect them against discrimination on the basis of religion caste, creed or colour. In USA there is Civil Rights Commission to enforce the increasing number of statutory provisions meant to counteract and combat discrimination in every form and in every sphere of life and to achieve a new form of national integration, so is the Human Rights Commission and the Ministry of Multi-culturalism, in Canada. In Britain, there is an elaborate legal machinery provided by the Race Relations Act. In USSR there is more comprehensively and strictly controlled socio-economic and legal framework as to attain a powerful form of integration between those who are culturally and racially so disparate as to be conceived of separate nationalities (though a move of disintegration has swept the country as a result of the twin policies of "Glasnost" and "Perestiroka" initiated by President Mikhail Gorbachov leading to the demand of independence by the constituent Republics of the USSR). The measure taken by our government in pursuance of the provisions of the constitution for the welfare of minorities have contributed substantially in raising their living standards but much more needs to be done to ameliorate their lot by floating new programmes and scheme to meet their special needs which have been thoroughly looked into and for meeting which a very comprehensive report has been submitted by High Power Panel headed by Dr. Gopal Singh.

The whole hearted implementation of the Prime-Minister's 15-Point programme for the welfare of minorities is a high national priority. Its review from time to time by the centre and state nodal officers and the National Integration Council has impelled the governments to initiate more effective measures for their educational economic and employment development and promotion of communal harmony but the achievements made so far in these fields leave much to be desired.

The Minorities Commission claims to have done whatever could be possible under the existing organisational structure and administrative set up and the resources made available to it. To make the commission to perform its function more effectively, it deserves to be granted constitutional status, statutory powers of investigation and the appointment of Commissioner for Linguistic Minorities or its integration with the Minorities Commission, appointment of State level minorities commission etc.

The suggestions made by the Minorities Commission in respect of national integration and secular values though commendable have not been able to yield the desired results. As a matter of fact, communalism has aggravated with the announcement of the implementation of Mandal Commission's Report and Babri Masjid Ram Janambhoomi controversy by the vested interests with a view to create favourable vote banks, and in the process our ideas of national integration, communal harmony, casteless society, social justice etc. have become the first causalities-Communal riots have occurred on an unprecedented scale in the recent past.

Communalism is not of recent origin in India. It has been allowed to be exploited for long in the calculated and pernincious pursuit of power by almost all politicians. No leader on either side of the fence hesitates to put self before countrymen and play communal politics at some time or the other. In fact, politics has come to be based practically on caste, religion and language and few leaders are willing to break the vicious circle. The generality of politicians are power hungry and are unwilling to shed communalism. Consequently one sees daily the debris of secularism in one city or another.

Gandhiji saw religion as a strong unifying force. He told the contending religious groups that "true religion should have nothing to do with activities such as riots or territorial divisions of the country. Nehru regarded as dangerous the alliance of religion and politics in the shape of communalism. But there is no going away from the fact that Secularism is what holds the variety of religious, cultures and traditions India together. Thus for our survival as a nation we must take courage in both hands. This calls for concerted and sincere efforts by the leaders of all political parties to promote a secular way of life and shed the hangover (divide and rule) policy of the British rule. All the political parties should be unanimous in condemning those who let the country drift into recurrent communal disasters. They should whole heartedly support the efforts aimed at curbing the menace which is eating into the vitals of our democratic secular fabric.

National Integration Council was set up in 1961 by Pt. Jawaharlal Nehru to find ways and means of combating the evils of communalism, casteism, regionalism etc. which were working against the unity and integrity of the nation. It has been reconstituted several times after its birth-as a rule with the change of regime in Delhi. It has been unable to achieve its objectives. New dimensions have been added to communalism in Punjab where efforts have been made to create ill will between Hindus and Sikhs and thank God that these have not yet succeeded in causing Hindu-Sikh riots on communal lines. Casteism has been encouraged by the Janata Dal's passionate backing of the Mandal Commission's Report and regionalism has taken a highly dangerous form in certain states and is the very anti-thesis of national integration as manifested in Kashmir's demand for independence, the campaign for Sikh Homeland and insurgency in Assam founded on the premise for an independent state. We have the moved to national disruption rather than integration. A ritualistic approach to national integration will not do any more. Enough speeches, worded in holy phrases have been made by our leaders in the past. Dissatisfaction among the sections of populations in the concerned states would have to be removed by taking appropriate concrete steps to guard the country against separatists and secessionists.

It is alleged that the minorities are being appeased, they have been given more than equal rights and privileges in the Constitution, the majority are not getting their due, the minorities are being given more than their snare and perhaps pampered in the bargain. On the other hand it is contended that the Muslims are more badly off than most other communities, around 3 per cent of them are to be found in the All India Services, their representation in the army, police and other services, is much lower than their proportion in the population. When the 1986 policy on education was being formulated, it was discovered that they were educationally the most backward in he country.

Bharatiya Janata Party stands for the abolition of the Minorities' Commission and its substitution by Human Rights Commission for all citizens of India irrespective of their religion, caste or creed, scrapping of Article 370 granting special status to Kashmir to bring back the state to the Indian mainstream, adoption of uniform civil code for all Indians irrespective of their religion, caste or creed, promotion of all languages and repeal of Muslim Women's Act to restore to Muslim women their dignity and right to justice that other Indian women have. The solution lies in appreciating the selfless struggle of Mahatma Gandhi to bring love among Hindus and Muslims. Symbolically, the thought of Rama of the Hindus to be the same as Rahim of the Muslims and never accepted the separation of Hindus and Muslims and became a martyr to this cause. We may rescue from the fratricidal quarrel the harmonious co-existence of the faiths by adhering to traditions of tolerance and togetherness emphasized by Gandhi.

9

Empowerment of the Unprivileged

The declared aim of the Constitution is to uplift the backward classes so that they may enter the main stream of national life as early as possible. Article 14 has accepted equality as the foundation of social justice. Every one is equal before law. But the structure of Indian society (including Hindus, Muslims, Christians) is based on caste hierarchy and inequality. This is the basic contradiction in the current Indian situation even four decades after the adoption of the Constitution. The social structure is based on caste and all the social, educational and economic disabilities arise as a result of the practice of caste inequality. Each caste is structured on the basis of endogamy and so preserves its identity. The people belonging to the caste want to preserve *caste identity* but fight against *caste hierarchy.* Further, each caste wants to rise up and claim equality with the castes above but is against the castes below coming up. So each caste whether "backward" or "more backward" or "depressed" desires that the reservation of seats in colleges and jobs in the government should be on the *caste* basis. But the "advanced castes", *while preserving the caste identity,* desire that the principle of equality should operate so that with the advantages of education and influence they are enjoying, they can maintain their forward status and give only lip sympathy for the upliftment of the masses. The concepts of "equal opportunity" and "social justice" sound hollow when we take into account the realities of social life. Backward *castes* exist in reality but the

Constitution speaks only of Backward *classes.* As a result any move by the State Governments to develop criteria on the basis of caste are struck down by the courts as they violate the Constitution. The only way by which some of the State Governments try to overcome the situation is by drawing up lists of castes which are backward; but this is not an easy problem since the "advanced backward castes" desire to be included in the list; as they are politically powerful their claims cannot be laid aside by any democratic government.

Constitutional Ambiguity

The Supreme Court in its various judgements has pointed out that while caste may be of some relevance, it cannot be the sole or even the dominant criterion. It has also suggested that if the whole caste is backward, it is more appropriate to put it in the Scheduled Caste list. But no caste can be said to be "completely" backward. Nor do any of these castes desire to be listed along with the Scheduled Castes.

As Justice Subba Rao (1973) pointed out the State should avoid the following pitfalls in their pursuit to improve the lot of the backward classes: "*(a)* in the name of backward classes the really advanced classes or castes should not be allowed to get benefits; *(b)* in the name of upliftment of backward classes, caste system shall not be perpetuated; (c) backwardness shall not be allowed to become a vested right; *(d)* the upliftment of backward classes shall not be allowed to suppress brilliance, for a country which neglects brilliance will ultimately deteriorate in quality."

Dr. Anirudh Prasad in his classic treatise *"Reservation Policy and Practice in India"* made the following suggestions to resolve the problem:

1. Reservation as such in the form of Quo system should be done away barring for unimpeachable backward classes like Scheduled Castes and Scheduled Tribes for few more years with a time bound programme.

   The problem of the Scheduled Castes and Scheduled Tribes is *sui generis.* The considerations and reasons which led the founding fathers to make compromise still exist and therefore reservation for S.Cs. and S.Ts. both in representative bodies and services should continue for another twenty years. In meantime, political parties should try to win the confidence of S.Cs. and S.Ts. by nominating them from unreserved constituencies. And, S.Cs. and S.Ts. should also develop a sense of initiative and independent standing because one decade concession conceded by a staunch supporter of their cause like Dr. B.R. Ambedkar and given constitution should not remain in perpetuity. Rigorous efforts should be made to educate their children properly. Reservation for them should not be end of governmental responsibility. Emphasis should be put on better initial education and additional coaching with full educational and financial assistance at upper classes level. A declaration should be made that after two decades there would be no reservation in the form of quota system. After this period only enabling provision should be there to assist them in preparation for fair competition.

2. Economic criteria should be adopted not to allow benefit to a so-called economically backward class but as an elimination process to eliminate those beneficiaries of preferential treatment whose family's annual income exceeds, to say, Rs. 40,000 per annum. States should follow Kerala Scheme involved and upheld in *K.S. Jayashree* v. *State of Kerala,* of course with revision of the income limit. Thus, the reservation scheme should be based on inbuilt self-abolition principle and not on self-perpetuation principle. Creamy layer of S.Cs. and S.Ts. in higher services must be eliminated from benefit. To make it more clear the wards of an S.C. or S.T. M.L.A. or M.P. a Union Minister or a Minister in a State Cabinet, an I.A.S. or I.P.S. or I.F.S. or P.C.S. or P.C.S. (J), a well placed teacher in a University or a Degree College or an employee in Group 'A' or Group 'B' services must not be allowed to eat away the reservational cake which is meant for their brethren who are at the rock bottom level of poverty.

3. Reservation should be restricted to the stage of the initial appoint, as after appointment every employee including

those belonging to the classes enjoying reservational benefit become member of one and the same class and there should be guarantee that "among the equals, provisions should be equal and shall be administered equally". And discrimination will breed injustice not only among equals but against the society by giving undue weightage to incompetent employee and thereby creating job dissatisfaction among others affecting efficiency in service.

4. Methods should be devised as to ensure that not only few castes members among the Scheduled Castes or O.B.Cs. grab most of the fruits of preferential treatment and thereby create new upper caste among themselves.
5. Reservational benefit should not go unevaluated. The beneficiary of compensatory justice getting benefit for past injustices done to him by unidentifiable persons, should not be allowed to do injustice with his own kinsmen. In other words, persons practicing injustice by deserting their wives and other intra S.Cs. and S.Ts. injustices should be deprived of reservational benefit. They must not be allowed to have best of both the worlds—claiming justice against others and doing injustice themselves.
6. Caste should never be recognised as criteria of identifying backwardness and backwardness must be of that terrible backwardness of the type from which Scheduled Castes and Schedule Tribes people suffer. In respect of O.B.C. the Courts should apply the strict scrutiny test.
7. For O.B.C. there should be no quota system. If they need protective discrimination, the preferential treatment other than reservation of seats, e.g., scholarship, concession in upper age limit for competitive examinations and special coaching should be awarded.
8. Reservations on the ground of residential requirements under Article 16 (3) should be abolished. It does help the parochialism demanding 'sons of the soil' theory's application in jobs and in admissions to medical and engineering colleges.
9. In order to inspire the confidence of S.Cs., S.Ts. and O.B.Cs.,

and with a view to develop a sense of security without reservation, the dominant or upper castes have to leave the way of their vested interest's protection through untold, unofficial reservations what the author has termed as destructive discrimination.

10. Without indulging in controversies that Indian society has for ages maintained and is still maintaining implicit reservation for upper castes in general and dominant caste in particular on the one hand, and making explicit reservation for depressed classes on the other, the common endeavour of all should be to ask for jobs for all and governmental policy should aim at that objective.
11. There should be no nservational quota for economically backwards, as the constitution does not intend to award compensatory discrimination benefit to such a backward class. The reasons are obvious. First, the Constitution speaks of socially and educationally backward class. It is cumulative backwardness—both social and educational, which attracts preferential treatment and upper caste poor can in no sense be regarded as socially backward. Second, economic backwardness is not result of injustice done in past against such people and therefore, no compensatory justice or corrective justice programme is warranted. Third, it involves false income certification and influential non-tax payers will grab the benefit and the real poor will be left as before.
12. Barring military and defence personnel reservation of seats should not be done in favour of any other category of beneficiaries not specifically warranted under Articles of the Constitution itself. Thus:
    (a) there should be no reservation in favour of the wards of political sufferers any more after four and half decades of our independence. Political sufferers have been compensated for more than a reasonable period and have been enjoying prestigious position with societal honour and therefore, there are no more disadvantaged or they do not suffer from that terrible backwardness which warrants special treatments;

(b) there should be no reservation of seats or any concessionary assistance to the wards of representatives of the people. They are emerging and have already emerged as new elite class. Their children get education in best educational institutions and they are most advantaged and in no sense disadvantaged to attract preferential treatment;

(c) there should be no reservation of seats for admissions in educational institutions for the wards of institution's employees. The reasons are obvious. First, public education is ultimately financed by general people and therefore, there should no discrimination in admissions between the ordinary students and wards of the employees of the institutions. Second, wards of the employees of the institution are placed better than others. They remain with employee, may have easy access to teachers and therefore, are in advantageous position in comparison to others. Though the Courts have disallowed preferential treatment in favour of the wards of employees of an institution, still in most of the educational institutions there are 5 per cent to 10 per cent weightage granted for the wards of the employees of the institution it should be scraped;

(d) at least after half century of the functioning of our constitution, the whole country should be treated as one unit for admissions purposes and for the purpose of jobs and outside state nomination need not be exercised. Fair competition will ensure fairly meritorious students from outside State and nomination breeds less meritorious donational candidates representing a State in poor shape;

(e) there should be no reservation on account of geographical location of an area except cease fire range. Indiscriminate concession will frustrate the objective. Even in Hill areas and Uttrakhand there may be wealthy and socially forward people getting their children educated in better institutions elsewhere and therefore indiscriminate preferential treatment may result into the utilisation of benefits by creamy layer of the inhabitants of those areas and therefore, elimination process should be made effective in relation to the inhabitants of those areas too. District-wise and unit-wise reservation have already been discouraged by the Courts, the institutional preferences should also be done away, because after all they recognize place of birth and residence in roundabout way as a basis of discrimination; and

(f) as far as possible, dereservation policy should be adopted in top and merit requiring services. In Class I services and in super specialities subject admissions there should not be any reservation. Suitability for the job and efficiency consideration should govern the decision of selection committees and not the reservation. That is to say, in nursery school jobs and for maternity jobs women can be preferred to the maximum but not in cases of superintendent of Jails having duties to deal the hardened criminals. Now table needs to be turned and merit and efficiency should be prime concern and reservation consciousness should disappear.

13. With anxiety and languish, if Article 15(4), providing for special provisions and not for reservational quota with underlying object to prepare the disadvantaged classes through facilities of freeship, scholarship, free boarding and lodging, special coaching, upper age concession for competition and so on, to face, the challenges of life, on footing equal to others, is not going to be accepted as Yug Dharma of the Indian society and instead, the crutches of reservations are to perpetuate, the extent to which protective discrimination through quota system is operated (which is injurious both to national cause of cohesion and international competitism) should be restricted to the minimum and rarest of the cases. The issue for determination should no more be how much is too much? Instead, it should be how less is too less? The vigil and elimination process should work with effective family planning

measures so that percentage of the beneficiaries of compensatory discrimination does not increase in a way as to demand more and more reservational benefits, the elimination process should work with diminishing return and not with increasing claims and perpetuating trend.

Reservation on Economic Criteria

It is clear that caste cannot be a criterion to help the backward classes to come up because it is ascriptive (based on birth); it is a group characteristic; and because it helps the powerful members of those castes to exploit the concessions for their own benefit. It is also clear that mere economic criterion by itself is not sufficient because it ignores the vital social fact.

One thing is clear. The bulk of the members of the backward classes are illiterate and unskilled. Using these criteria the following suggestions may be made:

Primary and Secondary Education

(a) Every individual who is the child of an illiterate person is entitled to educational concessions.

(b) Every individual who is the child of an unskilled worker is entitled to educational concessions.

(c) Every individual who is the child of a person following the traditional occupations like hair-cutting, washing clothes, shoe-making, sweeping, etc., is entitled to educational concessions.

Negatively the following suggestions may be made:

(d) No child of a person employed in Class I or II of government service or an organized industry or an institution, is entitled to educational concessions, because the income of such a person is about six to eight times the per capita income in the country.

(e) No child of an educated person, however poor is entitled to these educational concessions.

Bibliography

Aurora, G.S. : *Tribe, Caste, Class Encounters,* Administrative Staff College of India, Hyderabad, 1972.

Baden-Powell : *Land System of British India*, Oxford, 1892.

Bailey, F.G. : *Caste and Economic Frontier*, Oxford, 1884.

Beteille, A. : *Caste, Class and Power*, Barkeley, 1964.

Bhatt, Anil : Caste, *Class and Politics: An Empirical Profile of Social Stratification* in *Modern India*, Manohar Book Service, New Delhi, 1975.

Bipin Chandra : *The Rise and Growth of Economic Nationalism in India*, Delhi, 1977.

Brass, Paul R. : *Language, Religion and Politics in India,* Vikas Publishing House, New Delhi, 1975.

Chaudhury, B.B. : *Growth of Community Agriculture in Bengal,* Calcutta, 1964.

Chopra, P.N. : *Social and Cultural History of India*, Sterling, 1979.

Cohn, B.S. : *Structural Change in Indian Rural Society*, London, 1969.

Das, Durga : *India from Curzon to Nehru*, London, 1969.

Das, R.K. : *The Labour Movement in India*, Berlin, 1923.

Durkheim, E. : *The Division of Labour in Society,* Macmillan Company, New York, 1933.

Dutt, N.K. : *Origin and Growth of Caste in India*, Calcutta, 1931.

Edward, M. : *British India*, London, 1967.

Farquher J.N. : *Modern Religious Movement in India*, OUP, New Delhi, 1914.

Gadgil, D.R. : *The Industrial Evolution of India*, OUP, New Delhi, 1942.

Ghose, K. : *Agricultural Labourers in India*, Indian Pub., Calcutta, 1967.

Ghurye, G.S. : *Caste, Class in India*, Bombay, 1950.

Giri, V.V. : *Labour Problems in Indian Industries*, APH, Bombay, 1958.

Gough, Kathleen : *Class Developments in India*, McGill University Press, Montreal, 1975.

Hutton, J.H. : *Castes in India*, Oxford, 1961.

Imtiaz, A. : *Caste and Stratification among Muslim in India*, Monohar Book Service, Delhi, 2001.

Joshi, V.C. : *Sri Aurobindo: An Interpretation*, Delhi, 1973.

Kothari, Rajni : *Caste in Indian Politics*, Orient Longman, Delhi, 1970.

Lokanathan, P.S. : *Industrialisation*, Oxford, 1946.

Lynch, Owen M. : *The Politics of Untouchability*, Columbia University Press, New York, 1966.

Majumdar, D.N. : *An Introduction to Social Anthropology*, APH, Bombay, 1960.

—*Caste and Communication in an Indian Village*, Asia Publishing House, Bombay, 1958.

Marriott, McKim : *Caste Ranking and Community Structures*, University of Chicago Press, Chicago, 1955.

Mehortra, S.N. : *Labour Problem in India*, Delhi, 1981.

Mehta, S.C. : *Caste in India*, New Delhi, 1965.

Nehru, J. : *The Discovery of India*, Calcutta, 1946.

O' Malley, L.S.S. : *Modern India and the West*, OUP, London, 1941.

Pocock, David F. : *Mind Body and Wealth: A Study of Relief and Practice in an Indian Village*, Blackwell, London, 1974.

Prasad, N. : *The Myth of Caste System*, Patna, 1957.

Revri, C. : *Indian Trade Union Movement*, Orient Longman, New Delhi, 1972.

Shelvankar, K.S. : *The Problem of India*, London, 1940.

Smith, D.E. : *India as a Secular State*, Princeton, 1963.

Thapar, Romesh : *Tribe, Caste and Religion in India*, The Macmillan Company of India Ltd., New Delhi, 1977.

Unnithan, T.K.N. : *Sociology for India*, Prentice Hall of India, New Delhi, 1967.

Verba, S., and Ahmed, B. : *Caste, Race and Politics: A Comparative Study of India and the United States*, Sage Publications, Berkeley Hills, 1971.

Weber, Max : *Essays in Sociology*, Routledge and Kegan Paul Ltd., London, 1952.

Index

□□□